# EDGAR Master
## OF tHE KENNEDY
## SLOW BURN

## by Bill Cassara

# EDGAR Master
## OF tHE KENNEDY
## Slow Burn

# by Bill Cassara

BearManor Media
2005

Edgar Kennedy: Master of the Slow Burn
© 2005 by Bill Cassara

For information, address:
**BearManor Media**
P. O. Box 750
Boalsburg, PA 16827

bearmanormedia.com

Cover design by John Teehan

Typesetting and layout by John Teehan

Published in the USA by BearManor Media

ISBN—1-59393-018-6

(1931) RKO
Mr. Average Man *publicity shot*

**KENNEDY** - English, Irish, Scottish
"Misshapen Head," from the Gaelic name Cinne'idigh.

*"A comedian's life is just one slap after another—
some on the back and some on the face"*

– Edgar Kennedy (1-22-38)

# Table of Contents

# Acknowledgements

DEDICATED TO MY TWO CHILDREN: Diana Cassara and Douglas Cassara. You are both beautiful and precious, long may you continue the gift of reading and laughter.

I would like to especially acknowledge my beautiful muse, Michelle Benton, who inspired me and gave me confidence just when I needed it most.

Filmography: It has generally been acknowledged that Edgar Kennedy appeared in close to 500 films. Until fairly recently, only about 300 titles were confirmed. The below gentlemen contributed heavily by confirming additional titles: the late Richard Braff, Leo Brooks, Dennis Campa III, Rich Finegan, Cole Johnston, Tony Hawes, Gary Hammonds, Leonard Maltin, Brent Walker.

Four gentlemen who greatly encouraged this project but did not live to see it in print: Raymond Daum, Ivan Deach, Tony Hawes, Eldon Root.

*The Biggest Edgar* "Average Man" *Kennedy fan in the world: Shorty Caruso*

The following authors helped with inspiration and/or advice: Richard Bann, Michael F. Blake, Richard Braff, Leo Brooks, Andy Edmonds, Mike Esslinger, Ron Fields, Sam Gill, Neil Hotelling, David Kiehn, Leonard Maltin, Dr. John McCabe, Randy Skretvedt, Warren M. Sherk, Brent Walker.

Research Contributors: Richard Bann, Bill Cappello, Richard Finegan, Gary Hammonds, Howard Strohn, Brent Walker.

Special Thanks to: Melodie Bahou, Michael Bainter, Kimm Benton, Tommy Bond, Tommy Bupp, Jr., Shorty Caruso, Mary Jane and Janet Cassara, Susan Clark, *Classic Images* (Bob King), Phyllis Coates, Doris Day, Wendy Deach, Derry Deane, Dorothy DeBorba, Bevis Faversham, Joan Fontaine, Teresa Gallagher, Nancy Logan Johnston, Lois Laurel Hawes, Larry Edmonds Bookstore, Paul Lisy, Roselle and Jeff Lowrance, the late Terry Melcher, Robin Nakhjavan, Rose Patrick, Neil Shaw, Gene Townsend Jr., Linda Ward, Jeffrey Weissman, Sam White, Bart Williams.

Sons of the Desert pals: Alex Bartosh, Gary Cohen, John & Janet Duff, Richard Greene, Del Kempster, Roger Gordon, Tom Hawthorn, Lori Jones, Kay Lotah, Kathy Luhman, Paul Mular, Bob Satterfield, Henry (Butch) Sorenson, Alison and Dave Stevenson, Dwain Smith, Tracy Tolzmann, the Wileys (Jimmy, Sr. Kris, and Jimmy, Jr.)

Fellow Midnight Patrol members: Dave Allard, Dave Cotter, Tom Crompton, Frank Goulette, Francis Hedley, Gloria Mattos Hughes, Jim Maley, Mary May & Fred Vareen and the late Lois Roberts.

Libraries: The Church of Jesus Christ of Latter Day Saints (Seaside, Ca), King City Library, Margaret Herrick Library (Harry Garvin, Kristine Krueger), Marin County Library, Marin County Historical Library, Monterey City Library, Monterey County Parks and Recreation Dept., Monterey County Historical Society, Monterey County Film Commission, Oakland City Library, John Steinbeck (Salinas) Library, San Antonio Historic Society, San Francisco City Library, San Jose State University Library, University of California at Los Angeles (Film and Archives), University of Southern California (Ned Comstock of the Doheny Library), Wisconsin Center for Film and Television Research (Dorinda Hartmann).

My Biggest Supporters: Colleen Deach, whose vision and encouragement made this book a reality. Her love for her dad greatly moved me. This project could not have been done without her. Lois Laurel Hawes, your kindness and generous sharing was a dream come true. Mark and Glenn Kennedy, you guys have inherited the very essence of your grandfather: unselfishness, a zest for life and an appreciation of friendship.

Boyhood Chums: Lloyd Beardsley, Bill Burton, Ted Meece, Randy Smith, Charlie Thorsell, Nolan Zane. Thanks for your friendship all these years, guys.

Special recognition goes to Gary Hammonds who unselfishly shared some of his found treasures hidden in long lost articles from the Los Angeles newspapers. Bill Cappello who helped run down every lead I could give him, with sometimes-instant results, and to Christina McKillip, who did many hours of hand searching at the recorders' office. Rich Finegan proved to be an excellent resource, as did Cole Johnston. Both of these gentlemen shared everything they had, from photographs to reviews. Their desire to contribute helped to make this book complete.

Special thanks to my father, the late Sam Cassara, who took me to see *When Comedy Was King* in 1960 at the Studio Theatre in downtown San Jose, California. He instilled the appreciation of laughter at the film comedy greats, especially Laurel & Hardy. Special recognition to the late Tony Hawes who encouraged me and mentored me. He was truly an ambassador for all mankind. I wish he could see this book in its final form. Ivan Deach, a true gentleman. He would help coax memories from his wife, Colleen, and, with great pride, help to facilitate the stories into my consciousness.

Thanks, also, to Dr. John McCabe who, as the "Exhausted Ruler" and founder of the "Sons of the Desert," helped increase my appreciation of Laurel and Hardy and, more important, helped me to make lifelong friends through this great organization. It was this foundation that allowed me to reacquaint myself with the Kings of Comedy and rediscover the role of Edgar Kennedy during his Roach era. All of this led to the glorious friendship of Lois Laurel and her dear husband, Tony Hawes. Without them this book would not exist.

Special acknowledgment also goes to Leonard Maltin, who authored many film books, but his two-reel comedy book greatly educated me and created a thirst for knowledge. The same goes for author Sam Gill who coauthored *Clown Princess and Court Jesters*. It too laid the foundation for my appreciation of the silent clowns and inspired me to write about Edgar. Meeting him was truly an inspiration. Lastly, sincere thanks to my dear old friend Kit Parker (and his wife Donna) of Kit Parker Films. He has always encouraged my dreams and helped me in so many ways with this book that I'll always be indebted to him. What a pal!

# Prologue

Ned Comstock, the film archivist at the Doheny Library at the University of Southern California, answered the phone. The call was yet another person who wanted to write a book on an old Hollywood movie star. "Who are you writing about?" Ned asked. Without any further introduction, I confidently spoke the name of Edgar Kennedy.

There was a pregnant pause of about three seconds. This was not the rounding up of the usual suspects of controversial celebrities: Clark Gable, Charlie Chaplin, Marilyn Monroe, Jean Harlow, Fatty Arbuckle and their ilk. Ned curiously replied, *"…Why Edgar Kennedy?"*

Why Edgar Kennedy, indeed. Edgar died at the top of his game back in 1948, but, since then, Hollywood has barely bothered reflecting on one of its film pioneers. Biographical information about his long and bumpy road to success has always been scarce and has been generally limited to his films.

Edgar Kennedy appeared in more than 400 films spanning four decades. He was one of the first to be honored (posthumously) with a star enshrining his name on the "Hollywood Walk of Fame." Known as "The Master of the Slow Burn," he had many other monikers over the years: "Mr. Average Man," "Kennedy the Cop," "Uncle Edgar," "One Punch Kennedy," and even "The Human Donald Duck."

An original Keystone Kop, Edgar predated the arrival of Charlie Chaplin and Fatty Arbuckle in the Keystone Comedies for Mack Sennett. He played foil to Laurel and Hardy, the Marx Brothers, W.C. Fields, Eddie Cantor and Harold Lloyd. Edgar also played memorable characters in prestigious Hollywood films, working with Clark Gable, Carole Lombard,

Jimmy Stewart, Claudette Colbert, Dick Powell and John Wayne. He saw the rise of Frank Capra, Jean Harlow, Betty Grable, Ginger Rogers, Lucille Ball and Doris Day.

Edgar starred in his own short comedy series for RKO, which spanned seventeen years. These "Average Man" short comedies established films' first all-talking situation comedy series. They fathered a genre emulated by radio program "families" and later television sitcoms.

A screen clown for most of his career, with some notable exceptions, Edgar also directed many comedies himself. After years of anonymity, he finally hit pay dirt by developing a character that was much put upon by others. He would seemingly *simmer* in frustration over life's annoyances, determined not to let it bother him. As the tension would mount, Edgar's pent-up impatience often *boiled* over. Unable to hold it in, he might finally *ignite* in anger, resigning himself to fate by emphatically wiping his face with his left hand. His stock-in-trade grimace and "Slow-Burn" made him one of the movies' most recognizable faces, until death claimed him at the peak of his career at age fifty-eight.

Now, more than half a century after Edgar Kennedy's death, the embers of interest in his life have been rekindled. Rare family photographs and stories, provided by Edgar's only daughter, have been shared with the author. Archival research has revealed never-known details about his childhood, professional boxing career and the evolution of his film legacy.

Edgar Livingston Kennedy never had the opportunity to tell his life memoirs, but, with the cooperation of his family, combined with gumshoe efforts, the story can now be shared.

# Introduction

Edgar Kennedy's perpetually perturbed, round Irish face filled the screen. Except for the slightest wisp of hair that stubbornly protruded from his frontal lobe, his follicles had retreated to form a horseshoe ring surrounding his cranium. This large, burly man's movie character usually had good intentions, but was beaten down by the wrath of his meddling mother-in-law, his conniving brother-in-law and his ceaselessly talking wife. He was America's beloved "Average Man," who justifiably could go into comic fits of rage. The angrier he became, the harder audiences would laugh.

Ed-Grrrr Kennedy became known as the movie's maddest man, with a TNT temper. He usually harnessed it at the conclusion of the comedy by bringing his meaty left hand to his head, then deliberately dragged it s-l-o-w-l-y downward over his face like a window shade. The "Slow-Burn" gesture became a symbolic white flag of defeat. He was a master at it.

Edgar's prolific film output and his signature trademark "Slow-Burn" mannerism made him one of America's most familiar faces. Indeed, B.R. Crisler of the *New York Times* wrote in 1936: "People who never heard of Clark Gable and wouldn't care about him if they had, know Kennedy and love him, for, in his 'Mr. Average Man' series for Pathe and RKO, he has created a character as universally comprehensible as Chaplin's little clown, and twice as real."

He had already been in movies for 26 years, when, on February 3, 1938, an official "biography" was released by the publicity department of Paramount Pictures. The main purpose was to promote the studio's most recent movie releases and create word pictures of the trials and tribulations of Edgar Kennedy's life. It is unknown if Edgar was even consulted

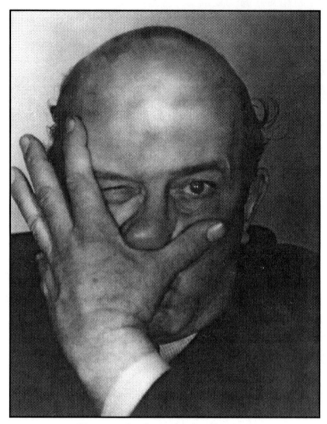

(From author's personal collection)

on the finished contents; most of the information was wrong, or at best, greatly exaggerated.

Edgar Kennedy was sitting in a dark corner of a movie sound stage, speaking of life, the movies and himself, he was very unhappy indeed.

As Edgar reviewed his past, he saw himself as a kind of Pagliacci; frustrated, bedeviled and ridiculous. He spoke of his valuable "slow-burn," and recalled how this gesture that made him famous was born of a moment of despair that has pursued him ever since.

He would like to play heavies. But they keep him in rowdy farce, keep him smiting himself in the brow and wiping his face distractedly with one hand in the "slow-burn." "You know," he confides, "when I do that burn I am RE-

ALLY burning. I get so dam' sick of having to do it!"

Kennedy relates how the celebrated burn originated long ago when he dropped around to a casting office looking for something to do. "Nothing today," they told him for about the twentieth straight time. Up went his hand and smote his brow. Down came the palm, along his pan, quivering with impotent rage and leaving an expression of premeditated murder.

The boys in the casting office roared. "You do that in a picture and we'll get you something sure!" they told him enthusiastically. The next day Edgar was escorted out to a movie set to perform his burn for a director. It landed him a job as a Keystone Kop.

But that's getting a little ahead of his story. Edgar had come to Hollywood some time before, had made the rounds of the studios day after day, and nobody had invited him into any of them. Finally one flip young man to whom he had applied many times before asked what he thought he could do anyway. "Do!" roared Edgar. "I can lick anybody in this studio including you!"

There was a gleam in the young man's eye when he told our Edgar to report back at 10 in the morning. Edgar reported back and found three hulking Piltdown men awaiting him. The young man in the casting office suggested that since he thought he could lick anybody in the studio Edgar might start with the reception committee. Edgar did—and knocked out all three of them.

"When I was through," he grins; "I told them about me having been heavyweight champ of the Pacific Coast." Which is what he once was.

Edgar was born in Monterey County, California. He attended San Rafael High School, which is in Marin County, and made the boxing team. After graduation he kept on boxing, turned professional, and held the Coast heavyweight title for the better part of 1911-12.

When the United States entered the World War, Edgar tried to enlist but was turned down for 'physical disability.' He couldn't understand this rejection because it came just two weeks after he had kept his feet till the final bell in the battle with Jack Dempsey. When the fourth draft came along Edgar took another crack at the army, and this time was accepted.

They put him into a uniform and sent him to Vancouver barracks, where Edgar became a Corporal and an instructor of boxing. He strove hard for promotion and made Sergeant, they put him to work driving a gurney wagon. He stayed there till after the Armistice, but yearned to get over to France and show what he could do!

After the war Edgar went back to boxing for awhile, then into Ferris Hartman's light opera company in San Francisco. Later he went into vaudeville and musical comedy. Then he went to Hollywood and walked into the picture business over the insensate bodies of the reception committee.

"Sometimes," he says, "I wonder what I saw in the movies anyhow. Sometimes I think I should have stayed with the boxing racket. Maybe I could have been a manager or something. But I keep on staying, hoping someday they'll let me ACT!" "Oh Ed," came a voice from another corner of the sound stage. "Me?" inquired Edgar. "Yeah. We're ready for you, Ed. This is the scene where you get in there and burn up. Ready?"

The Kennedy hand smote the Kennedy brow. Down came the palm along the Kennedy pan, leaving an expression of premeditated murder. And what Edgar Kennedy said cannot be repeated here.

The above document was carefully crafted to reinforce the public's perception of Edgar as the loveable but befuddled victim of others, complete with the inevitable "Slow-Burn." To his fans, Edgar Kennedy the film star and the private person were one and the same. That perception was not discouraged by the studios.

There were many such mini-biographies of Edgar, from virtually every studio in Hollywood. They each contained varied succinct "facts" to entertain, not necessarily inform. Such blithering, though written with a germ of truth, was built on contradictions. The basics of the above biography were reprinted as needed for the rest of his life and beyond. Even his obituary writers would reuse the information, not minding if it was correct or not.

Was Edgar Kennedy a Keystone Kop for Mack Sennett? Yes. There were many variations that told of the colorful way Edgar fought his way into the movie business. According to the unnamed publicity writer, Edgar started in the movies after serving in the World War. Well, the Armistice was in 1918 and Edgar was already a seven-year veteran of the movies by then. Did Edgar fight Jack Dempsey? Sort of. Did Edgar really invent the "slow-burn" out of exasperation when he was turned down by the "boys at the casting department?" Poppycock.

Edgar's hard knocks of life, combined with his intimate knowledge of the workings of the camera, helped pave his way to fame. And now, here is the true story of Edgar Kennedy: the man, the myth and the mirth.

# 1.
# It Happened In Monterey

Edgar Livingston Kennedy was jubilantly received into this world on April 26, 1890 by his parents, Annie and Neil Kennedy. He was born in a small farmhouse in Monterey County, California.

Health concerns for mother and baby were always present in such a pioneer environment. However, there was a particular reason to be cautious with this new baby. Preceding Edgar in birth was a sister named Veratina, born in June of 1888. She was a weak baby and struggled for her life, only to succumb in September of that same year. All of the hopes and dreams of Annie and Neil rested on little Edgar.

Neil Kennedy was born in 1843 in Canada. He eventually immigrated to California, where he settled in Grass Valley, some 70 miles northeast of Sacramento. Neil became a schoolteacher in the area while in his 30s.

Annie Quinn was the daughter of Mary Cassidy and Jonathan Quinn of New York. She was born on July 4, 1856 in California. Mary was formally educated and was an accomplished artist and musician. Jonathan was a carpenter.

Eventually the Quinns landed in Grass Valley, after seven months of tortuous travel across the country. Annie Quinn and her sister Margaret (Martha) were born in a cabin that their father built. Mary taught school and gave the girls a firm foundation and appreciation for education.

Annie was sixteen when she first met Neil Kennedy in 1872; he was 13 years her senior. She cultivated a crush on him that lasted years. According to family legend, Neil slowly worked up the courage to propose. Annie accepted. Jonathan built them a cabin on his land, where they lived for the next two years.

According to the 1880 census, Neil and "Anna" Kennedy had moved to nearby Nevada City, California, a former boomtown, during the Gold Rush

(From author's collection)

era of 1849. There was a time when Nevada City had the third highest population in the state (after San Francisco and Sacramento). The city incorporated in the 1850s and originally was named "Nevada." When the state of Nevada entered into the union, the townsfolk decided to add "City" onto the name of Nevada to distinguish it from the state.

Neil had been teaching at Nevada City High School since 1878 and in 1880 became the school's principal. Annie became a schoolteacher at the same institute of higher learning in 1881. The Kennedys had accomplished much and conceivably could have lived the rest of their lives there very comfortably, but Neil and Annie had bigger plans.

On April 18, 1882, Neil was sworn in as a Citizen of the United States. He received his naturalization papers from the Superior Court of the County of Nevada, California after denouncing "all allegiance and fidelity to every foreign Prince, Potentate, State or Sovereignty whatever, and particularly to

Victoria, Queen of Great Britain and Ireland."

Upon becoming a U. S. citizen, Neil applied for a homestead land grant from the government. Meanwhile, Martha wound up marrying Neil's best friend, John McCormick. The four of them shared dreams of property, prosperity and parenthood.

By 1886, Mr. and Mrs. Neil Kennedy had moved to San Francisco where they resided at 132 6th Street. Neil found a job as a bookkeeper and taught school for the Lincoln Evening Classes at 4095 18th Street. Annie became pregnant late in the year of 1887.

On December 29, 1887 there was more good news; Neil Kennedy was finally granted a homestead opportunity from the Land Office at San Francisco. After paying $16 for administrative costs, Neil was awarded 160 acres in the very southern region of Monterey County.

This area of the county was very sparse in population. The closest big city was Salinas, some 90 miles north. Monterey, the former Spanish and Mexican capital of California, was even further away along the coast.

The Kennedy homestead was between the new town of Bradley (est. 1886) and Pleyto. Each township was about eight miles away in the opposite direction. Pleyto was a stagecoach stop for points north and south and featured a dance hall, store, livery barn and blacksmith shop. Bradley had become part of the railroad line connection for San Miguel, and other cities leading to Los Angeles. Destinations north included San Ardo, King City, Salinas, San Jose and San Francisco.

The 160-acre Kennedy homestead actually bordered the county line of San Luis Obispo in central California. The area just south of the property was generally referred to as Bee Rock, so named by the natives of the area because of beehives that existed in the rocky crevices of the mountains.

The Pacific Ocean is approximately 40 miles due west, with the Diablo mountain range rising up just inland from the coast. In 1769, The Spanish explorer, Portola, wrote in his journal describing the nearby Nacimiento and

Neil Kennedy, Edgar's dad
(Courtesy Kennedy Family)

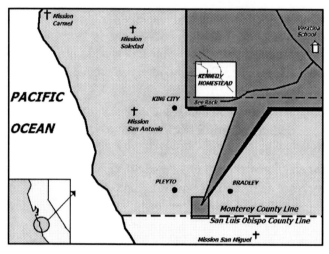

(Map drawn by Neil Shaw)

San Antonio Rivers. These were the lands of the Salinan Indians when the Spanish arrived. Pedro Fages of the Portola expedition reported: "There are bears, deer, antelope, wild sheep, rabbits, squirrels, etc. Among the birds no species is lacking. Quail and very blue ring-doves and turtle doves, swallows and calendar-larks are seen here. Of fish in fresh water there are large trout."[1]

Under conditions of the land grant, the homesteaders had five years to improve the land to be self-sustaining. Despite complications that travel might have on Annie's pregnancy, the Kennedys felt an urgency to get to their homestead so that the baby could be born on the new land. They waited for the first signs of spring, then ventured south with the McCormicks. They arrived at their new homestead in March of 1888. Neil, John and other homesteaders (Edward D. Spanow, Ernest Rideout and his family) started building a structure for the new neighbors to live in. With a pioneer spirit of helping each other out, the first home was completed for the expectant Kennedys. McCormick was able to purchase land adjoining the Kennedy land boundaries so they could be neighbors. Work then began immediately for the McCormicks, who already had a young son named Samuel.

It was now the end of April, and the Kennedy wood house was surrounded by wild natural grass and flowers that seemed even more beautiful as spring settled in. The land was groomed for ranching, with cattle and farm animals grazing the rich and fertile earth. A well was completed, but even more work had to be done in the coming five years.

---

1.  *History of Southern Monterey County* by Robert B. Johnston

Just prior to the Kennedys arriving, a new post office was established in south Monterey County. The opening on September 5, 1887 was a community event in which the founder of the township of Pleyto, Lauson H. Ward, was named Postmaster of a new post office to serve the area. It was located on the Old Stage Road, eight miles southwest of Bradley. Pleyto had only one building, which served as the general store and post office. The community named it Nacimiento, and it was the social cornerstone of the area.

Everything was progressing as planned when Annie gave birth to their first child, Veratina, in June. With the rugged challenges, and lack of medical care, little Veratina became weaker by the day. After only about three months, she finally gave up her fight for life. The small community of homesteaders mourned the loss. On November 7, 1888, the township decided to honor the child by changing the name of the post office from Nacimiento to Veratina. Annie Kennedy was appointed the Postmistress.

When little Edgar was born, Annie and Neil swelled with parental pride. They redoubled their efforts to tame their land and make it prosperous. The Kennedys also wanted to contribute to the community by offering their services as educators, if a school could ever be built.

It was decided to build a school on the Branch Ranch off the county road, just a couple of parcels over from the Kennedy land. The McCormicks and all of the other men in the area helped with the construction. They used fine lumber from the plentiful trees in the area to build the sturdy one-room schoolhouse. When it was finished, it was an inspiration in its setting.

According to the *Salinas Californian* of March 16, 1893, Neil Kennedy was the teacher and Annie served as Clerk of the Board. The same newspaper, in the July 30, 1896-edition, printed that the state school money apportionment to the Veratina was $6 per child. There were 12 children in the classroom of all ages. Apparently, Neil and Annie were unpaid volunteers.

Life was a challenge, but was very rewarding. Young Edgar thrived in this nurturing educational environment. And he actually enjoyed his chores on the ranch. His special love was hunting and fishing, much-needed skills on the homestead.

Edgar learned to ride a horse almost as soon as he could walk. He competed with plentiful mountain lions in the region for wild game to bring home to eat. Fish were also abundant in nearby rivers and creeks. It was an ideal setting for the boy and he matured quickly. Even Huck Finn never had it so good.

Throughout his entire life, Edgar never forgot his wonderful experiences growing up. He always considered himself a transplanted rancher and farmer, no matter how successful he was in the movies. In one interview he gave later in life, the subject of his birthplace came up. He typically mentioned that he was born on a farm in Monterey County. When pressed to name exactly where in Monterey County, he responded, "in Veratina, California." Other than the post office, which closed in 1895, there are no references to Veratina on any California map. This must have kept the interviewer busy scanning the contemporary maps of the time to locate Veratina. In rural Monterey County in the 1890s, the people of southern Monterey County routinely identified themselves with the closest post office, since there were no nearby cities.

On April 16, 1894, Neil Kennedy filed a form with the government articulating that he had cultivated the land as promised. In a "Homestead Proof—Testimony of Claimant" form, Neil described his land: "I first built my house and established an actual residence upon this land on April 29, 1888. I have a dwelling house (6 rooms), a barn, outhouses, and 5 acres of fencing." In addition, the Kennedys had a well, an orchard of fruit trees, cattle for grazing and chicken coops for chickens and turkeys. Neil wrote that he had "lived on the land continuously with my wife and two children." The above facts had to be posted in the local paper, in this case, *The Bradley Mercury* (now defunct). This procedure was necessary in case someone wanted to dispute the claim and block the transfer of land.

Edgar was ten years old when his father suddenly became ill and died of pneumonia. Neil was only 57 years old, but he had accomplished much: He had become a citizen, acquired and cultivated his own property, and helped to further education. Most important, he left a son to carry on the family name. Edgar's world as he knew it would change forever. He was now the man of the house.

Despite their best efforts, farming the land and Annie's school teaching took a toll on them. Edgar tried to convince Annie that if he could quit school, they would be able to keep up the land. Annie wouldn't hear of it. She valued a solid education for her son and was a very determined woman.

Annie sold her cattle and leased out her land. Fortunately, John McCormick still had ties to San Francisco. He often stayed in the City to work at the Golden State and Miner's Iron Works on First Street in order to support his wife and family in Monterey County. Complications arose when he broke his leg in an industrial accident in 1900. Nevertheless, later that year, McCormick welcomed Annie and Edgar when they arrived by train into San Francisco from southern Monterey County. It was a northward journey of almost two hundred miles.

# 2.
# San Francisco

With hard capital from the sale of livestock, Annie bought a large boardinghouse occupied by tenants at 511 Bryant Street. Near 3rd St.; the house was right in the middle of the Irish section of town. St. Patrick's Church became their parish, where Edgar most likely learned to sing in the church choir.

The closest public elementary school to Edgar's house was the Rincon Grammar School, just off 2nd St. between Harrison and Bryant. Little is known about his early school days because of the destruction of all records from the 1906 earthquake and fire. Annie thought this was a perfect environment for Edgar to learn in. She also hoped that the surrogate family of boarders would embrace Edgar and help condition him to this strange new world. Annie was very adept at cooking, and socializing came easy for her.

San Francisco in 1900 had 360,000 people living in the city, and was the center of culture in California. This infamous city with its Barbary Coast reputation was fascinating to young Edgar. There was a sense of excitement and even danger living so near the waterfront. This area of working-class citizens was referred to fondly as "South of the Slot" by San Franciscans. It was unofficially named because the dividing line was Market Street where the cable lines pulled the cable cars.

As described by San Francisco native Jack London, for an article in the *Saturday Evening Post* in May of 1909: "Old San Francisco, before the earthquake, was divided midway by a Slot. The Slot was an iron crack that ran along the center of Market Street, and from The Slot arose the burr of the ceaseless, endless cable that was hitched at will to the cars it dragged up and down. In truth, there were two slots, but in the quick grammar of the time was saved by calling them, and much more that they stood for, 'The Slot.' North of The Slot were the theaters, hotels, and shopping district, the banks and the staid, respectable business houses. South of the Slot were the factories, slums, laundries, machine shops, boiler works, and the abodes of the working class."

Edgar's immediate neighborhood, however, was very middle class at the turn of the century. Perpendicular to Edgar's house on 3rd and Bryant was South Park, one of the first exclusive living areas in the city in 1852. It bordered Bryant and Brannan and Third and Second Streets on very flat land.

> "In the early days of the city, Rincon Hill with its spectacular views was the first choice of the elite of San Francisco to build their homes. Rincon is the Spanish word for 'corner.' Rincon Point formed a natural crescent-shape overlooking the water's edge extending north. Rincon Hill in its glory days ascended to one hundred feet high and extended from Folsom Street to Bryant and from Spear to Third. The hundred foot high foothill was quite accessible by horse and buggy. The views of the bay were extraordinary. Below the hill from First Street to Third, the area was referred to as 'Happy Valley.' At the foot of Howard Street, at First, stood the San FranciscoGas Works, the wastes giving the nearby area the name Tar Flat."[2]

In adulthood, Edgar often made specific reference to his neighborhood, describing it as "South of the Slot" in general, but living in the "Tar Flats" in particular. Those terms have little meaning in contemporary San Francisco.

With the advent of cable car technology (in 1876), the elite of San Francisco started to vacate Rincon Hill for even higher ground. The 100-foot-high grade was eventually bulldozed down after the ravaging earthquake and fire of 1906. The landfill effectively extended the shoreline and now makes up the base of the San Francisco-Oakland Bay Bridge and the San Francisco Giant's ballpark.

Gradually, South of Market or "South of the Slot" became a workingman's district. Many of the Irish clustered around St. Patrick's church, (dating from 1870) on Mission Street near Third.

Many successful people, including future Mayor Jim Rolph, future Police Chief Dan O'Brien, David Warfield (of The Warfield Theatres) and other dignitaries, grew up in this area, but none so famous as the

---

2. *A Vistit to Rincon Hill and South Park* by Albert Shumate

writer Jack London. London was born on 615 Third Street, between Bryant and Brannan St., on January 12, 1878. The residence was right around the corner from Edgar's home. As Jack London started to become famous, the neighborhood swelled with pride at his literary achievements and the publication of *The Sea Wolf* (1904). London went on to pen *The Call of the Wild, The Iron Heel*, as well as 28 other novels and many newspaper accounts of the day. Edgar sought out and enjoyed reading Jack London adventure novels throughout his life.

One of the boarders at the Kennedy's was George Barker, who originally came from England. He had a daughter named Irene, who was eight years old in 1900. For Irene, Annie was almost the mother she never knew. And for Annie, Irene was so bright and energetic, she sometimes imagined that Veratina would have been just like her. Irene followed Edgar around like he was her big brother.

In the next few years, life was an adventure for Edgar, being in the largest city in California offered many life experiences on the streets.

By 1903, widow Annie was listed in the City Directory as "Kennedy, Mrs. Anna, Furnished Rms., 511 Bryant St." Annie was delighted to be involved in the church and in the community, but something was missing. She longed to be a schoolteacher once again.

Annie participated in charity work at San Quentin. It was located twelve miles north of the City, accessible by ferryboat. Eventually, a low-paying position was offered to Annie to teach the prisoners.

San Quentin, "The Big House," was the infamous State prison (still in use) for hardened felony convicts. Once sentenced, they were forgotten by society. Their monotonous existence was brightened only by an occasional visitor, if one was lucky. Annie Kennedy bestowed upon the prisoners a sense of hope in the form of education. The mostly ignorant convicts embraced the opportunity to learn, as many of them were driven to crime because of their illiteracy.

Annie didn't judge them, but she instead taught them the basics of education, with some successes and some failures. But it was her love and enthusiasm for teaching that won over these lost souls. Ever appreciative, the convicts made a wooden cribbage board to present to Annie. It remains in the family today as a cherished heirloom.

# 3.
# San Rafael

To get physically closer to her work, Annie and Edgar took residence at 201 E Street in San Rafael, California. They lived there during the fall of 1904 and the spring of 1905. San Rafael is 17 miles north of San Francisco in Marin County. San Quentin is five miles south of San Rafael.

Edgar was enrolled at San Rafael High School. He was away from his newfound friends in San Francisco, but was anxious to help support himself and his mother. Edgar was aware that his grandfather Quinn had been a carpenter by trade. He learned enough carpentry skills from George Barker to list himself as a carpenter in the City Directory of 1905. Of course, Annie made sure that school came first.

Though painfully shy[3] the first year of this new school, Edgar excelled in his educational endeavors, and he was a standout in drama studies. A mere freshman, on April 14, 1905, Edgar was cast in the lead of the annual school production of William Shakespeare's *A Midsummer Night's Dream*. This play is considered a comedy version of Shakespeare's own *Romeo and Juliet*.

The story of *Pyramus and Thisbe* was based on Greek mythology. In the tale, a young man and a lovely young maiden are in love, but their marriage is opposed by their parents. Both of their homes are adjoined, and the two lovers can speak to each other through a crevice in the dividing wall. One night they plan a secret rendezvous outside. Thisbe is first to arrive, but is frightened by a lion whose paws and jaws are bloody from his prior prey. She flees and inadvertently drops her mantle, which the lion mauls. When Pyramus arrives, he surmises that Thisbe has been slain. In grief, he kills himself. Thisbe returns and, seeing her true love dead, takes her own life with his sword.

---

3. *The Marin High School 1905* (Courtesy of the Marin Historical Library)

Shakespeare used a portion of the above scenario for his *Midsummer Night's Dream*. In a "play within a play" sequence, Pyramus, Thisbe and especially the lion are portrayed by actors who play their scenes so badly, they were outrageously funny to the audience.

The local San Rafael newspaper, *The Marin Journal*, reported in their "High School Notes" section:

> A very entertaining program was given by the students of the High School last Friday afternoon. Many of the parents and friends were present and the assembly hall of the school was well filled.
>
> Everyone was then summoned by one of the girls dressed in a green costume to assemble in the tennis court where the junior class would present the play of Pyramus and Thisbe. The scene was made very effective by the background of roses and foliage. All the characters were well taken and the junior class certainly deserves great credit as they are the first class who has given anything of its kind in their first year.

In a role that he was born to play, Edgar portrayed the lion in *Pyramus and Thisbe*, despite being a mere freshman. Even at the age of 15 he was a big kid and physically imposing in his handmade burlap costume. The look was made even more complete with fake blood on his paws and chin. Edgar relished performing the comic heavy. The highlight of the skit was when Edgar reassured the audience (in lion garb) by telling them that, despite his bloody paws and mouth, no one was really harmed. The laughter and applause Edgar received no doubt inspired him to pursue what eventually would be his chosen profession, acting.

The following account was published in the yearbook:

> The school and friends were invited to seats in the tennis court to watch the play, by Dolly Cushing, on behalf of the junior class. The invitation was coached very prettily in old English, and the spectators adjourned to the court readily to witness 'ye lamentable and doleful tragedy of 'Pyramus and Thisbe.'

Edgar as the Lion in *A Midsummer's Night Dream* (1905)
(Courtesy Kennedy Family)

Estelle Turner, as Qunice, gave the prologue and introduced the actors. The scene, then followed where Pyramus and Thisbe, clad in classical Greek garments, in the persons of Mildred Wood and Margaret Brennfleck, amorously discoursed through the 'sweet and amiable wall.' The dialogue went off with spirit. The sweetness of this scene was rudely changed in the next by the advent of Lion. He, concealing Edgar Kennedy, under burlap, fur rugs and gore, first assured the terrified audience that he was perfectly harmless, and then rushed in and, having scared Thisbe so that she dropped her mantle, mouthed it till it was bloody. Then followed the affecting scene where Pyramus, and then Thisbe, returned and most tragically avowed their faithfulness unto death and killed themselves.

The entire play went off well, and was a great success. The acting was really fine, and the congratulations received by those taking part in the 'tragedy' were well merited.

It was a memorable year for Edgar in San Rafael, but in the early spring, Annie received a letter from her sister Margaret explaining that her husband, John McCormick, had suddenly died at their homestead property back in Monterey County. Margaret soon realized the same problem that Annie did earlier; with no husband to man the hard chores, the family could not keep up with the demands of the ranch.

Annie had every intention of eventually moving back to San Francisco and encouraged Margaret to make the move to the big city. Margaret moved her family into the vacated boardinghouse at 511 Bryant Street and ran it on behalf of her sister. Edgar was thrilled; his very favorite cousin was Walter McCormick. The two were as close as brothers their whole life.

During the Easter break at school in 1905, Edgar decided to go back to the old homestead and check on his family and aunt's property. He ventured south by train all by himself and could hardly wait to visit his old stomping grounds. Every morning while he was there, he took his rifle and mounted his horse and met up with the local boys with whom he grew up. He would sometimes go exploring by himself, always discovering something new. On this trip, Edgar spent one of the nights at the McCormick's empty home. He had been away for over five years now, and he didn't realize how much he missed being a cowboy.

It was during this trip that Edgar wrote to Walter. The letter was reconstructed in the form of an essay for his school yearbook. The freshman was acknowledged in the yearbook for his writing skills and won a third place finish in a writing contest. It included an award of $2.

A hundred years later, this essay has been rediscovered in a crumbling 1905 yearbook at the Marin County Historical Library. This wonderful telling of a day-in-the-life of this long-ago 15-year-old boy is really a time capsule. Reading it, one can see the metamorphosis of a boy turning into a man. This is a time of Edgar's life that was previously undocumented, long before any Hollywood publicity writer fictionalized his background.

Edgar Kennedy, class of '08
Third Prize Story

> My Dear Walter:
>     Well, here I am, this beautiful morning, in the very room in which you were born. I can hardly take time to write, I am so very anxious to be hunting. I have longed

for this, my first hunting trip, for many years. Before I came here, I thought I could shoot anything that my eyes rested upon, from an elephant to an ant, but somehow or another, I do not shoot everything I see. Maybe I spend too much time in admiring them. At any rate, they get out of the range of my gun pretty often. I have discovered two very important things about animals; in the first place, they seem to be afraid of man, also that they do not travel on beaten tracks. I saw two deer, yesterday, trotting over the hill. I did not get either of them, and waited for hours, thinking the rest of the herd would follow, only to be disappointed. There is a good deal of difference between shooting at a target and at a live animal, isn't there?

This is a beautiful place and I wish I could live here always. I bet you will return here when you have completed your education. My hammock swings between the two large locust trees that the boys told me you planted when you were five years of age. It is hard to believe, they are so immense. They are now a mass of beautiful white flowers, and at a distance look as though they were covered with snow. Last evening as Harry and Sam were returning from town, they saw me and drove up to the house. When they found I was a friend of yours, they could not show me enough attention, and so we planned a real hunting trip for tomorrow, but before I tell you of it, I must whisper something to you, I am almost afraid to put it on paper for fear it will miscarry. Do you remember a large rock, up the first canyon, about a mile from the house, that seems to be the covering of a spring? Well, I was strolling along up that way a few days ago, with the thermometer at about one hundred and ten. I became very thirsty and, noticing this rock, thought I had found a spring and would refresh myself. I got down on my knees to pull the grass back and, instead of seeing water, there were two immense eyes peering straight at me, as much as to say, what do you want? I straightened up suddenly, and decided that I was neither thirsty for water nor blood. I do not know how it happened, but when I realized where I was, I was in a tree about fifty feet from the rock. The gun was safe, but somehow I wished it were in the tree, too. I looked down and saw a lovely lioness and three cubs. For the first time since I left home, I thought the city would look good to me again. Well, I sat up in that tree watching the beautiful creatures for about two hours. The time did seem a little long, but then I had nothing else to do, so it did not matter. After a time they returned to the rock. I concluded they were asleep and would not come out for a while. I crawled down as stealthily as I could, so as not to disturb the dear little things, got my gun and waited till I got home for a drink. On my way home I got three cottontails, and was glad to see the house again. It is strange what a queer feeling comes over one when you find yourself so very near a lion. They must have hypnotic power. The boys told me that there was a family of lions somewhere up the canyon, and that the farmers had lost great numbers of sheep, hogs and calves, and forming a hunting party they had scoured the country for weeks, but could not get onto their lair, and that a well-to-do farmer had at last offered fifty dollars for the skin of the lioness. You bet, I did not relate my experience of the day, but I resolved then and there, to get that fifty dollars and, if I were so fortunate, then mother could join me here and have a vacation, too. I could not sleep that night thinking how it was possible now to get mother here, and how easy it would be to make that fifty dollars. It took me fourteen months to save twenty dollars, so that I might come here and, just think, I could make fifty dollars in less that fourteen seconds. Gee, what a long night it was. I thought morning would never come. The boys were on hand at four in the morning, but I was ready and straining my eyes looking for them an hour before that time. They expected to find me in bed and, slipping quietly to my window, were about to throw a chicken in the room to awake and scare me, when they discovered me strapping on my leggings. We started down the creek looking for tracks when Sam hollered, "Come, boys, quick." He had found what he supposed the track of a lion. However, it was soon lost. Then we agreed to take different courses, but were all to meet at a certain point. I went up the canyon (for I knew something they did not know), Henry to the left, and Sam to the right. I had not gone very far when my horse gave a sudden and tremendous jump and threw me head down over an embankment. When I recovered sufficiently to see where I was, I found myself about one hundred yards from the spring where I had for the last two days been watching for that lioness. I heard a terrible roar, and springing to my feet, grabbed my gun, pulled the trigger and oh— Well, I started on a dead run, a run for my life, in the direction of the place where we had agreed to meet. I covered a mile in four minutes and did not have time to look back, and my gun, yes, I had left that too. When I came up to the boys, who had been watching the whole performance from the top of a hill, they were about exhausted from laughing, and maybe they did not jeer me. They yelled as if in one voice, "Why didn't you shoot? There is fifty dollars on that animal." They had a heap of fun at my expense, dared me to get my gun, but I was too tired just then to walk down the hill and then I did not need it at that time either. I knew the gun was safe. Next day we all started again for that same poor animal. I let the boys go ahead and secured a few cottontails. After a three-hour walk we were near this famous rock again. We were all thirsty and Sam suggested that we go and get a drink. They knew that there was water there. They hollered to me to join them. I let them go first. They dropped down about the same time, one to remove the grass, the other to wait his turn. They had hardly touched the ground, when, like magic, they arose, left their guns and were making for the house at a two-forty pace. Now it was my turn to laugh. I ha-ha-ed so loud that it brought the family out. My gun was ready, for I expected this, and before I gave up, had shot the lion, lioness and one cub, and trapped the other two cubs. The boys hearing the three shots in succession, and then not seeing me, had concluded that I was shooting from a tree, and the reason I didn't not come home was that the enraged animals were hovering about and I was afraid to come down. After they recovered from their great scare, they had considerable sport imagining me up a treetop.

They were lying resting under a shade tree when I got in sight and had, as they told me, just about got their minds made up to go in search of me, and their guns. Imagine the surprise when they saw me dragging myself along under my heavy burden of the three skins, three guns and two cubs. Well, it would take about six sheets of paper to write their exclamations. Then they said, 'How was it that you ran yesterday and were so brave today?' I replied 'When I was thrown from the horse yesterday, my gun was discharged, and it was the last shell in the repeater. I had forgotten that, and when I pulled the trigger to shoot, realized my situation. There was nothing to do but run. What did you do with a loaded gun? Let's all laugh.' Well, instead of fifty dollars, I got one hundred and fifty, and mother will be here tomorrow night.

It is clear in this essay that Edgar was trying to reassure young Walter that his relocation in San Francisco would ensure a good education. He also beckoned him to return afterward to the paradise of land in which they were both born. Although Edgar's words were scripted for Walter, they were in a sense also for himself. He, of course, was echoing Annie's point of view when she convinced her son of his educational needs. Edgar really did intend to return to the ranch when he grew up. Although he enjoyed living in the city, he enjoyed more so the outdoors and the freedom of ranch life.

Happily, Edgar, Annie, her sister, Walter and his siblings were reunited in the fall of 1905 on Bryant St. in San Francisco. Both families lived together in the huge house. Annie secured a job as a public school teacher and Edgar was enrolled in a nearby public school. Edgar's best pal was Stanley Kelly. The Kellys were staunch Irish descendants, steeped in San Francisco tradition. Stan's grandfather was one of the original founders of Hibernia Bank in the City.

According to Edgar's daughter, Colleen Deach, "Stan was tall, slender, sandy-haired and had a smile that dazzled all. He was gallant, smart and wild as they come. Mrs. Kelly was grateful for my dad's calm."

Then there was a beautiful neighborhood girl named Polly. Colleen said that "Polly may have been an early heartthrob of my father's, but he was vying with his best friend for her affections and it was no contest. Polly was a petite Irish lassie with strawberry blonde hair, a wonderfully soft, kind face and bright blue eyes that bore right through you. She, my dad and Stan were constant companions." Apparently, they both competed over her until eventually Stan won out. He married Polly in 1915 after he graduated from law school. Edgar had lifelong affection for the Kellys.

Colleen said, "When I knew the Kellys, they were married and had two kids of their own, Stan, Jr. and Polly. Uncle Stan was a judge, and they lived in Burlingame. It was a place we all loved to visit. My dad was always ready for one of Polly's dinners, and Aunty Belinda [Polly's aunt], was my dad's favorite partner for an Irish jig."

Edgar was surrounded with the family and close friends whose companionship he craved. Everything was coming together in his world until April 18, 1906, when it literally fell apart.

# 4.
# The San Francisco Earthquake

The McCormicks and the Kennedys were jostled awake at 5:18 A.M. by a violent shaking of the earth. Every other family in San Francisco and the outer regions was shaken by the same tremors. The noise was deafening, and the very structure of the house was in jeopardy of collapsing. Many buildings succumbed. Families poured out into the streets for fear of being crushed by their own homes.

If the giant quake wasn't enough, it was followed by what some say was even more devastating, the fire that ensued. With no water main to fight the fire, impetuous Edgar, 20 days before his 16th birthday, volunteered to help fight the flames. He, Stan Kelly and a bevy of other San Franciscans fought bravely with the only weapons they had, buckets of water from the bay. It was one of the many "bucket brigades," hundreds more like them also attempted to extinguish the fire. Unfortunately, it was like fighting the Devil himself. The fire spread over the next few days with reckless abandon, wherever the winds blew.

Young Edgar had no idea that thirty years later he would appear in a talking movie entitled *San Francisco* which commemorated the disaster and that he would be portraying the sheriff. There was little to dream about at this point: the fires, earthquakes, human suffering, and the problem of how to survive to the next day, were the only things in the minds of the people of the city.

It was too much of a strain for the San Francisco Police Department to try to protect the whole city. The Army and the National Guard, with orders to "shoot to kill" if they witnessed any looting, were called in for emergency duty. The three mentioned entities split up the city into 1/3 section each, to establish their presence. By now, the fire department's only weapon to stymie the path of the flames was dynamite. With their limited resources, all efforts were concentrated on Nob Hill, where the mansions of the rich were.

The people "south of the slot" were helpless to contain the fire. It incinerated every wood building in its path to cinders. The only exception was the nearby San Francisco Mint on 5th and Mission. The fortified-mortared building was constructed in 1874 to resist fire and was successful in protecting its contents from harm. It did not necessarily discourage some opportunists from trying to force their way inside to steal the gold and paper money. Many were shot on sight, no questions asked.

Exhausted families had no other shelter than pup tents supplied to them at various parks in the City. With an estimated 300,000 people suddenly homeless, hordes of people stayed at Golden Gate Park. Many South of the Slot dwellers had to suffice by staying in the open area of South Park. Others left the city to Oakland for temporary shelter.

Then there were the many visitors who, the night before, slept in the plentiful hotel rooms in the city. One well-documented celebrity was the great Italian tenor, Enrico Caruso. The previous night, the great singer performed with the Metropolitan Opera Company at the Grand Opera House singing *Carmen*. Sitting in a box listening was famed actor John Barrymore.[4] "The Great Profile," as he was later known, was still in his tuxedo from the prior evening when he finally retired in his bed at the St. Francis Hotel. When the earthquake hit, it threw Barrymore across the room and ultimately out on the streets. Allegedly, Diamond Jim Brady, who witnessed this, would forever tell the story of how Barrymore "dressed for an earthquake."

Caruso was lucky to escape alive, reluctant as he was to leave his fine clothes and liquor. The "Great One" was just another survivor wandering the streets hoping to get out. The great tenor vowed never to return to San Francisco for the rest of his life.

Everyone was in shock at what happened. Some folks remembered the warnings that San Francisco would suffer the wrath of God for being a hot bed of sin and vice. For this modern city of Sodom and Gomorra, it was surely divine punishment. But if that was so, then why was St. Patrick's church demolished? And why was part of the Barbary Coast with its gambling, red lights and alcohol spared? None of this made sense to anyone in San Francisco, and it really didn't matter anyway. Just being alive was blessed enough.

---

4.   *Damned in Paradise* The Life of John Barrymore

Many thousands of people lost their lives in the fire and earthquake. Some people were never to be heard from again. Such was the case of George Barker, their former boarder at 511 Bryant Street. His daughter, little Irene, was spared despite suffering the loss of an eye from an unrelated accident. Annie nurtured and took care of her as her own. Without any formalities or legal papers, Annie adopted Irene as part of the family. Edgar was overjoyed to have a sister. He adored her for the rest of his life.

Seemingly the entire city was leveled in the destruction. With its density, the Chinatown section suffered the most damage and fatalities, but the neighborhoods "South of the Slot" suffered the second most in the city. The whole area burned to the ground. There was nothing left of the houses on Bryant St. to salvage, even the birth home of Jack London went up in flames.

Jack London was commissioned by the *San Francisco Chronicle* to cover the earthquake and its aftermath for the local paper. The building that housed the *Chronicle* also suffered major damage but London and other reporters were able to wire their stories to other destinations for print.

Every able-bodied person helped with the rebuilding of San Francisco. Whether it was cleaning up the debris, tending to the wounded or distributing food, the inhabitants impressed the world with their resolve. Edgar was already talented as a carpenter, but he learned masonry and assisted with anything needed. He had a strong back and was getting stronger.

The schools were in shambles. Nevertheless, some teachers took to educating their students outside. Thousands of people left the city in the aftermath, but the Kennedys did not. There was work to be done, so much work that Edgar convinced Annie that he didn't need to continue his formal education. Annie couldn't argue with him this time, besides, she could always school him informally at home. Edgar was a ready pupil and thirsted for knowledge at every opportunity from then on. Education was not something to be taken for granted; it was a privilege. Whatever books Edgar could get his hands on, he read.

Edgar had just turned 16 and was now mature beyond his years. He had seen and experienced things most people couldn't even imagine. He was now the main breadwinner at home. His carpentry skills were much sought after, but none so much as the owners of the famous "Cliff House" on the beach in San Francisco. Edgar helped rebuild the roof of the landmark building.

Another celebrated event in San Francisco was the building of a new modern Dreamland Athletic Club walking distance from the Cliff House. It contained a health spa and two swimming pools, one with fresh water and one with salt water piped in from the Pacific Ocean. It is unknown if Edgar helped with the construction of the Dreamland Athletic Club, but the facility would be very important to him in a few years.

The Kennedys and McCormicks now depended on each other even more than before. They moved to a couple of different addresses in the City, but in 1909 they eventually settled at 2156-2158 Market Street between Church and Dolores. The dwelling was a tenement structure, three stories high with a basement, and brand new in 1907. The 1910 census identified Margaret McCormick as the head of the house at the above address. Living in the same dwelling was Annie, Edgar and Irene, as well as Margaret's children Samuel, Walter and Marie.

The whole city rebuilt public buildings, houses, schools, churches and places of entertainment. San Francisco had always been a Mecca for live theatre on its many stages, but there were also concerts in the parks. Edgar's large appearance contradicted his sweet Irish tenor singing voice. Edgar sang whenever the opportunity presented itself. For the next few years, Edgar made weekend jaunts to San Jose, Oakland, Berkeley and communities around the San Francisco Bay to sing the songs of the day, mostly from the chorus.

# 5.
# Show Business Start:
# An Irish Tenor

In February of 1909, the San Rafael weekly newspaper, *The Marin Journal*, announced that "Edgar Kennedy a former San Rafael lad had left to New York City to study grand opera singing." This serious study most likely took some serious money to finance.

The time Edgar spent in New York was apparently short-lived. According to an interview Edgar gave the *New York Times* in 1936, Edgar started in show business as a singer in an amusement park chorus in Oakland in 1909 (Idora Park). Later in life, he never talked to the press about his formal opera training. Edgar always downplayed his singing ability, saying that he "couldn't carry a tune." Edgar rarely brought up this part of his life to the Hollywood publicists, interviewers, or even his offspring. Suffice to say Edgar never made a living as a grand opera singer.

Edgar had the opportunity to take in Broadway shows of the day. One such show made its debut on 1-25-09 at the Broadway Theatre, *A Stubborn Cinderella*, and starred a young man named John Barrymore. This play would later become instrumental to Edgar.

When Edgar returned home from his singing lessons, he was hired by Ferris Hartman who was directing opera and comic operettas at Idora Park in Oakland. Hartman was the former director of opera at the Tivoli vaudeville house.

Although Idora Park was just across San Francisco Bay, most San Franciscans shunned it. They considered Oakland a rural community and certainly not on a par with the rich theatre tradition that San Francisco offered. That all changed after the San Francisco Earthquake. Since virtually every theatre had been destroyed, if one wanted top notch entertainment, Idora Park in Oakland offered it.

Idora Park was built in 1903 and was located between 56th and 58th Streets, from Telegraph to Broadway. Unfortunately it was torn down in

1929, but in its prime, Idora Park was hailed as the second-best amusement park in the country, after Coney Island. On the 17 acres, there was a large zoo, a scenic mini-railroad, a swimming pool, a carousel, a giant figure 8 roller coaster and a roller skating rink that was described as the "largest west of Chicago." Most important for Edgar was the big open-air amphitheatre and a second wooden structure that featured opera performances.

Described by the *Grizzly Bear* of September 1913: "Oakland's famous pleasure park is only a 30-minute ferry ride from San Francisco and has proven to be the Mecca of pleasure seekers in central Californian. The big amphitheatre is the only theatre of its kind in the United States where a season of 20 weeks of standard musical comedy can be given in the open air by a company of star singers and comedians. The stage is equipped to handle the most ambitious productions, and the audiences are accommodated in a big auditorium. The auditorium has been made comfortable by a great canopy, which comprises the greatest single stretch of canvas erected for such a purpose in the State." By 1913 Idora Park even had a structure to show "moving pictures."

There were many performances of Gilbert and Sullivan plays, including *The Mikado* and *The Pirates of Penzenze*, and also Victor Herbert operettas, along with visiting world-renowned singers from New York, Italy and other places. Edgar performed in many of these as part of the chorus.

According to a column from the *Berkley Daily Gazette* of 2-4-43 ("So We're Told" by Hal Johnson): "The big wooden opera house which featured the park was filled at every performance when the great operas were sung by all-star casts with best seats selling for a dollar and no tax. Comic opera was presented the rest of the park season. Manager Bert York booked the best musical talent for Idora. In order to bring some of the larger opera companies here, he had to arrange bookings between New York and California. After appearing in Idora Park, the opera companies filled engagements in Los Angeles and Portland and Seattle."

In 1910, now 20 years old, this strapping specimen of a man was garnering attention in a different field: boxing. Some people speculate on Edgar's growing up in the predominant Irish section of town and surmise that he had to be good with his fists to defend himself, especially with an Irish tenor voice. Such a scenario would have undoubtedly drawn attention of the local bullies wanting to take advantage of the situation. If Edgar had been lured into fighting, given his size and grace, it is with complete conjecture that Edgar was victorious on the streets more times than he lost.

During this era, San Francisco was considered to be the fight capital of the United States. It was the birthplace of former boxing champion "Gentleman Jim" Corbett, who reigned as heavyweight champion of the world in the 1890s. Edgar was a student of the sport and had plenty of chances to watch organized bouts in the twenty-plus athletic clubs in the city. Jack London wrote many articles in the *Chronicle* about the professional fights of the day. Edgar joined the San Francisco Athletic Club at Sixth and Shipley in the South-of-Market District. He worked out in the ring as often as he could when he was in town and in between performing commitments.

In 1908 a black man by the name of Jack Johnson knocked out Australian Tommy Burns to become the new boxing champion of the world. Some sportswriters fanned the flames of bigotry that were already present. Professional gamblers and spectators alike became obsessed with replacing Johnson with a white champion. Throughout the nation there was a cry for a "Great White Hope" to emerge.

In 1910 a $192,000 purse lured James J. Jeffries, a retired undefeated champion, to fight Johnson. It was originally scheduled for San Francisco, but just two weeks before the bout, it was abruptly moved to Reno,

Nevada. Jack London covered the fight in detail for the *Chronicle*. Johnson won the bout.

Edgar continued his singing commitment by touring with various musical troupes. The travel was exciting, but he was not getting the good parts, being relegated to the chorus only.

There was a brand-new form of entertainment for the masses that was expanding in 1911. The flickers were now projected onto screens where many people at once could enjoy the entertainment.

Like most small show business operations on the stage, actors quite frequently performed multiple jobs in preparation for a show. With Edgar's carpentry skills, he was often called upon to design and construct backdrop sets.

Movie studios during the era of 1911 were spread along the eastern seaboard. There were only a couple of film studios in all of Los Angeles at that time, one of which was the Selig Polyscope Company whose main studio was in Chicago.

In December of 1911 Edgar was in Chicago as part of the chorus for the musical *A Stubborn Cinderella*. It was performed at the College Theatre at Sheffield and Webster Avenue. This is the city in which the play originally opened on December 16, 1908 at the Princess Theatre.

The play contained eleven songs, including: "I've Lost My Heart But I Don't Care," "If They'd Only Let Poor Adam's Rib Alone," "Don't Be Cross With Me," "Don't Teach Me to Swim Alone."

Traveling in early musical troupe, circa early 1910s (Edgar center)
(Courtesy Kennedy Family)

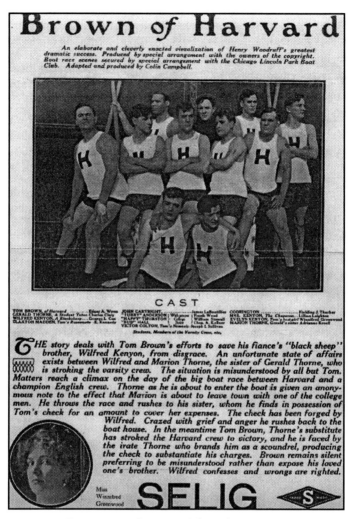

First screen role, 1911. Selig Polyscope Co.
(Courtesy Academy Arts & Sciences)

It was during this run that Edgar went to Selig's Chicago studio seeking out a part. With his bulging muscles and carved physique, Edgar was hired to perform in the one-reel short *Brown of Harvard*, as Clayton Maddox.

Edgar portrayed the collegian best friend of the lead character, Tom Brown (played by Edgar G. Wynn). *Brown of Harvard* was Edgar's first credited role in movies. It is possible that Edgar appeared in other Selig films, including those at their Edendale location, as uncredited extras but over the course of the years, few records, or films remain of any Selig product.

Scoop Conlan confirmed in 1934, in his article "They'll Fool You These Boys," Edgar's beginnings with Selig, adding, "After trying the extra list at the old Selig Studio in Edendale with scant success, he walked across the street and pestered Mack Sennett."

Edgar once reminisced that he would do his time in the "bullpen." That's the area where prospective extras would congregate and hope to be chosen as a bit player. They sometimes would receive a dollar a day with a lunch.

He explained years later that a high voice was fine for the chorus, but it rarely generated into leading parts. Edgar said he was always worried that he'd be "fired with that voice of mine." He figured if he broke into movies (which were silent then), his voice wouldn't matter. Stage acting proved to be sporadic, at best, and was unreliable as a steady source of income.

Moviemaking was a mere novelty back then, with no guarantee of a consistent income. Edgar was goal-oriented and was not opposed to hard work, he perceived that professional boxing led to instant fame and fortune.

People had always encouraged Edgar to pursue boxing as an occupation, and not only because of his size. Edgar had always followed the sport and San Francisco was the hotbed of boxing in the country. Edgar was named "Kid Kennedy" during his amateur days.

# 6.
# Boxing

In 1912, Edgar returned home to San Francisco to train for a chance at representing the United States at the Olympic boxing matches later that year. Edgar trained in earnest at the San Francisco Athletic Club. There was special attention given to the big amateur. He was a 6-footer, considered quite large for the day. Anything over 165 pounds was classified as a heavyweight. Edgar was coached by Alec Geggains, a legendary trainer.

The *San Francisco Chronicle* reported on April 24, 1912 that "San Francisco will have its first strictly amateur boxing show in years Saturday afternoon. Phil Wand, who has been handling the details of the show, the purpose of which is to raise funds to send the American team to the Olympic games in Stockholm, made up his pugilistic card last night. The main event will be between Edgar Kennedy of the San Francisco Club and Jim Long of the Olympic Club, two husky heavyweights. They are well known to local followers of pugilistic sport and it may come to pass that a 'white hope' is uncovered." Phil White elaborated, "The boys have all been tried out and have proved that they know how to box. They loom up like a mighty fine array of boxers, and who knows but what another Jimmy Britt, James J. Corbett or other champions may not be developed out of the material?"

The day of the fight finally arrived, April 27, 1912. Saturday morning's paper, *The San Francisco Chronicle,* had headlines updating their readers with details about the Titanic that sunk twelve days earlier. The sport pages reported, "If you want to see some *simon-pure*[5] amateur boxing matches, in which the contestants will be at one another hammer and tongs, take a run out to Coffroth's open air arena, Eighth and Howard Streets this afternoon. Commencing at 2 o'clock, nine rounds will be staged

---

5. *Simon-pure:* A long lost sporting reference to a clean fight or sporting event, usually associated with new or fresh athletes.

under the supervision of the Olympic Club, the proceeds to go to the Olympic Games fund. The main bout of the afternoon will be between James Long of the Olympic Club and Ed Kennedy of the San Francisco Club." General admission was 50 cents while reserve seating was $1.00.

Jimmy Whalen, a boxing columnist for the *Sunday San Francisco Chronicle*, wrote about the fight:

> A new 'White Hope' in the burly form of Ed Kennedy of the San Francisco Club (located at 317 6th St.) was brought to the fore at the auspices of the Olympic Club (524 Post St.) yesterday at Coffroth's open-air arena. Kennedy gained a host of admirers by knocking out Jim Long of the Olympic Club in two rounds. Long did not shape up such a formidable gladiator for he looked fat and out of condition; but that Kennedy showed enough ring ability to warrant the prediction that he will give a lot of the heavy-weights in these parts a lot of trouble. In the first round Kennedy pumped in many a straight left to Long's jaw and stomach, and in the second round he dropped his man twice with hard rights to the jaw. The second wallop landed Long flat on the mat and he was out for several minutes.

Joe Murphy of the *San Francisco Call-Bulletin* reported:

> Edgar Kennedy, a medium-sized heavyweight of the San Francisco Club, displayed a flash of class yesterday in the amateur boxing tournament conducted under the auspices of the Olympic club by knocking out Jim Long of the Olympic Club in two rounds in clever fashion. The knockout was of the 18 karat variety, as a right cross to the point turned Long around and he fell face forward on the canvas. There was no doubt that Long would take the count, though it is doubtful if the referee would have allowed the contest to go on had Long regained his feet. The bout did not last two rounds, but there was plenty of action in it while the men were on their feet. Long had the advantage in weight, but Kennedy proved the cleverer and he seemed to carry a finishing wallop in his right

mitt. He seemed to know more about the game, as he took the lead from the outset and near the end of the first round he had Long decidedly groggy. Kennedy kept pegging his left hand into Long's face and body, and when the opportunity presented itself, he would whip across his right hand, and it usually found its mark. Long was game and never flinched under punishment, but fought back gamely and tried hard to score a decisive blow. He seemed to be up against it, as Kennedy seemed able to protect himself.

Edgar later accepted a gold timepiece from the Olympic Club that was engraved: "To Edgar Kennedy, the P.A.A. [Pacific Athletic Association] amateur heavyweight champion 4-26-12." The watch had the distinct flying "O" insignia of the Olympic Club. The date was significant for even though Edgar won the match on April 27; he had the date engraved for the day before, his 22nd birthday. Edgar wore that watch proudly for the rest of his life.

Another event was unfolding across town in the theatre district. *The San Francisco Chronicle* announced:

> **"London comedians lead new bill at Empress. Sparkling Farce Returns to Amuse Devotees of Vaudeville"**: Fred Karno's London comedians, with Charles Chaplin in the leading role, returned to the Empress Theater yesterday afternoon as the headline attraction on a sparking bill, with a new farce entitled, 'The Wow Wows.' It is based on the experience of a camper, whose stingy propensities bring him into disfavor with his fellow campers.

Edgar didn't realize it at the time, but in another two years, he would be working in motion pictures with Chaplin. The understudy to Charlie Chaplin during that period was Stan Laurel. He would also be a significant player to Edgar's career in the late 1920s.

Another account of the same boxing match was written by Bill Henry of the *Los Angeles Times*, 8-15-37, some 25 years after, when Edgar was a famous film star.

Edgar learned to box up in San Francisco and won the Pacific Coast heavyweight championship in his one and only amateur fight. They prepped him at the Olympic Club for two hours before they ever let him fight and in the course of that time Ed became an astoundingly clever boxer. He won the title in his lunch hour as he had a job driving for a boss who didn't think much of fighting and wouldn't let him off work to do his scrapping. When Ed got a chance to fight for the amateur title, he just arranged to take his lunch hour at the time scheduled for the bout and hustled over to the arena; knocked out his opponent, collected a handsome gold watch and the title and hustled back to work. Next time you see him ask to see his trophy of his proudest possession.

The Olympic Club accepted Edgar into their membership after his successful bout. Edgar pondered his future as a boxer. He qualified to continue in the Olympic Club's goal in promoting a local representative for the Olympic games. That would entail Edgar to remain an amateur until after Stockholm. It would also mean that in any ensuing bout, Edgar would only qualify for a medal, trophy certificate or another watch. There were slicker methods in which the manager of his fighter would sometimes resell an item to obtain cash, but that was not good enough for a future heavyweight champion of the world. Edgar had the size, speed and savvy to excel in professional boxing.

Many people became interested in Edgar's potential, not excluding the local gamblers. Al Aren became Edgar's manager. His goal was to take his young charge slowly along to build confidence and experience.

To ease the pressure and expectations of his first professional fight, Aren took Edgar up to Sacramento to fight under the assumed name of Bob Mason. The strategy was simple; if "Mason" lost, no one would be able to associate him with Kennedy. However, if "Mason" won he would proclaim his true name.

The bout was originally scheduled between two African-American fighters: Rufus Cameron, the "Black Bear Cat," from Los Angeles, against Joe Collier of Sacramento for four rounds in the preliminary heavyweight scrap. "Both of these boys weigh over 190 and have terrific kicks," said *The Sacramento Bee* on May 20, 1912.

For reasons unknown, Collier was unable to make the bout. Kennedy was inserted under the name of Mason and fought his first professional fight on May 20, 1912.

On May 21, 1912, *The Sacramento Union* wrote, "Rufus Cameron, colored, lost to Bob Mason [Kennedy] in a hard hitting slugging match that was more comical than scientific. Mason was somewhat fat but was a surprise, and shows class. Cameron tried hard, but tired."

*The Sacramento Bee* reported in a more matter-of-fact style, "In the heavyweight preliminary Bob Mason, white, won from Rufus Cameron, colored. Cameron looked like the winner until the fourth round and then a few blows made him so weak he could scarcely stand up."

Edgar returned to San Francisco and, on August 9, was pitted for a "four-round spat" against Al Williams. *The San Francisco Chronicle* observed,"They are looking for great things from big Ed Kennedy, the local giant who won the recent Olympic Club tournament. He is to start against Al Williams of Cleveland, who Spider Kelly says is the best white hope in the business. Kennedy is rather shy on experience, but he is clever and has a fair punch, and besides he is willing to take a chance. Williams has met Flynn and Stewart and other notables and knows the game thoroughly."

The next day the *San Francisco Chronicle* showcased the results:

### KENNEDY SHOWS BEST OF HEAVY-WEIGHTS AT DREAMLAND

Before a capacity audience at Dreamland last night, Ed Kennedy, former Olympic Club Member and amateur heavy-weight of the Pacific Coast, demonstrated his superiority over Al Williams, Spider Kelly's white hope in four rounds of fast boxing. Kennedy showed the making of a fighter. He took a lot of punishment, but came back strong and delivered blows that put Williams a shade to the bad. Although scheduled as one of the minor events on the Observatory Club's card, the Kennedy-Williams mill proved the star attraction. Referee Bert McCullough's decision giving Kennedy the fight was well received.

The *Chronicle* further editorialized the fight in their 8-11-12 edition:

Eight 'hopes' appeared at Dreamland last Friday night, some of them white and some black, but the only boy who gave any promise was Ed Kennedy. The former Olympic Club champion has had two professional fights and he gives promise of a good future, if properly handled. Kennedy is green when it comes to the ring game, but he is naturally clever, quick for a big man and seems fast to pick up things he should know. He may never make a champion, but champions have had worse beginnings than this game lad.

One uncredited sports newspaper article made this observation:

If Kennedy can keep up the lick he has set he is bound to become a very popular heavyweight. He is far and away cleverer than any of the heavyweights that have shown around here in some time, and many of the fans who have seen him in action are of the opinion that he will be a top-notcher within a year if he is taken along the right trail.

Alec Greggains, one of the greatest boxing instructors in the world, was Kennedy's mentor while the latter was learning his trade, and it can be said for Kennedy that he was just as apt a pupil as Greggains was a teacher. He's one of the few white heavyweights we have seen in years who really knows anything about boxing.

Kennedy was gaining quite a local following. He next participated in a bout at the Dreamland Rink on August 30, 1912. Rebuilt after the 1906 earthquake, it was considered to be the Madison Square Garden of boxing in San Francisco. Promoters claimed it had the seating capacity of five thousand on the main floor and another two thousand could be accommodated in the gallery. It featured a return match between Kennedy and Williams. Williams won the return match.

Reported *The San Francisco Chronicle*:

The surprise of the night was the fashion in which Williams came back to drop Kennedy. The last time they met Kennedy went about as he pleased. Last night Williams outpointed Kennedy for the fore part of the round, although Kennedy worked in a couple of good lefts. Finally Williams worked Kennedy into a corner and swung a hard right flush to the jaw. Kennedy went to the floor like a log, stood up at the count of nine, was handed another punch that sent him reeling against the ropes and then Referee Hayes, assisted by the police, stopped the bout. Kennedy was still unconscious when he was taken to his corner.

Although Williams checked the upward spurt of Kennedy, the latter isn't at all discouraged over the defeat and is anxious to fight his way back to the place which he formerly occupied. A return match with Williams is what he is after, as he feels that it was simply one of those unfortunate haymakers which occasionally crops up in a boxer's career that caused his unexpected defeat at the hands of Kelly's fighter.

During the rest of 1912, Edgar concentrated on his new boxing profession which took him all over California. That is not to say that Edgar won every bout. He suffered a few loses, but he gained knowledge with each match. Edgar was taught boxing scientifically. As a result, most of the street fighters he fought against were simply outclassed. The most used word to describe Kennedy back in this era was "clever." It was the highest form of compliment given to any boxer.

On 1-25-13, *The San Francisco Chronicle* reported on another local match: "The semi-windup will bring together Ed Kennedy and Sailor Schaefer. The latter hails from Vallejo and will make his first appearance here. He is a likely looking chap with a hard punch and a reputation for gameness. Kennedy up to the time that he met defeat at the hands of Williams, was going along nicely, and it was thought with experience he would develop into a real white hope."

The next day the same paper wrote, "Heavy-weight Ed Kennedy was a winner over Mark O'Donnell. The bout wasn't a particularly fast one, but Kennedy hammered O'Donnell into submission with body punches. The Portlander was about all in when the last gong sounded."

Edgar's manager lined up a fight in Taft, California, just outside of Bakersfield. Taft, in 1912, was an oil town with big husky men maintaining the massive pumping machines and refineries. The gruesomely long days were not for the weak. The menfolk of the town loved their boxing

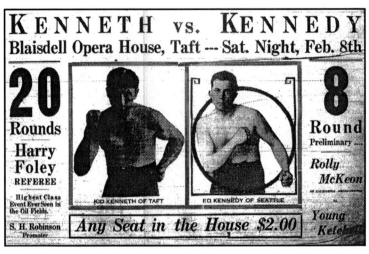

Kenneth vs. Kennedy

and when Saturday night came around, most of them were ringside for the entertainment. Of course nearly everyone placed bets on who they hoped would be the winner.

In January, Edgar had easily won over his last opponent in San Francisco in six rounds. By this time Edgar had quite a few professional bouts under his belt. Edgar's manager decided to take him out of town and pile up some easy wins for his professional record. He also decided to refer to Edgar in more colorful terms: Ed "Lightning" Kennedy. Allegedly, his left hand was so quick it was like a lightning bolt, and "strikes but once."

Whomever Edgar was to fight, it was supposed to be easy pickings. It was arranged for Edgar to fight the local favorite "Kid Kenneth," a big husky oil worker. There was plenty of early publicity for "Kenneth vs. Kennedy," in what was scheduled as a 20-round fight Saturday, February 8, 1913.

Kid Kenneth trained at Robinson's on the floor above a bar of the same name. Edgar trained at Wood's Gym. Edgar's reported training routine included running ten miles each morning and afternoon. He also sparred with three different boxers for a total of seven rounds daily.

## Can Whip Him Says Kennedy

Ed Kennedy is hard at work training for the 20-round go with Kid Kenneth on Saturday. Ten miles on the road each morning and each afternoon; after about an hour's work with gym apparatus, he does the mitts for a three-round go with Ikey Cohen; two rounds with Kid Rose and two rounds with Young Ketchell.

Kennedy told a Driller man that he realizes that he is up against a tough proposition and consequently is taking no chances. " I can whip him though," said Kennedy.

The Kenneth-Kennedy twenty round match at the Blafsdell was perhaps a disappointment to the crowd of fans who crowded the house on Saturday night and at the same time it proved to be more or less of a revelation. Ed Kennedy is a good boy and an exceptionally clever boxer but Kid Kenneth proved himself so far superior as a ring general that Kennedy didn't have even a look in. If Kenneth would allow Kennedy to box him, Kennedy would stand a good show of winning on points, but Kenneth was too foxy and made Kennedy fight and fight hard. In the first round Kenneth had his man groggy with a succession of rights and lefts to the face and considering Kennedy's dazed condition had an opportunity to knock him out before the gong sounded. In the second round, Kennedy succeeded in keeping away and through clever boxing and blocking made things about even for the round. The third and last round were all Kenneth's and after chasing his man all around the ring landed a right to the jaw and Kennedy went down like an ox and after the count of nine was carried to his corner still unconscious.

Under the title "Post Mortems," Kid Kenneth said, "Kennedy is a good man and better than I thought; he has a punch and is a clever boxer. He is a better man, by far, than big Al Kaufman. I managed to get him in the first round otherwise the fight would have lasted longer."

Edgar said, "The best man won and I want to say that Kenneth is the cleverest man I have met; he is a clean fighter and a good one in every way and I am proud to have him as a friend even if he did 'clean me' good and plenty tonight. I believe he would stand a good chance with McCarty and I consider it no disgrace to be whipped by a man like Kenneth."

Years later in an interview with the *New York Times'* A.H. Weiler in 1942, Edgar reminisced about that fight. "I thought I'd kill the guy, but as it turned out, between the second and fourth rounds I was on my back eight times before he put me away. He was the most gentlemanly fighter I ever knew, he would knock you down, then wait in his corner till you got up, then knock you down again." This was a far cry from other boxers of the era. Jack Dempsey, for instance, was known for hovering over his prey once he knocked them down. He would taunt his opponent and challenge him to get up so he could finish them off. The rules for retreating to their corner after a knockdown did not occur until the 1920s.

This was Edgar's last professional bout, although he always had boxing to fall back on. In later years, Edgar told stories of when he was stranded in cities where musical shows he was performing in folded. Often as a preliminary to the main fight, local boxing arenas would welcome challengers to box a professional for a round. If the challenger defeated the professional or even lasted the round, he could be eligible to win a cash prize up to $50.

On 7-18-16, *The Los Angeles Times* announced:

> A monster benefit will be held at Jack Doyle's Vernon arena tonight for the widow and children of the late Rudy Unholz, one of the game's bravest boxers ever known. All the boxers and wrestlers in southern California have volunteered their services free of charge. Charlie Murray of the Keystone has charge of the show and every cent will go to the widow and children.
>
> The boxing end of the programme will bring back many an old-time boxer. Among those who will climb back out of the shadows of old Vernon like George Memsic, Len Lauder, Danny Webster and Al Kaufman. There will be other boxers, too, such as Kid Dalton and *Ed Kennedy*. There will also be a battle royal—one of those old-time kinds that used to open Uncle Tom McCarey's shows. Charlie Chaplin has consented to referee one of the bouts, so the management says.

# 7.
# Mack Sennett's College of Comedy

It was now Sunday, February 13, 1912. Edgar was nursing a black eye and was hurting from the beating he received at the hands of Kid Kenneth. He realized the odds were slim for him to be successful in professional boxing. He pondered his fate as he left town to go 100 miles south to Los Angeles, but not for boxing.

There are many versions of how Edgar broke into the movies. In the *Chicago Daily News*, on March 29, 1937, Clark Rodenbach gave one, after interviewing Edgar: "It was in 1912 that this big fellow (then a pugilist), with a magnificent black eye from a long fight walked into a Hollywood studio and demanded a job."

Also in 1937, Harry Morrison of the *Indianapolis Times* interviewed Edgar:

> A high tenor voice and a handy pair of dukes drove and helped Edgar Kennedy, slow-burn artist, into the movies. "I was the romantic lead in a road company," he said, "then I graduated to chorus boy, and I mean graduated. You got paid every week. The only trouble was I couldn't be very romantic with that voice, so I decided to get into the movies. You didn't need a voice then. All you needed was to be crazy."
>
> Mr. Kennedy says he got that way from fighting; he was amateur heavyweight champion of the Pacific Coast in 1912. He turned professional and got knocked out. "I had a little money, so I went over to the Mack Sennett lot and hit him for a job. I asked him once a day for five days and didn't get anywhere. The next day I got him by the lapel and told him I was going to bother him once a day for two years. He said: 'what can you do?' And I said, for one thing, I can lick any-

body on this lot." The next day Mr. Kennedy fought three electricians, knocked them all out and got a job.

From Roger Carroll's article/interview in *Motion Picture Magazine,* August of 1942, entitled "Looking Back with a Keystone Kop," Edgar entertained his reading audience with this version:

"I went on the stage in 1909 with the ambition to be a great dramatic actor. But my voice, what there was of it, was pretty high. I was working under an awful handicap. Every time I got fired, I always had to wonder if I'd ever be able to get another job—with that voice. But finally I saw a possible solution to my problem. 'Now if I could get in the movies,' I said to myself, 'it wouldn't matter what my voice was like, audiences couldn't hear me.' So I came down to Los Angeles, and started wandering around with some actors who seemed to know where all the studios were." [In those days, the studios were scattered all over East Los Angeles, Hollywood was just a hick suburb.] "One day we were out on Alessandro Street in Edendale and I said, 'What's this studio we're going past, and why are we going past it?' They said, 'Oh, that's the Mack Sennett Studio. It's a new company, and we don't know whether they'll pay off or not. We aren't going to bother look-

Keystone/Sennett Studios
(Author's collection)

ing there.' But I figured that if other guys were staying away from Sennett's, that was one place where there might be a chance for a willing guy like me. So I sneaked back, walked in, and applied for a job."

An interview by Harry Mines of the *Los Angeles Illustrated Daily*, on 9-19-32, revealed: "Edgar had always wanted to be the heavyweight champion of the world. But three years [sic] of socks and more socks in the jaw and black eyes had sort of robbed Mr. Kennedy of his enthusiasm. He decided to look for something more peaceful. So he arrived at Sennett's where he met

At Keystone
(Courtesy Kennedy Family)

Fred Mace, one of Sennett's assistants, who told him to come back the following morning with his boxing gloves. Edgar obliged, and bright and early the next day he found himself lined up to battle 19 sinister looking mugs, invited by Mr. Mace for the occasion. After doing damage to the fourth mug, Mace and Kennedy came to an agreement whereby the former was to become manager with a guarantee of $15.00 a week. Mace used the fighting contract for publicity purposes by challenging all famous heavyweights, including Jack Johnson, Jess Willard and Young Al Kaufman."

It was this latter interview that was probably closest to the truth, if for no other reason that it was one of the earliest versions given by Edgar, himself. Edgar certainly would have included Fred Mace out of respect, later columnists might not have recognized the name, for Mace had died in New York City on 2-21-17 at the age of thirty-eight. Fred Mace was one of the actors that Sennett had taken west with him from the Biograph Studios (New York) in 1912. Edgar had always referred to Mace as "the star" of Sennett's during the early days.

With Edgar's boxing prowess and Mace's influence, Edgar was signed on as a stock actor. Coy Watson, Jr., who had worked at the Keystone Studios as a child actor (and authored the book *The Keystone Kid*), remembered hearing a story from his dad. The Watson family lived right next door to the studio and Mr. Watson often was hired at the lot. Coy, Jr. elaborated: "Keystone was a small company back then [1913] and my father would come home and tell the family about the new people when they were hired." Coy, Jr. remembers his father telling him later in life when "Ed was hired as a stock actor, he was allowed to share a dressing room with another comedian. That was a big deal to the actors who made it into stock." Proud of his new promotion, Edgar jokingly went around the lot that day like a big shot saying "you can call me *Mister* Kennedy now." Coy, Jr. said that his dad liked Edgar, "he was a good guy."

According to the Roger Carroll interview, Edgar received a big increase in salary. "The pay was munificent: $3.00 a day. After a while, I even got a guarantee of five day's work at $3.00 a day. That was really something. When I got that, I jumped off the end of the Venice pier or did anything else they asked me to do. In the beginning, they cast me as a comedy heavy, with a false mustache hiding my broad Irish pan. They didn't think of me as a comedian at all. I became one by accident. I overemphasized the drama a bit—knocking myself out, trying to be an actor. And people laughed. So Sennett said, 'From now on, you're a comic.'"

There is one more version from Mack Sennett, himself, that might have relevance as to how Edgar broke into the movies. It is not as glamorous a story. According to Sennett's autobiography, *The King of Comedy*, Sennett was one-third owner with Charles O. Bauman and Adam Kessel, forming the Keystone Comedies in 1912. The migration west of movie studios wasn't only because of the sunlight and cheap land, it was because Thomas Edison invented a camera and had a patent on the use of it. Movie companies were forced to rent from his company until the patents company trust was challenged in 1917.

> So far as Kessel and Bauman and Mack Sennett were concerned, this merely meant that we had to become bootleggers. Any time we were shooting, the Patents Com-

pany might break us up and take our camera away. We posted guards.

I'll have to explain the prizefighters. I had the lot jumping with gentlemen who were quick with their dukes as my answer to Thomas A. Edison. The patent companies headed by Edison, and including Vitagraph, Biograph, Thanhouser, Kalem, and Selig, had all the legitimate motion-picture cameras tied up tighter than an alimony settlement dictated by Greg Bautzer. Their snoops, spies, detectives, and deputy sheriffs sought every opportunity to seize my bootlegged cameras, so I protected the company the best I could by putting up some professional fists. They all considered themselves actors.

Sennett reminisced in a very entertaining way how out of work vaudevillians, boxers and circus clowns found their way into his study and found work. While that statement may be true, one has to be careful not to swallow wholehartedly all his colorful claims. Sennett said he always had the idea since the Biograph days of using policemen as the foil for his comedies. Sennett claimed cops were the ultimate authority figures and thus would get the biggest laughs if an errant pie found their face. He said this concept gave birth to the Keystone Kops, complete with a wild chase ending.

Sennett was not the first to introduce cops as authority figures or as comedians. Circus clowns, since before the turn of the century, used comic policemen in their skits. As early as 1909 the French had already utilized the chase and cops in mass pursuit. Sennett claimed that Mabel Normand threw the first custard pie on film at Ben Turpin in 1913. Unfortunately, Mr. Sennett had to rely on his memory of events more than 40 years prior to his 1956 autobiography. The first pie thrown in a Keystone film *A Noise from the Deep*. Fatty Arbuckle is credited with the inspiration of the gag and the tossing of the custard-baked delicacy.

Ben Turpin, he of the crossed eyes and neck like a giraffe, wasn't hired by Sennett until 1916. Turpin already had years of experience in the movies, most notably working with Chaplin at the Essannay Studios during 1915. This didn't stop Sennett from claiming to have "discovered" Turpin while the comedian was a janitor. Turpin took a pie in the face as early as 1909 in "Mr. Flip."

Mack Sennett would make one think that The Keystone Kops was an idea of his that was a full-blown comedy concept with an immediate impact. In Sennett's autobiography he named "the seven original Keystone Kops" as:

1. Georgie Jesky
2. Mack Riley
3. Charlie Avery
4. Edgar Kennedy
5. Slim Summerville
6. Bobby Dunn
7. Hank Mann

It must be mentioned that both Mann and Sennett collaborated to compile this list, strictly by memory. The fact that they were listed in Sennett's autobiography has served as "proof" to its legitimacy. Authors quote this resource whenever the original Keystone Kops are mentioned. There were so many Kops over the years, that probably no two people could come up with an all-inclusive list.

The above seven indeed all appeared as Kops, but never at the same time in any movie. Author Gene Fowler, in his 1934 biography of Mack Sennett, *Father Goose*, was equally colorful describing the Keystone comedies and the original Keystone Kops. Fowler wrote that after producing a "masterpiece" of 750 feet of film entitled *The Grand Army of the Republic*, Sennett could now afford the luxury of an automobile. Once purchased, he was "arrested for speeding," but the District Attorney squared matters for him. This apparently was the impetus needed, for, according to Fowler, he claimed Sennett announced he was going to create a comedy police force. He appointed Ford Sterling Chief. The rest of the "original" Keystone flatfeet were: Billy Hauber, Billy Gilbert, Slim Summerville, Bobby Dunn, Charles Avery and Charlie Parrott.

The Fowler list is even further off than Sennett's, which is amazing since it was written in 1933. How then does one define "an original" Keystone Kop? This author suggests that anyone in a cop role appearing in a Keystone comedy from 1912-16 qualifies as an original. In 1916, the Keystone studios were no more, having merged into Triangle-Keystone Comedies.

Any comedy produced after that date was, in a sense, a parody of the original Koppers. Even Hal Roach lampooned them, with Will Rogers in a Ford Sterling impersonation. It was done so well in sustained action, that Robert Youngson in his comedy documentary, *Golden Age of Comedy*, included it as an example of the Keystone Kops. The film *Keystone Hotel* is another example where some of the original Kops reprised their roles. Ben Turpin starred, and was supported by Ford Sterling, Chester Conklin, Hank Mann and even Vivian Oakland. The film was released in 1935, some 20 years past the prime era. It is from these two movies, and the later *Hollywood Cavalcade* (1939), that most of the posed stills of the "Keystone Kops" were shot.

Edgar weighed in with this interview for *Motion Picture* magazine (August 1940):

> "Looking Back with a Keystone Kop" Edgar elaborated from memory. "It's hard to remember which were the original five, besides myself. One, I know, was Fred Mace; he was Sennett's big star then. Another was Nick Cogley—he was the original Chief of Police, later succeeded by Ford Sterling. I think Roscoe Arbuckle was in there too. And maybe Eddie Cline. Eddie worked in the butcher shop next door, until we drafted him to be a Kop. Now he's a director.
>
> "There are several top directors—dignified ones, included—who were Keystone Kops when I first knew them. Frank Lloyd, for example, and Wesley Ruggles, and Eddie Sutherland, and William Seiter,* and Mal St. Clair. Charlie Chaplin was a Keystone Kop a few times, but he got star billing whenever he joined the force; he was a 'shabby genteel' Kop, in a class by himself. Wally (Wallace) Beery was a Kop. Any number of great silent day comics started as Kops. Ben Turpin, for instance, and Al St. John, and Chester Conklin, and Hank Mann, and Mack Swain, and Little Billy Gilbert, and James Finlayson, and Lige Conley, and George Jeske, and Slim Summerville, and…well, if you've got all day, I can go on naming 'em all day. There were that many.
>
> "The Kops got underway about 1915 or 1916 [sic]—a year or two before the Bathing Beauties—and for six or seven years Sennett never made a picture without them. They were

*Algy on the Force*, Edgar top left
(Courtesy of Academy of Arts & Sciences)

that popular. They were a constant source of joy to all the
people in the world who like to see cops take bumps."

Edgar made a somewhat revealing comment, in retrospect, about the
Kops. "They would probably be going yet if police departments here and
there hadn't been so sensitive."

The truth is that the Keystone Kops was a slow evolution depicting a
comic force. Often, *Hoffmeyer's Legacy* (12-23-12) is mentioned as the
first appearance of the Keystone Kops. Unfortunately, no print of that
title exists today to verify that claim. Another title that carries that same
claim is *Bangville Police* (4-24-13). In some lists *Hoffmeyer's Legacy* and
*Bangville Police* are listed together as a retitled release. In some existing
filmographies Edgar is credited for being in both. It is doubtful that Edgar
was in *Hoffmeyer's Legacy*, seeing how he was still boxing in San Francisco
during the time of production. In *Bangville Police*, available prints are
clear that the film has only one cop in the whole movie. Fred Mace re-
ceives a phone call at the police station all right, but there is no gaggle of
uniformed cops responding. Instead, town folk of all shapes, sizes and

gender respond to Mabel Normand's frantic phone call. Edgar portrays a farmer armed with a pitchfork.

The most significant aspect about this film is that both Edgar and actress Dot Farley share a scene, albeit a group shot for the ending. Dot Farley, eighteen years in the future, would team up with Edgar to play his mother-in-law in his "Average Man" series. She was only eight years his senior. Author Kalton C. Lahue called her "the ugliest woman in pictures." Dot was on the Sennett lot only until making *Bangville Police*, when she left to make movies for the Albuquerque Film Manufacturing Company.

Farley freelanced during the years at various studios and met up with Edgar again in a Fox Sunshine comedy, *Self Made Lady*. She returned to the Sennett lot in 1920 and was a stand out, particularly when playing with Ben Turpin. As part of her comic repertoire, Dot had perfected crossing her eyes for the cameras whenever a scene called for it. In *A Small Town Idol* (1921), for Sennett, she portrayed Turpin's mother where, naturally, they are both cross-eyed. Interestingly, Ben Turpin was some 13 years Dot Farley's senior.

In *Algy on the Force* (5-13-13) a photograph exists of Edgar dressed in a contemporary policeman's uniform with a few other cops. They are wear-

Keystone Kops in *Clutches of the Gang*. Edgar front center w/ mustache next to Ford Sterling (Chief). Fatty Arbuckle far right
(Courtesy Academy Arts & Sciences)

ing eight-cornered formal hats, not the outdated (even for 1913) high-crowned hats more popular at the turn of the century.

Comic policemen, or rather policemen, put in funny situations became a staple of the Keystone comedies. More and more cops were the butts of the jokes while they plunged off the pier into water, were dragged behind speeding vehicles, fell off cliffs, and were pelted with objects or other indignities. Ever present throughout the comedies were a multitude of death defying acts culminating in a chase of some kind.

As a stock player, Edgar was playing villains, comic heavies, cops and even handsome suitors. Oversized mustaches, face make-up, wigs and other exaggerated features and clothes were expected for character portrayals. Each actor was expected to apply their own makeup. Stock players were supposed to be unrecognizable from one comedy to another, often depicting different characters in the same film.

The Keystone comedies of 1913 produced a prodigious amount of titles on a monthly basis. It was also a time of growing pains and turnover of personnel. Fred Mace left. But Sennett hired an actor he later claimed he discovered, Roscoe "Fatty" Arbuckle. It was nonsense, of course. Arbuckle appeared in movies for Universal and at Selig Polyscope Company periodically from 1909 to April of 1913. Arbuckle's first appearance for Sennett was in *The Gangsters* in May of 1913. Arbuckle soon rose to a favorite at Sennett's by the end of the year.

The comic policemen, later referred to as "The Keystone Kops," were prominently featured *In the Clutches of the Gang* (1-17-14). In this short, the Kops were: Ford Sterling, Edgar Kennedy, Fatty Arbuckle, Al St. John and Hank Mann.

The above comedians all wore what came to be known as the traditional Keystone police uniforms with the high crown hats. They worked as a team, or rather as an *anti*-team, seemingly going in opposite directions at once.

The throwing of pies became a comic staple on the Keystone lot. The throwing of the "first" pie as a historic event was loosely reenacted in a 1939 Fox film called *Hollywood Cavalcade*, about early silent comedies. This sequence in the film was without dialogue and featured Buster Keaton as a Keystone Kop (he never was one). For this feature film, many Sennett alumni made an appearance as a Kop. Edgar was conspicuous by his absence. Edgar Kennedy, in later years, once claimed that he had been pelted by more pies than any other human in the movies.

Slim Summerville
(Courtesy of the Kennedy Family)

Another turning point for the success of the Keystone comedies was when Sennett hired Charlie Chaplin in December of 1913. Sennett was quoted often over the years that when he first hired actors, they had to prove themselves by first being a Keystone Kop. There are no photos or film credits to support that Chaplin ever portrayed a Keystone Kop.[6]

In June of 1914 a landmark film for Edgar was being made on the Sennett lot. It was called *The Knockout*, a Fatty Arbuckle vehicle that he directed himself. In this two-reeler, Fatty was a challenger in the fight ring

6. Chaplin did don a policeman's uniform for Mutual Films in 1916.

against the champion, "Cyclone Flynn." Edgar played it straight (without makeup and thinning, slicked back hair) and gave us a glimpse of what he looked like in prime shape. Naturally, Edgar perfectly portrayed a champion boxer and took comic pratfalls besides.

The referee was played by that up-and-comer Charlie Chaplin. The fight scenes were executed with great comic precision, with the referee frequently the inadvertent victim of numerous blows. After the fight scene, Fatty acquires a gun and fires a never-ending series of shots in any and all directions.

This film was also significant in that it was the film debut of Slim Summerville. This 6-foot 7-inch beanpole usually played the country rube, but, like the other stock actors, he was often called upon to play any kind of character.

Edgar claimed in an interview ("Looking Back at a Keystone Kop") that it was he "who got Slim Summerville into the movies, and it will probably illustrate something about those days to tell you how that came about. The last fight I put on was up in Taft, California—which was where I first laid eyes on Slim. He was a big, lanky country bumpkin, but he had a quick wit. I had been down here about six months, working for Sennett, when I saw Slim in the distance one day, walking along the street. I yelled 'Hey, Slim.' He took one quick look over his shoulder, and started running in the opposite direction. He didn't know what I might be wanting with him and he wasn't staying around to find out. He ducked into the lobby of the hotel, and I trailed him. He was hiding in a phone booth. When I got close, he finally recognized me, and was as glad to see me as I was to see him. I took him to Sennett's and asked to try him out...That's how a lot of people broke into the movies in those days—just walking in and asking for a tryout." Edgar further added, "He was so funny looking with that frame, I wanted to take him back with me and put him in the movies as a Keystone Kop."

Slim Summerville was identified by Mack Sennett as an "original" Keystone Kop although his first role was as a crowd extra in *The Knockout*. It was released on June 11, 1914, a full 16 months after Edgar joined Keystone.

Chaplin made 34 films for Sennett in his only year at that studio. Edgar was in 11 of them:

> *His Favorite Pastime*
> *Cruel, Cruel Love*
> *The Star Boarder*
> *Mabel at the Wheel*

*Twenty Minutes of Love*
*Caught in a Cabaret*
*The Knockout*
*Mabel's Busy Day*
*Tillie's Punctured Romance*
*Getting Acquainted*
*A Film Johnnie*

Sennett continued to crank out comedy shorts to the laugh-starved public. On November 14 in the same year, a landmark in film comedy was established with the release of the first feature comedy film, *Tillie's Punctured Romance*. Charlie Chaplin played the male lead, but was not considered a great enough name for such an investment; the film cost $200,000 to produce. The name of the film was decided after securing stage star Marie Dressler fresh from a popular stage show called *Tillie's Nightmare*. Every contract player Sennett had was in the picture except Fatty Arbuckle, allegedly at the demand of Dressler. Chaplin did not play the little tramp character he was experimenting with; he played a city slicker, a cad reminiscent of the stage melodramas. Surprisingly, it was Chaplin that got the notices from critics and the public. It paved the way for other studios to try and steal Sennett's new star. He eventually went to Essanay studios.

Edgar Kennedy did not play a Kop in *Tillie's Punctured Romance*, although they showed up in force at the end of the Santa Monica Pier. Edgar played it straight as the restaurant owner. Edgar's versatility was his strength. He could play any character as needed.

> You could get a job if you could do anything. And once you got a job, the trick was to be able to do anything.
>
> You might play a Police Chief in one picture and an ordinary cop in the next, or vice-versa. Or you might have to play a crook and a cop in the same picture, with the two of you chasing each other. You might have to put on five or six different make-ups in one day—and there weren't any make-up experts around to help you. You did everything yourself, and how well you did it determined whether or not you got the part. So you became resourceful, or else.

Another thing. They didn't have close-ups then. They hadn't been invented [sic]. You had to figure out broad motions to attract attention to what you were doing. You played every scene as if you were playing to the last row in the balcony...of a theater the size of Radio City Music Hall. Those were the days when all the tricks of scene stealing were developed.

We didn't have any gag-writers. All of us were our own gagmen. And another thing. We didn't have any scripts to go by. Every picture was written on the cuff—if somebody had a clean cuff. We'd start with just one germ of an idea, and hope it would turn out to be an epidemic. For instance, someone would suggest a situation such as a guy under a bed with a bomb in his hand. The Old Man would say, 'It sounds good. Get going. The cameraman's waitin.' We were supposed to decide extemporaneously how to get a guy under a bed with a bomb in his hand, and how to get him out again, and build up to a fast chase. Every comedy had to have a breakneck chase at the end, with one complicated mishap delaying the pursuers—the Kops...I didn't have time to register a 'slow-burn' in those days. Things moved too fast.

On 11-19-14 Edgar even played the Police Chief in *The Noise of Bombs*. He wore a huge mustache and, quite frankly, the stock players were seemingly interchangeable. There were drawbacks to being a stock player. Without a consistent screen image, there was little chance the public would notice him. Edgar didn't care about that at this juncture in his life, he was content just to be steadily employed at this laugh factory. He was getting regular pay raises, was well liked and respected. Edgar was absorbing an education in comedy that would pay dividends for the rest of his life.

On 11-23-14, *The Los Angeles Record* published this interesting little news account:

> Realism in moving pictures reached a climax today when a comedy fight scene was so vividly acted in front of the Oriental Café at Fifth and Main that the cops were deceived.
>
> A riot call was fired in to headquarters. A half a dozen

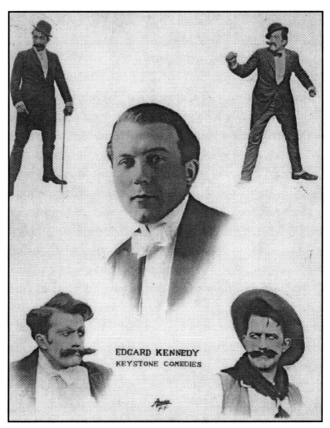

EDGARD KENNEDY
KEYSTONE COMEDIES

Photo montage of Edgar roles, circa 1915
(Author's collection)

large patrolmen, flourishing saps, dashed up in the patrol
wagon and 'pinched' the movie actors: Big Ed Kennedy,
Mack Swain, Charlie Parrott, Miss Brockwell and Director Jones of the Keystone Comedy Co.

Jones thought that the ornate front of the Oriental Café
would make a fine location, so he put Kennedy, Swain, Parrott
and Miss Brockwell to work there. In full makeup they cavorted over the sidewalk, while a big crowd gathered. Big Ed
Kennedy, who is some box-fighter, was supposed to be cleaning up the place. His flailing arms, rising ever and anon over
the heads of the excited spectators, moved some hysterical
person to flash the 'hurry up' sign to Central.

Ten minutes after the sensational 'pinch'—explanations
had been made, the blushing cops, suggestively tapping

their own conks, fell back on either hand, and movie people returned to their choice location to complete the enactment of the strenuous situation.

At the beginning of 1915, Sennett lost Chaplin to Essanay Studios where his legend status began to grow even more. To replace the void, Sennett teamed Arbuckle with Mabel Normand, and continued to direct. Sennett always had the philosophy that it takes in-house experience to know how to make a Sennett comedy. Outsiders were not welcome.

Fred Mace, who was so influential in obtaining Edgar a job at Sennett, returned to the Keystone fold in July of 1915. He had left Sennett in April 1913 in an effort to establish the Fred Mace Feature Film Company. A near broken man, Mace appeared in only seven comedies when, in December of 1915, he was found dead in a New York hotel, the victim of an alleged stroke.

During 1915, San Francisco welcomed the world in hosting "The Panama-San Francisco Exposition." Sennett sent a movie crew that included his two biggest stars, Fatty Arbuckle and Mabel Normand, to the City for three weeks in April. Edgar went with the entourage. During the filming of *Fatty and Mabel at the World's Fair*, Mayor Rolph personally escorted the two stars throughout San Francisco. No one could foresee the scandal that would ruin the career of Fatty in this very city in 1921.

Work started the first week of April for the Keystone comedy *Wished on Mabel*. It was filmed in San Francisco with the running title of *The Golden Gate Story*. Edgar played the cop in the park. Wearing a standard police uniform, Edgar portrayed a typical Sennett cop; that is to say, not too bright, and all too quick at seeking justice at the end of his billy-club. Still, the crook got what was coming to him at the end thanks to Edgar's reluctant diligence. After completion of the two-reeler, the crew took the ferry boat ride eleven miles across the San Francisco Bay to Oakland for another shoot.

# 8.
# Idora Park

The Sennett crew decided to make a comedy at Idora Park in Oakland, the same park where Edgar debuted as a professional actor. It was a nostalgic return for not only Edgar, but Roscoe Arbuckle as well. Fatty Arbuckle grew up in San Jose, just 40 miles south, and often came to the park as a spectator and, later, a performer.

In the *Oakland Tribune*, 4-12-15, a small news account announced:

> Movie Celebrities to Invade Idora Park—Mabel Normand, 'Fatty' Arbuckle and other movie celebrities, will use the trees and lawns, the bears and ostriches, the scenic railways and fun devices of Idora Park this week as a background for a Keystone film farce comedy. The photographs will be taken during the afternoons of the present week when the weather is good, and it is anticipated that some of the crowds at the park will be commandeered into the company to make fun on the screen.
>
> Roscoe Arbuckle, who is to be the hero of one of the comedies, has declared that he will ride a bear, if he has to use up a ton of peanuts to get into the ursine graces. One of the members of the company is going to escape by diving into the tank with one of Carver's diving horses.
>
> There's going to be a wreck in one of the cars on 'The Race' Thru the Clouds' when Fatty tries to win the heroine's hand by overloading a train.
>
> Arbuckle was formerly a member of the Idora musical comedy company and when a setting was wanted for a movie laid in a big amusement park he suggested Idora.

Candid shot at Idor Park, Edgar w/ unknown woman.
"Mabel's Wilfull Way" (circa 1915)

The Keystone people made the negotiations and the plans have been made for great doings all this week in making the films. The pictures will be taken between 1 and 4 o'clock every afternoon, when the light is good. It is anticipated that a number of moving picture fans will take the opportunity of seeing how a motion picture is filmed."

The *Oakland Tribune* took out ads [*see insert*] granting access to the park for their customers to watch the "Keystone Film Company make one of their clever new plays. They will film their scenes at Idora Park every afternoon this week. Miss Normand, Arbuckle and all the rest of the famous comedy company will be on hand and the spectators will have a chance to see Keystones as they are made."

There was no script per se going into production. The working title was at times *The Park Story, The Idora Park Story* and *The Race for Life*; it was finally titled *Mabel's Willful Way*. Starting production at the park created some logistical problems. It was pre-announced in the *Oakland Tribune* that "Mabel Normand will make the dive into the giant tank from the back of one of Carver's horses while the villain, foiled at the moment of triumph, grates his teeth and opens fire with a large caliber revolver on the swimming maiden. The police rush to the rescue. They are about to seize the villain when he springs into space and dies a horrible, but comedy death in the tank.

"'Fatty' Arbuckle will be the hero. Of course there is no horse in existence that could bear his weight, but he will dash gallantly to the rescue on either a motor truck or in a cart drawn by a couple of elephants.

"The excitement will be fierce while it lasts. Thrills will be frequent and obvious. There will be desperate dashes through the clouds by the fair Mabel. She will fall off the theatre building."

During the one week of production, the above scenario proved difficult to actually shoot in the constraints of a working park. The story was scaled down, but it offered Edgar a chance to perform as the love rival without his usual heavy make-up. One sequence in particular showcased Edgar deftly handling a cane (*a la* Chaplin) while running up and down the stairs of the Idora Park gateway.

As the film was wrapped up, this article appeared in the *Oakland Enquirer* on 4-17-15:

(Courtesy *Oakland Tribune*)

Mabel Normand shot at Idora Park
(Courtesy Kennedy Family)

Fatty Arbuckle acted before an admiring crowd at Idora Park yesterday in the making of a Keystone farce comedy film. Mabel Normand slid down the mountain slide in the face of an artificial gale, made by several electric fans, which sent her skirts flying.

A rough and tumble scenario is being filmed at Idora. It tells the adventures of a merry maid who escapes from her parents in Idora Park, is followed by a fat admirer and a thin admirer who fight. Policemen, park attendants, diving horses, bears and instrumentalists in the band are minor characters. The Keystone stars and the cameraman say they will have completed their labors before the sun goes down tomorrow night. They will be at it all day long.

The crowds followed them yesterday for a short time to let the crowds see the Carver diving horses perform. Each scene has to be rehearsed and gone over again and again in the 'movies' to get every detail perfect. And every time a pie was smashed in the face of one of the Keystone artists, the crowed cheered.

Fatty Arbuckle at Idora Park
(Courtesy Kennedy Family)

The article continues by making this strange point: "It is more fun making movies than seeing them. According to the throngs of visitors. Many of them 'got into the picture.' The films will be produced at theaters in the bay region and elsewhere. Those who were brought into the 'movie' will watch anxiously to see themselves on the screen. Dancing in the Grill Garden, the Carver Diving Horses, and the Pelz Exposition Band continue the big attractions at Idora."

Unfortunately, there were no other followup articles written about the film making, nor the "local boy makes good" angle with Edgar or Fatty reminiscing about their professional beginnings. If Oakland was blase about the film production, it might have been because just a few miles south of them in Niles (between Oakland and San Jose), Charlie Chaplin was making comedies for the Essanay Studios all during 1915.[7]

While being afforded the opportunity to return to San Francisco, Edgar was dismayed when he discovered that his mother had suffered a slight stroke. Fortunately it was not a debilitating one, but he wanted to bring his mother back to live near him in Los Angeles.

During 1914 Edgar was living at 1126 Trenton St. in Los Angeles. He moved in 1915 to 1746 Alessandra in Edendale. It was just walking distance from the studio (1712 Alessandra). With a doting son, Annie made steady progress in her health. However, she was overweight, and it was of major concern to her doctors. Edgar moved his mom into her own house on 1453 Alvarado to make himself available for her throughout the day.

Edgar always claimed in later years that it was his mother that inspired an open house to whomever wanted to drop by. On December 1915 the tradition continued with Annie in Los Angeles.

By this time Edgar's adopted sister, Irene, was employed as a seamstress when she met a candymaker named William Brunnenkant in the San Francisco area. They married and had a son born on November 12, 1913. Irene insisted that they name the boy after Annie's father. There was no arguing; the child was named Neil Mathews Brunnenkant. They started a candy store together in Los Angeles and, with Irene's help, the business thrived. When there was a need for a baby on the set, often Edgar would use the Brunnenkant baby.[8]

On July 7, 1916, just three days after her 61st birthday, Annie suffered a serious stroke. She was in paralysis, with obvious brain damage. There was little medical science could do. She was not expected to live more than a few days.

Annie was placed into a hospital where she was made as comfortable as could be expected. She lasted until 9:30 a.m. on January 29, 1917, when she finally succumbed. This obituary appeared the next day in the *Los Angeles Times*:

"**KENNEDY,** Fannie [sic] beloved mother of Edgar L. Kennedy, Mrs. Irene Brunnenkamp [sic], and devoted sister of Mrs. Margaret McCormick,

---

7. Chaplin often went to Idora Park to use the skating rink and may have given him inspiration for the later "The Rink" comedy classic short.
8. Neil Brunnenkant later became a cutter and stayed in the business. He died on 11-12-97 in L.A.

Edgar (sporting a toupee) has his arm around his mother at the top of stairs from their house on 1746 Allesandra (now Glendale Blvd) in Edendale. (Circa 1915) Also in photo: Walter McCormick, Irene Brunnenkant, Slim Summerville, Tom Forman, Ruth King, Hank Mann, Edwin Frazee, Joseph Singleton. (Courtesy Kennedy Family)

aged 60 years. Funeral Wednesday, January 31 at 8:30 a.m. from the parlors of Cunningham & O'Connor, 1031 South Grand Avenue. Interment, private, at Hollywood Cemetery." The cemetery was also known as Hollywood Memorial Park, which is now known as Hollywood Forever.

Edgar was forever indebted to a dear friend of his, Bert Henderson. It was he who sat by his mother's side while Edgar was at work. Edgar never forgot his kindness; Bert later became a family institution.

Edgar carried a special grief for his mother. According to Edgar's daughter, Colleen Deach, "My father couldn't talk about his mother without getting choked up." He rarely mentioned her for the rest of his life.

Free from the responsibilities of taking care of his mother, Edgar turned his attention to the Great War being fought in Europe. If one can believe the studio biographies written years later, Edgar "tried to enlist four dif-

*Love's False Faces* (1919)
w/ Jimmy Finlayson, Edgar (*on knees*),Chester Conklin

ferent times, but was turned down because of 'flat feet.' The fourth doctor eventually realized the mistake and cleared him for military duty." Edgar enlisted into the Army on June 28, 1918. He wanted to serve his country and see the world, especially France, to see some action. It was not to be.

1916 saw another major change at the Keystone studios. Mack Sennett, Thomas Ince and D.W. Griffith formed Triangle-Keystone Comedies. In July of 1916 Fatty Arbuckle was lured away for more money with the chance to produce and act in his own comedies for Schenck's Comique Film Corporation.

Sennett by now had developed a reputation as a stingy developer of talent that he couldn't (or wouldn't) keep. Chaplin, Arbuckle and Mabel Normand left. By 1917 Ford Sterling went to work at the Fox Studios where in March, the Sunshine Comedy unit began. The vice-president and General Manager was former cameraman and director Henry Lehrman. Other Keystone veterans were also lured to the new unit, included Hank Mann, Charles Parrot (Chase), and Edgar Kennedy. By 1919 Slim Summerville and Chester Conklin joined the ranks. Despite the fact that Sennett usually referred to the defectors as "traitors," Edgar continued to work for both Fox and Sennett in supporting comedy roles.

# 9.
# You're In the Army Now

Edgar was stationed at Vancouver Barracks in Vancouver, Washington. It was the home of the Spruce Division (part of the Signal Corp.), Third Division, Seventh Brigade, 21st Infantry. There were 39,000 soldiers on the post, and most of the draftees were put to work in the lumber mills. The YMCA was also represented on post. There were news clubs, glee clubs, and boxing on post for entertainment and training. Edgar, at 6 feet 2 inches, was considered a hulking figure of a man in 1918. Years later in a publicity release, Edgar downplayed his role in the Army. He told them that he drove a gurney wagon. This was a name that the soldiers called the medical wagons (both horse-drawn and motorized) that carried the wounded and dead back to the aid stations. Units of Special Services people, such as cooks, office personnel, would drive these gurney wagons in battle. At the Vancouver Barracks, Special Services included athletes and entertainers.

With his expertise as a professional boxer, it was decided that Edgar could provide far more service to Uncle Sam as a trainer than he could as an infantryman. He worked the raw troops into fighting men. Boxing was a huge sport during this time and the manly art was considered para-

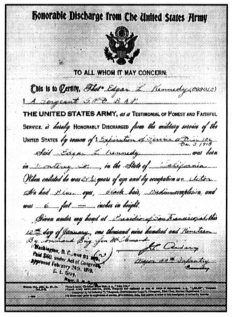

Honorable Discharge papers
(Courtesy Kennedy Family)

mount to defense and conditioning.

Also stationed at Vancouver Barracks was another actor from the film colony, Tom Forman, who socialized with Edgar before the war. Forman was married to Ruth King, who would soon play a major part in Edgar's life.

Forman had been a contract player for Famous Players-Lasky. Forman was assigned to the Company of Coast Artillery, comprised almost entirely of motion picture folks. The unit was commanded by Ted Duncan (another Lasky actor) and a Lieutenant named Walter Long.[9]

TOM FORMAN

Tom Forman (circa 1919)
(Author's collection)

9. Walter Long played a slave in blackface in "Birth of a Nation" and later played "heavy" roles supporting Laurel and Hardy.

*The Los Angeles Times* reported this item, 10-12-17: "Mrs. Ruth King Forman, who earns $65 a week and made no request for alimony, was granted a decree of divorce yesterday from Thomas Powers Forman, a motion picture actor, now a Lieutenant in the Coast Artillery. She charged cruelty. Once, after a quarrel, Mrs. Forman testified, she locked herself in a room to avoid her husband, but he broke in the door with a chair and the flying glass cut her arm, leaving a scar. He also threatened her with a revolver, she declared."

*Motion Picture Magazine* quoted Tom Forman in June 1919:

> You know, I was kind of shy about being a motion picture actor when I went into the army. Men from other walks of life seemed to me to look down upon it, but I hadn't been in the army long before I was doggone proud of the fact, because in my mind and in the opinion of thousands of others the pictures did as much to turn out the army we did as anything else, if not more.
>
> Forman earned his chevron stripes and became a Sergeant. He was put in charge of building a motion picture theater to be used for the amusement of the men.
>
> We had motion pictures to study, with pictures showing the movements of guns, the effect of explosives, the explaining of maneuvers and other things. Seeing these on the screen, the soldier could understand them in about a quarter of the time that was required to get 'em into his head by word of mouth. As for keeping up the army moral, it was the greatest thing in the world. After a solder had paid his Liberty Bond appropriation, his allotment to his home and his insurance money, he didn't have any great amount of cash left to spend in amusement. The canteen and the saloon were fortunately closed to him, and he would sure look forward to the nightly picture show, which only cost him a nickel to see, and he had something to talk about the next day.

Before the war, Forman played leading roles opposite Mae Murray, Blanche Sweet, Fannie Ward, Marie Doro, Vivian Martin and others. His last picture before entering the army was *Hashimura Toga*, with Sessue Hayakawa.

After the war, Forman was immediately cast in a Cecil B. DeMille production, *For Better for Worse*. In his role as a romantic lead, Forman's character marries the beautiful Gloria Swanson.

Forman started to sour on being an actor. In a February 1921 interview for *Motion Picture Magazine*, he explained that the "director gets more money than anybody unless it is the star, and a star never expects to retain his following for more than six or eight years. The public is notoriously fickle. An actor is only so much putty in the hands of his director. He has no will of his own! You know a director never gets the credit he deserves when the picture is good, but he gets the blame when the picture is bad…but I prefer to be the man behind the gun." The words of a bitter man? It was a strangely prophetic statement. Tom Forman killed himself with a gun in November of 1926 at the home of his parents in Venice, California. He shot himself through the heart with a 45-caliber revolver while in the bathroom. Ironically, it was the day before he was slated to direct *The Wreck* for Columbia.

Ruth L. King was a strikingly beautiful stage actress with aspirations of movie acting. King filed for divorce from her husband, Tom Forman in 1916; the divorce was granted the following year.

It is unknown how Edgar and Ruth King met, although it is likely it was because of, or in spite of, Tom Forman. Edgar became serious with the former Iowa girl and married her on April 27, 1919 in Riverside, California. The famous Mission Inn was a destination of Hollywood notables. It was a beautifully built replica of California Missions and had wonderful orange trees surrounding the area.

Edgar turned 28 the day after getting married, Ruth was 24. The best man was Edgar's cousin, good old Walter McCormick. The Matron of Honor was Betty Weldi. It was eight years to the day that Edgar won the Pacific Coast amateur boxing championship.

On January 12, 1919, Edgar received an honorable discharge with the rank of Sergeant. With a new enthusiasm, Edgar happily returned to work where he was welcomed by Mack Sennett.

Edgar appeared in only five films in 1918 before he went into the service, one was a landmark feature film that starred Mable Normand, *Mickey*, and Mack Sennett produced it. While it may seem on the surface that this was a return to old times, it was anything but. *Mickey* had numerous delays finding a financier and was eventually shown to a limited market. However, *Mickey* turned out to be a commercial and critical success. Undoubtedly, one of the reasons Sennett produced a starring vehicle for Mable Normand was to try and woo her back as his fiancé. Mable had also vacated the Sennett lot to go on to greener pastures. She had never forgiven Sennett for an incident when, unannounced, she interrupted her fiancé in a compromising position with her best friend, the "eternally ever popular Mae Busch." *Mickey* was directed by old standby F. Richard Jones, a veteran of the Sennett Studios and soon to be an executive with the Hal Roach Studios.

After the war, Edgar continued to work in relative obscurity. One example was Mack Sennett's second feature-length comedy burlesque, *Yankee Doodle in Berlin*. In Sennett's autobiography, he claimed that he opened the film-run in San Francisco, making this the first ever out of town premiere. *The San Francisco Chronicle*:

> Musical comedy invades the realm of the silver sheet this week in Mack Sennett's burlesque showing at the Tivoli Theater. The play is a combination of the old one-reel comedy props. It is probably the best burlesque on the Crown Prince and the Kaiser, the Kaiser's wife andthe royal entourage that has been put on the screen and the captions are laughable.
>
> Mack Sennett gathers together as his cast most of the comedy stars one is used to seeing in the Sennett pictures, and many of the widely advertised 'Diving Beauties.' These last add to the appearance of the show a cinema musical comedy by appearing both in picture and in person as the chorus, a very pretty if a trifle generously displayed chorus.

Vera Reynolds, one of the beauties of the film, appeared in person. The film starred Charlie Murray as an American soldier. Charlie was no spring chicken in 1919; he was middle-aged. Edgar played a bumbling German soldier.

At least Edgar received screen credit for appearing in the movie. Such was often not the case during the years between 1918 to 1923. Existing filmographies typically reflect only a handful of movies Edgar made during this period.

Song sheet for *Yankee Doodle in Berlin*

Edgar certainly was not a star; he was a struggling actor trying to make a buck. What worked well for him as a stock actor, with many different screen images, did not bode well for him in face recognition. Since Edgar never developed a consistent character, it was hard to sell himself as anything other than a supporting comedian or heavy.

There are uncredited titles for films that Edgar appeared in during the years 1918 to 1923. It happened at Sennetts and again at Fox and Universal; Edgar's first name was often shortened to "Ed." This was further complicated when it was assumed by whomever was typing the credits that Ed was the short version of Edward. Indeed, there are many credits that include Edward Kennedy at both studios. It was the same person.

# 10.
# Kennedy vs. Dempsey

Edgar finally got a chance to box the Heavy Weight Champ of the ring, alas it was for movies only. The sequence of events started on December 14, 1919, the *Los Angeles Times* ran a story about the newly crowned Boxing Heavyweight Champion of the World, Jack Dempsey. In an attempt to cash in on the popularity of the new champ, Dempsey agreed to make a movie serial to a salary of $185,000 for only twelve weeks of work.

*The Adventures of Daredevil Jack* was shot at the Brunton Studios on Melrose Avenue. The director assigned to the task was W.S. (Woody) Van Dyke. A former protégé of D.W. Griffith, Van Dyke was getting quite a reputation as an "action" director. As years went on, Van Dyke was responsible for directing such notable films as *Manhattan Melodrama, The Thin Man, Naughty Marietta, Rose Marie, San Francisco, Rosalie* and *Marie Antoinette*, among others.

The champ knew how to box all right, but his acting skills were dismal. He couldn't pull a punch and there were not too many actors who could take one. Van Dyke knew just the right person, Edgar Kennedy. Here was a person that was not just an actor, but someone who had experience in professional boxing. Even more important, Edgar had the respect of Dempsey.

Although Van Dyke and Edgar were friends, this was their first film association together. Both men's professional lives would often co-mingle throughout their careers. Van Dyke went on to become one of Edgar's most cherished friends and closest confidants.[10]

According to Jack Dempsey, in his autobiography *Dempsey*, "From the time I arrived in Hollywood, everyone made a big fuss over me. My hair

---

10. *Woody Van Dyke was a protégé' of the great Director D.W. Griffith (Birth of a Nation and Intolerance fame). Van Dyke directed Edgar in numerous films, the most famous being San Francisco.*

was wrong, and my nose was wrong, so they called in Lon Chaney to do a complete overhaul. He put putty on my nose to straighten it out, puttied my ears and penciled my brows. He put rouge on my face and goo on my head. Everyone stared when I finally walked out of the dressing room.

"Once everyone had a good laugh when Edgar Kennedy knocked off my putty nose. Two minutes later I accidentally knocked off his toupee and everyone laughed even more—everyone except Kennedy and Van Dyke, who had no time to spare."

*Van Dyke and the Mythical City Hollywood,* a book written by Robert C. Cannom, elaborates: "One day Van Dyke was having trouble with close-ups because of his star's slightly deformed nose so he decided to fix it up with putty. Dempsey's nose turned out fine; and the champ looked like a Roman gladiator until, in the next scene, Edgar Kennedy knocked the 'putty' across the room. In the shot it looked like the champ's nose was flying through the air. Not to be outdone, Dempsey measured one just right and Kennedy's toupee landed in the rafters."

Three photographs still exist of one of the staged fights with Edgar. In front of an impressive set that might actually be an outdoor arena in front of a huge crowd, Edgar and Dempsey are squaring off in the ring. Dempsey's makeup makes him look a bit embalmed. The second photo depicts the fighters in action. Dempsey's hair reverted back to its original mop of untamed hair. The third photo, also an action shot, is of Edgar with his back on the mat. An obvious victim of Dempsey's killer punch—or just acting?

"Woody taught me how to pull a punch," Dempsey explained in his autobiography. "He had to; I kept knocking the other actors out cold, and the studio's doctor had issued a complaint against me. Pulling punches was a damn sight harder than fighting professionally. I was often ragged at the end of the day from not throwing punches."

In a curious asterisk to Edgar's career, it was often mentioned that Edgar had "once fought with Jack Dempsey for 14 rounds. Dempsey won the decision." Most of Edgar's obituaries mention that "fact," as did some columnists during the height of his career. There are many inconsistencies to the story.

According to *Ring* magazine, only two fighters ever went past 14 rounds with Dempsey, and Kennedy was not one of them. Furthermore, there was no such thing as "14 rounders." So how could a fight be over via a decision? An existing photograph clearly shows Edgar on the mat while

Edgar Kennedy, boxing for the film *Daredevil Jack*, vs. Dempsey
(Courtesy Kennedy Family)

the referee is holding up Dempsey's hand declaring him the winner. Looks like a clear knockout, with the audience in jubilation.

Further complicating the events is Edgar himself. In one studio press release, Edgar made a reference to his frustration about getting rejected for military duty because of physical reasons. Edgar was quoted as saying: "And I just went toe-to-toe with Jack Dempsey and they call me unfit?"

That would put the date of their "fight" in 1917 or early 1918. Those years would make it highly unlikely, seeing that Edgar was five years older than Dempsey and had not boxed professionally since early 1913. There are two independent sources that identify the Dempsey-Kennedy fight as "for the cameras only." A May 5, 1941 Feg Murray "Seein' Stars" Sunday comics feature showcasing Hollywood stars illustrated two boxers with the caption "Edgar Kennedy was Pacific Coast Heavy Weight Champion in 1911 and in 1912 [sic], fought 14 rounds with Jack Dempsey for a movie."

This story was published by the *Los Angeles Times* while making the series in 1920: "Ed Kennedy, ex-heavyweight champion in the story the Jack Dempsey company is making at Universal Studios has fully recovered from the effects of his recent battle with the champion and is once more in training. He has another fight with Dempsey at the close of the picture now being filmed. Kennedy also claims the distinction of being the only man in the world who has knocked Jack Dempsey down three times in as many rounds. This happened in the fight just before Jack delivered a K.O. to Kennedy."

There are no known complete prints that exist of *Daredevil Jack*, with the exception of the first few reels of the series. The films are stored at the University of California at Los Angeles; unfortunately, the boxing sequences are not included. As a result of this filmed fight, both Edgar and Dempsey considered each other lifelong pals.

Edgar was "discovered" in another boxing theme a few years later. "He Raised the Mask," Oct. 14, 1923, *The Los Angeles Times*:

> "Born-of a comedy prize fight picture—a new tragedian!"
>
> This is the strange rise to recognition of Ed Kennedy, to be featured as "Lem Beeman," perhaps the most tragic figure ever put on a screen, in Perley Poore Sheehan's production of his own story, "Innocent," soon to start at Universal City. Lem Beeman is a country telegraph operator who accidentally shoots his best friend. He cannot leave his switchboard to aid his dying friend—the limited instructions are due at the wire, and failure to get them might mean a wreck. The remembrance fairly sears his soul through the years. And this tragic part will be played by the man who up to now has been known principally as "Ptomaine Tommy," the fighting camp cook in "The Leather Pushers."

Sheehand, the author, did not even know his name when he chose Kennedy for the part. He approached Fred Datig, the casting director for the information. "There's a fellow in the fight pictures," he said, "who is cast as a roughneck cook—doing a comedy role. I want him—don't know his name but that fellow is one of the greatest tragedians I've ever seen."

"Why—that's Ed Kennedy, he does comedy," said Datig. "He does comedy because he's told to—but give him a chance at tragedy and watch him!" asserted Sheehan. Kennedy was sent for and cast for the new picture. Rehearsals followed—for Sheehan is rehearsing his play just as a stage play is rehearsed, and will do so for days before the cameras grind. After the first rehearsal the studio was agog with excitement. Sheehan was right—Kennedy proved the surprise of the year.

On November 2, 1923, the *Los Angeles Times* wrote this tongue-in-cheek article:

Former Fighter to Leave Screen and Try Fistic Arena Again. Edgar Kennedy, former Coast heavyweight champion, and now a picture player, is to enter the ring again. According to his manger, Hayden Stevenson.

Stevenson plays the fight manager in *The Leather Pushers* at Universal City, and used to handle fighters. Kennedy wants him to remain with him. "I know I can come back, and if the studios are going to close I don't care," says Kennedy. "I'll take on some of the best heavy-weights and I'll show that six years of acting can't down a good man."

"I'm Kennedy's manager—but I don't think he's any good. I'll take him get him bouts, but I've laid him a bet he'll lose 'em all." "Not so," says Kennedy. "I'll show this manager of mine that I can still fight—and it's going to cost him money to be convinced."

Stevenson in now in negotiations for the first bout and Kennedy will probably appear in his first fights locally. He has gone into training and expects to be in shape in two or three weeks.

# 11.
# Mrs. Edgar Kennedy

In 1920 Edgar and Ruth were recorded in the census as living at 1517 Scott Avenue in Los Angeles. According to the City Directory, Edgar had been listed as residing there as early as 1918. Also living at the residence was Hilma Miller (age 34), who is listed as a servant, along with her daughter, Vivian Miller (age 5). The Kennedys listed a boarder, Edwin London (age 29). Sometime during 1921 Edgar (listed as a photo player) moved to 1416 Fairfax in Los Angeles.

During the fall of 1921 Edgar was summoned by his old pal and Sennett alumni, William S. Campbell, who was directing *A Nick of Time Hero* at the Fine Arts Studio for Educational Pictures. Coy Watson, Jr., the star in this kid picture, remembers working with "Ed," but only briefly. Edgar's uncredited appearance had him speaking in title card to the little female lead, Doreen Turner. "How dare you be so happy on a day like this," says Edgar, wearing a mustache for the role.

In 1922 Edgar secured his first directing job at Fox Studios. In succession he made *The Fresh Heir, His Wife's Son, Safe in the Safe,* and *Step Lively Please.* By now, Edgar considered himself an experienced director and hoped he could establish himself as such.

By 1923 he was listed as living at 1616 Poinsettia in L.A. Something was indeed going on in Edgar's personal life; he was experiencing a rocky marriage with Ruth.

In the beginning of March 1923 Ruth left the house. In June of 1924 Edgar became the plaintiff seeking court action to dissolve the marriage. According to the Complaint for Divorce documents, "That on or about the first day of March 1923, in the City of Los Angeles,…the defendant [Ruth King Kennedy] disregarding the solemnity of her marriage vows and without any cause or excuse and against the wish and will of the plaintiff, left the plaintiff and their home, and deserted and abandoned the plaintiff, and ever since said date has continued to remain away from the plaintiff, and has refused to live or cohabit with the plaintiff, all against his wish and will, and without his consent..."

On May 20, 1924, Ruth was served with a "Complaint and Summons, and that the defendant has not answered said complaint." The affidavit further stated: "Affiant further states that he is about to leave the County of Los Angeles and will be absent for a number of months...that it is necessary for him to be absent because of business and that he is a motion picture director and cannot remain in the County of Los Angeles for the trial of the above entitled case. Affiant therefore asks that the above entitled action be set for immediate trial for the reasons above set forth."

Ruth did not bother to defend the accusations and failed to show up in court. Because there was no trial, an "Interlocutory Judgment of Divorce" was filed on June 13, 1924. Typical in California back then, it took approximately one year for a divorce to become final.

Starting in the year 1917, and throughout the years of being married to Edgar, Ruth appeared in twenty-two films. The years prior to marrying Edgar, she was mostly in westerns. Interestingly, three of the titles (all shot in 1917), *Land of Long Shadows*, *The Range Boss*, and *Men of the Desert*, were all directed by Edgar's future close associate W.S. Van Dyke.

During the years of marriage, and even until her last credited screen role, Ruth often portrayed a vamp character. Even the movie titles seem provocative: *Dangerous Love* (as the other woman), *The Devil's Pass Key* (Erich von Stroheim direction), *The Cheater Reformed*, *Scandal Proof*, *Driftin' Thru*, and, from 1926, *The Lady From Hell*.

In 1924, while Ruth was separated from Edgar, she had a very prestigious role in *He Who Gets Slapped*. This is one of the best roles of Lon Chaney's film career. The memorable images being Lon's character getting slapped as part of his clown act while his wife, Maria Beaumont (Ruth King) has an affair behind his back. It is a compelling dramatic silent film that set Chaney apart from the rest of his contemporaries. Ruth King was perfectly cast as the sadistic adulterous wife.

Edgar supplemented his income with stage appearances in various musical comedy revues. It was in one of those now forgotten shows that an event occurred that would change his life forever.

According to Colleen Deach, it was Ruth King who introduced her estranged husband to Colleen's future mother, a beautiful young dancer who went by the name of Patricia Allen. This alleged sweet Irish lass had a wonderful singing voice and a vivacious personality. She was a fairly recent widow who lost her young husband in the influenza epidemic of 1918. A romance ensued while Edgar and Ruth waited for the divorce to be finalized. In order to fully appreciate Edgar's later success, the strength of Patricia Allwyn, the future Mrs. Kennedy has to be acknowledged. She was so influential to Edgar's personal and professional career, that her background must be shared as well.

Colleen said her mother was slightly mysterious about her past, and always discouraged questions about the topic. Her mother only acknowledged that "she thought she was born in Wisconsin, and that her mother's name was Mary Tipler." Colleen didn't know her true age or her mom's maiden name.

Patricia would sometimes talk about her first husband to Larry and Colleen, but she always refused to divulge her first husband's name when asked. Grandson Mark Kennedy, who had always been intrigued with the mystery, persisted in questioning her every chance he got. She put him off over the years by telling him, "someday I'll tell you." This very private, dignified lady finally conceded to his request on her deathbed. She told Mark that her first husband's name was Ben Reader. Patricia Violet Kennedy died on May 24, 1977.

There has been some recent success in identifying Patricia's family background. It started with information obtained from a social security document turned in to the government in the 1940s. In her own hand, Patricia identified her mother as Mary Tipler, and wrote down her father's name as Fred Eichmann of Vinland, in Winnabago County, Wisconsin. Patricia listed her birth date as June 17, 1896 on the form. During census inquiries in later years, Patricia claimed 1898 as her birth year. In actuality, she was born in 1895.

A check of the 1900 census finds a family headed by Fred C. Eichmann living at 502 Caroline St. in the small city of Neesah, also of Winnabago County, Wisconsin. It was right next to another small community called Allentown. The head of the family was listed as a railroad brakeman on the Wisconsin line. His wife was identified as Mary Eichmann. Children are listed as: Lulu Tipler (age ten), Mabel Eichmann (eight), Fred Eichmann (six) and Violet [Patricia] (five).

In 1900 Neenah had a population of 5,954 and was primarily a paper mill town (the Kimberly-Clark Corporation), it was just outside of Allen-

Violet Eichmann a.k.a. Violet Reader a.k.a. Patsy Allen a.k.a. Patricia Allwyn.
(Courtesy Kennedy Family)

town. The Eichmanns lived at Neesah until around 1905. In the mean-
time, Mary encouraged little Violet to take dancing and singing lessons.
Violet soon attracted attention with her performing skills at school, and
became sought after in stage performances all over the area. It is unknown
if this show business passion by mother and daughter caused a rift with
Fred Eichmann. Eventually, in the teens, Mary Eichmann and her offspring were all living in Los Angeles. Violet, under the stage name of
Patricia Allen, or sometimes Patsy Allen, was dancing professionally.

Court records verify that on July 1, 1914 Violet M. Eichmann entered into matrimony with Benjamin Harrison Reader, formerly of Indi-
ana. She was 19, he was 26. It was the first marriage for both. They were

married at the local Justice of the Peace by D.W. Garwood at 141 S. Hollenbeck Street in the township of Belvedere, a suburb of Los Angeles. They settled down to live at 228 W. 28th Street in L.A.

Ben knew everything about machinery and mechanics, but his passion was aeroplane flying. Reader enlisted into the military service for the Great War and became a glamorous fighter pilot.

Mrs. Violet Reader worried throughout the conflict for his personal safety. Being in Europe, and in those flimsy flying machines, Violet was worried sick for her young husband. Finally Armistice was declared, and flying hero Ben Reader returned home.

Everything seemed to be falling into place. Ben got himself a job as a mechanic, they had a nice home; perhaps the Readers could finally start a family. It was not to be.

By 1918 the entire world was griped with the great influenza epidemic. Unlike other viruses before or since, this deadly assault was particularly brutal to the young and strong.

Both Violet and Ben came down with life threatening symptoms and were confined to bed. Mother Mary Tipler came to their house to be a nursemaid for the young couple. The pneumonia-like symptoms choked off the lungs. Ben fought for his life but weakened daily.

Inflicted with the virus, it took only five days to claim Ben Reader. On October 22, 1918, Ben died, a mere 30 years old. Violet was so deathly ill herself, she was incapable of leaving her own bed. There was great concern if she would survive. Fortunately, Ben had a brother and sister living in Los Angeles who took care of the burial. In a rare moment of retrospect when she was older, Patricia shared the concern she had of her fighting pilot during the war. "I worried sick about him everyday and was so relieved when he came back uninjured. Then he died at home shortly after returning of influenza." The irony never escaped her.

There was still widespread panic regarding this mysterious outbreak. Ironically, the day Reader's death was announced in the paper, the headlines in the *Los Angeles Express* proclaimed "Influenza Epidemic Slowing Down." There was also an announcement from the Health Department: "From now until further notice, there will be no more public funerals in the City of Los Angeles. The only ones allowed to attend are the immediate family of the deceased."

With hardly any veteran service pension for death benefits, Patricia Violet plunged into show business to support herself. She was often cast in musical revues during dinner shows, particularly in San Francisco and Los Angeles. At times the spelling of her name changed to Patricia Allyn. One undated write-up gives us a small glimpse into her past:

> Frances White, Ada Forman, and other Los Angeles celebrities who have taken the East by storm have a new Angeleno compatriot. The noted soubrette of half a dozen "Follies" engagements, and the dancer whose classic interpretations have set Gotham agog, have a rival or ally, which ever you choose to call it, in Patsy Allen, who has just returned with vaudeville and cabaret laurels. And now Patsy Allen, a Polytechnic product, whose mother, Mrs. R. Rader, lives at 4163 West Washington Street, has hit the bull's-eye of popular approval. She has just come back from a tour of a big vaudeville circuit, and last winter staged a revue at Harry Marquard's café in San Francisco. She is here for a short vacation, while considering the various offers that have been made to her by different vaudeville circuits, revue organizations and musical comedy producing companies. An enthusiastic rooter for the 'Poly' athletic teams, Miss Allen has been no less an enthusiast in behalf of Los Angeles during her recent tour of the footlights over the big time circuits.

Patricia Allen was the headliner for the *Fashion Revue of 1921*, at the Café Marquard in the Columbia Theater in San Francisco. A writeup in the San Francisco paper said, "Heading the performance is the clever Patsy Allen and her 'easy to look at' choristers. Miss Allen has a fetching way about her and puts her song and dance numbers over in a manner that never fails to win the plaudits of her audience." On September 13, 1922, "Patricia Allyn" signed a contract with Actor's Equity Association for Stock employment.

After this run, Patricia was recruited by the comedy team of Kolb and Dill. Clarence Kolb (1875-1964) and Max Dill (1878-1949) were the toast of San Francisco when they teamed up in the early 1900's to perform in musical revues and comedies.

Kolb and Dill soon were producing their own shows featuring themselves as "Dutch" comics. Clarence Kolb through the years appeared in his trademark Dutch makeup consisting of long chin whiskers and a comic

Dutch dialect. He was 6-foot-4, with seemingly rubber legs when dancing or when "intoxicated." Dill also spoke in Dutch dialect. His distinction was a huge rubber prop worn around the waist with an extra large coat to create the illusion of a hugely disproportionate fat stomach. Kolb would frequently convulse the audience by striking Dill's rotund target at any given excuse. The illusion was complete with the simultaneous sound of a bass drum coming from the orchestra pit.

A recent graduate of the Kolb and Dill musical comedies was Lon Chaney, Sr. who excelled in singing characters and eccentric dancing. Lon was also the stage manager for the frugal producers in their April 1913 production *Dutch*. After a quarrel backstage, Lon's wife, Cleva, allegedly attempted suicide by drinking mercury while on the wings of the stage during a Kolb and Dill performance.[11] The suicide attempt on stage ultimately led to Lon's dismissal. Unable to find stage work Lon was able to break into the movies and eventually became a star.

It was 1922, during Prohibition, that Kolb and Dill put together a comedy troupe in San Francisco to perform *Wet and Dry*. It was a two-act satire on the evil effects of drinking, complete with music. Patricia Allen was cast as Anna Kremait and, according to newspapers of the day, "scored a hit when she sang 'I'm Glad He's Irish.'" Kolb played the mayor with Dill portraying the local sheriff.

A newspaper columnist made the observation, "While opinions may differ as to whether there is anything funny about prohibition, and while we may not all agree that the bone-dry law is a comedy and not a tragedy, there can be but one opinion of Kolb and Dill's play. It is very amusing and a good vehicle—wagon in this case—for the two comedians."

Even in San Francisco, the subject matter and the lampooning of reformers and politicians proved its early downfall. The play met with critical and enthusiastic crowds, but the play was closed down because of the supposed mocking of the Volstead Act. Kolb and Dill subsequently took the entire company on the road where it was considered a great success all over the States of California and Oregon.

That year-long wait for the divorce to be granted had to be excruciating for all parties concerned. One thing was certain; Edgar had a new invigo-

---

11. *In 1956 the suicide attempt was recreated for the movie "The Man of a Thousand Faces,"* about Lon Chaney's life starring James Cagney. Amazingly, Clarence Kolb played himself in the film with an actor that took his long deceased partner's place. Kolb was more recognizable by then in frequent character roles in movies and in a recurring role as Mr. Honeywell on television's *"My Little Margie"* (1952-1955).

Photo Clarence Kolb & Max Dill
(Author's collection)

rated focus on life. Patricia gave him confidence and was a classy dish besides; she was a beautiful woman with dark brown hair and eyes. According to Edgar and Patricia's daughter, Colleen Deach, most men found her enchanting. She was intelligent, witty and had a magnetic personality.

In Edgar's eyes, his marriage to Ruth ended when she walked out on him on March 1, 1923. According to Colleen, "My parents always claimed August 22, 1924 as their wedding anniversary. There was talk about a 'Mexican Marriage' and then another one in Los Angeles. I have not a clue and I have no curiosity about the subject."

Colleen said the fact that her father was married before was a taboo subject. It was certainly not to be discussed in front of children. There was even a family rumor hinting that Edgar was a victim of blackballing. Added into the mix that some of Edgar's directorial credits were listed as E. Livingston Kennedy, further suggests that a low profile was necessary. Colleen was under the impression that the blackballing was allegedly caused by an influential "producer," possibly the father of Edgar's first wife, who was upset that Edgar was divorcing Ruth.

The family rumor is intriguing. Now that we know Edgar's original marriage was to actress Ruth King, formerly married to Tom Forman, the whole theory sounds far fetched. If Ruth's father was upset over Edgar's filing for divorce, what about Ruth walking out on him? Or how about the fact that she was married and divorced before?

There is another, more plausible, possibility; it was director/producer Tom Forman who was upset. But it couldn't be over Edgar's divorce filing. No, it would have to be because Ruth married Edgar on the rebound. Certainly Edgar's movie credits dried-up in the years he was married to Ruth. Was it really because of a "blacklist" or was it that Edgar and Ruth took to the road more often? Could Forman be that influential or that irrational? Just when some of this starts to make sense as a subplot, it was discovered that Tom Forman actually directed Edgar in *The People Versus Nancy Preston* in 1925. The question persists, though, why would this rumor even materialize?

Finally, on June 19, 1925, a Final Judgment of Divorce was granted. By then, Edgar and Patricia were well on their way raising the family that they both had wished for. The Kennedys were blessed by the birth of a son, named Larry Conrad Kennedy, on June 6, 1925. Daughter Colleen was born on November 29, 1926. By this time they were living at 1506 McCadden Place in Hollywood. It was in the strength of this nucleus of a family that Edgar found lifelong security and success.

Kennedy family on the set (circa 1930), Edgar left, Colleen, Larry, Patricia
(Courtesy of Kennedy Family)

Everything started falling into place. Patricia was beautiful, socially refined and a marvelous cook. She had an engaging personality and loved to entertain at home. Although Edgar suffered through the hard knocks of life up until this point, he never forgot what it meant to be down and hungry. For the rest of his life, Edgar surrounded himself with loyal friends and work. He doted on his new family; he treated Patricia "like a princess," Larry like a pal, and Colleen like daddy's little girl.

# 12.
# Directing Duties

After a six-year absence, Edgar returned to the Sennett Studios, only this time it was to direct comedies, holding on to the edict that to know how to make a Mack Sennett comedy, one had to be promoted from within the ranks. It was the chance Edgar had waited for. A ten-year veteran of movies, Edgar worked with the best of them and saw many rise to great artistic and commercial success as directors.

Serving his apprenticeship at the Sennett Studios, and getting his feet wet directing at Fox, gave Edgar a firm foundation in comedy. F. Richard Jones, the directing supervisor, hired Edgar (with Sennett's approval), and gave him an assignment to direct Ben Turpin, who by then was the star of the lot.

Edgar's directorial debut at Sennett began in May of 1924 on a Turpin comedy that, after many working titles, was eventually entitled *Three Foolish Weeks*. The storyline was a combined burlesque on Eleanor Glyn's *Three Weeks*, and the Erich von Stroheim-directed epic *Foolish Wives*. Another working title on the script called it *2 1/2 Weeks*.

Some publicity was generated by the Sennett Studios during this time for Turpin in the form of an article, "Are Crossed Eyes Bad Luck?" The unidentified original article quoted Turpin, "I often see people look at me and cross their fingers (to prevent their own eyes crossing)." Other information was put out as though Turpin was complaining. "I Want a New Character" he allegedly said. Turpin added a monocle *a la* Erich von Stroheim's screen portrayal as a Count in *Foolish Wives*.

Extra attention was taken with this short. Listed as a co-director was a veteran of seventeen other directed films, Reggie Morris. As usual, the production was supervised by F. Richard Jones. On June 10, 1924 there was a public preview of this two-reeler at the Empire Theatre, resulting in the title change.

Edgar w/ Ben Turpin (Sennett), circa early 1920's
(Courtesy Kennedy Family)

After many previews and some reediting, there was a successful reaction to *Three Foolish Wives* (the final title). Edgar was promptly assigned to direct another Ben Turpin vehicle with the working title of *The Turpin Story*. Credited with the storyline on this comedy was Arthur Ripley and Frank Capra. Edgar had known Ripley for years and would later contribute to Edgar's "Average Man" series for RKO. Capra was a young upstart with a short writing apprenticeship for the Hal Roach Studios before he was hired by Sennett as a gag man. After two uncredited shorts, *The Reel Virginian* became Capra's first screen credit as a scenario writer. Edgar Kennedy and Frank Capra are rarely linked together, but this short established them in the eyes of Sennett. Edgar proved himself as a comedy director and Capra was given more opportunities as a staff writer for comic scenarios.

Capra went on to the heights of directing later in his career after carefully crafting a screen persona for Harry Langdon at Sennett. He later enjoyed unprecedented and esteemed successes with *It Happened One Night*, *Lost Horizon*, and *It's a Wonderful Life*, just to name a few.

*The Turpin Story* eventually evolved into *The Reel Virginian*, a parody of the original 1902 novel *The Virginian* by Owen Wister, put to film as early as 1914, but was most recently filmed as a straight western in 1923. The director of *The Virginian* of 1923? None other than Tom Forman.

Publicity was released to the trade papers on 10-26-24: "Work began this week at the Mack Sennett Studios on Ben Turpin's burlesque of 'The Virginian.'" What the item did not mention is that Turpin broke his ankle while slipping on a grease spot during the first few days of production. Director Kennedy filmed around him like a veteran.

The finished product features the opening title "Medicine Bow, the toughest town in the west." Turpin is introduced as the Virginian holding four aces with a queen high, his rival poker player has four aces with a king high. Turpin is accused of cheating. (Close up of Turpin's face.) Then, there's a cut to a cue card in which Turpin mouths the famous catch phrase from the original novel: "If you want to call me that, *smile*." Turpin is looking at Trampis (his rival) but is pointing his gun at the other player.

In Sennett's *The King of Comedy*, he wrote that at no time were gag writers allowed to write a script, the directors were expected to be able to shoot without aid. There still exists a rough draft of *The Reel Virginian*, typed up with plenty of notes and signatures authorizing production to go ahead.

Unfortunately, nothing regarding this early liaison with Edgar Kennedy and Frank Capra ever made it to print. In Capra's autobiography, *The Name Above the Title*, there is only mention of his relationship to "old man" Sennett. There is, however, one gag that Capra and Sennett had a

*She Loved Him Plenty* Keystone—1918
W/Chas. Conklin, Ben Turpin, Edgar

disagreement on. Capra only referred to it as a Ben Turpin-Madeline Hurlock comedy, the title of which he forgot.

According to Capra, he got himself fired for suggesting an additional running gag involving a loosened wagon wheel. Every time Turpin makes a passionate play toward Hurlock, the wheel (as though it had a life of its own) precariously dangled near the cliff as it was rolling. In his book Capra explains, "the topper? When Ben stands up in the buggy and says dramatically 'Love me or I leap to my death!' the wheel falls off, the axle drops, throwing Ben over the cliff. Madeline rushes down the cliff, embraces the groggy Turpin and says in title card 'My hero. Don't die, I love you.' "

Capra was mortified when he told the gag to Sennett. "I don't like it, Frank, 'tain't funny. And don't go telling it to the director—what's his name? Lloyd Bacon? [It was actually Edgar]. You hear?" To prove a point, Sennett agreed to leave the gag in the previews and predicted the young upstart would learn his lesson. According to Capra, "the audience laughed all the way through the wheel routine."

Edgar as the Director of "Cupid's Boots" for Mack Sennett. Notice on his megaphone that his name is on it. This photo came from the Academy of Arts and Sciences and has not been seen before.

Although Ben Turpin and Hurlock teamed up in three comedy/love interest stories with Lloyd Bacon starting in 1925, further research contradicts Capra's recollections. Frank Capra's biographer, Joseph McBride, corrected Capra's memory by matching up the wheel gag to *The Reel Virginian* and properly identified the director as Ed Kennedy.

During this time, the Pathe Publicity Department expected their contract talent to fill out a generic questionnaire. Edgar Kennedy completed the form and submitted it. Fortunately, this document has been preserved in the Margaret Herrick Library in Beverly Hills and reveals a rare glimpse into Edgar's life in 1924. It was here that education institutions were revealed. Interestingly, Edgar wrote that he had a featured role in *Stubborn Cinderella* on stage and played P. Tomaine Tommy in the *Leather Pushers* with Reginald Denny. He mentioned his hobby was golf, that his preferred types of reading were "London" [Jack] and the *Exhibitors Herald* [*Motion Picture Herald*].

In a most provocative pronouncement, Edgar proudly wrote that he was a nephew of David Livingstone, the great African Explorer.[12] Continuing, Edgar listed that he had previously acted in Sennett Comedies "six years ago with Mabel Normand, Fred Mace, Ford Sterling, and was the first comedy heavy. Directing Ben Turpin at present." It is relevant to note that Edgar did not fill in the space asking "Married to." Under the category "Highest Ambition," Edgar wrote, "To make good comedies."

Credited as Ed Kennedy, his next directorial assignment with the megaphone was in Sennett's *Cupid's Boots* (running title: *Graves Story*). This time there were no coauthors; it listed the story by Frank Capra. The titles were by J.A. Waldron, one of which includes: "Darkness came because the sun had set and the moon was all in from being out the night before." Introducing a character, the title said: "Jasper Strong—Everyone knew he was rich because he only paid $109.00 for income tax."

The cast featured Ralph Graves and Andy Clyde. The production was supervised by F. Richard Jones. The script begins:

| | |
|---|---|
| **Open:** | In front of bootery. |
| **Dissolve:** | Into Ralph in full armor standing by brewery horse, in same posture as Sir Galahad. |
| **Iris:** | In—external shot of wind and lightning. |

12. The family believes that the connection is with Neil Kennedy's mother. Since it is unknown what her name or what providence of Canada Neil came from, continuing research has yet to verify that claim.

| | |
|---|---|
| **Pan:** | Down to upstairs window |
| **Dissolve:** | Girl tied to post |
| **Cut:** | To leader of the Heavys phoning (in close up). |

There were notes written at the preview: "Groves Cupid Boots." Delux Friday night. "That last rock sequence—it does not seem to get over. Think we lost a laugh by cutting out the dog pulling blanket over himself/this got a good laugh at the Bard's Theatre."

In Frank Capra's autobiography, he unfortunately didn't elaborate on working with Edgar or the films described above. But some 45 years after achieving the heights of all film successes, Capra reflected on the beginning of his career at Sennett's.

> The writers and directors knew that while Sennett was the heart, the body, and the name of the studio, Dick Jones was the brains. He assigned writers and directors, cast the parts, thought up and listened to story ideas, supervised the editing. Then, without appearing to do so, he had everything tried out on the old man. Although Sennett had no

Edgar directs *Hot Dog* w/ Arthur Lake (1926) Universal
(Photo Courtesy Sam Gill)

great sense of humor—as most of us commonly know it, his reaction to comedy was an infallible audience barometer. If Sennett laughed, audiences would laugh. If Sennett didn't laugh—well, rewrite it or re-shoot it, said Dick Jones.

It didn't take me long to sense that Dick Jones knew and understood more about comedy than anyone else on the lot. Its construction, the art of timing, the building of a gag, the surprise heaping of 'business on business' until you top it all off with the big one—the 'topper.' Dick Jones was my man. Leech-like I stuck to him night or day, sucking up his know-how. He lived alone at the Hollywood Athletic Club; young (late twenties), handsome, a married bachelor—married to his work.

The preceding was a rare insight into the daily routines of the Sennett factory. F. Richard Jones was more than happy to give all the credit to Sennett. Even hardcore film buffs hardly hear about Dick Jones; certainly not from the Sennett autobiography (except in describing him as his favorite director). The significance in all this, Capra pointed out, was that it was Jones who hired the directors and approved the storylines, not Sennett. Thus, it should forever be noted that F. Richard Jones was the one who directed numerous early Sennett shorts with Edgar appearing in them, and hired Edgar back as director.

In a bold move for the top spot in comedy film production, F. Richard Jones was recruited by Hal Roach to work at his studio as supervisor (not unlike the job he held at Sennett) in the spring of 1925. Jones paid immediate dividends to Roach by hiring Stan Laurel as a director.

In late 1925, Edgar went back to Universal to direct a one-reel "Bluebird" comedy called *Hot Dog*. It starred a young juvenile by the name of Arthur Lake. It is an obscure, long-lost film notable only because the adolescent Lake would years later portray Dagwood Bumstead in the "Blondie" movies series and on television. Even more interesting is that Edgar would become famous working with Arthur Lake's sister, Florence Lake, who portrayed Edgar's wife in the "Average Man" series. Edgar later appeared in one of the "Blondie" movies in 1940, *Blondie in Society*.

Only a *Moving Picture World* review (from January 30, 1926) by Sumner Smith gives us any indication what this missing film was about:

"This Blue Bird comedy features Arthur Lake. It is fairly entertaining. Arthur and Eddie compete for Betty at a picnic. Both take her home and both strive for the privilege when she announces she has lost the key and someone must enter by opening a window on the second story. Arthur runs foul of a bulldog, falls in the bathtub and, imagining ghosts, runs riot through the house. When at last he finds the front door, he also finds a note saying that Betty has decided to take a spin with Eddie."

So was Edgar a comic, a director, or a heavy? This short article from the *Los Angeles Times* of 7-12-25 identifies him as a great dramatic find!

> On completion of the role of 'Bill Sproat,' in '**My Old Dutch**,' which Laurence Trimble directed for Universal, Edgar Kennedy has been signed to play 'Geewhillaker Hayes' in the '**The Golden Princess**' for Paramount, with Betty Bronson, Neil Hamilton and other well known players.
>
> Kennedy was hailed by Trimble as the greatest discovery among 'heavies' in years, and first won note when Perley Poore Sheehan signed him as the hero of '**The Night Message**,' proclaiming him as a dramatic find. Kennedy started as a comic opera comedian and then became a screen comedy director. He played 'Ptomaine Tommy' throughout the '**Leather Pushers**' series. He is now at Bishop on location with the Badger unit. He is also slated for a role with Raymond Griffith.

In 1925 Edgar was just a hard-working stiff trying to build on his successes. He had the respect of his peers, but he was a virtual unknown in the public's eye.

With the success of *Cupid's Boots*, Universal Studios hired him as a director. Edgar wasn't tied down to any long-term contracts and was starting to enjoy the fruits of his success. On October 17, 1925, in *The Moving Picture World*, a small news release was printed: "**Kennedy to Direct 'U' Comedies**. Edgar Kennedy, well-known actor and director, has discarded his makeup box for the megaphone once more. He has been signed by Universal to direct Arthur Lake and Eddie Clayton in the next series of 'Sweet Sixteen' comedies, according to announcement from Scott Darling, Universal comedy supervisor."

On October 6, 1926, the *Los Angeles Record* printed a little item on Edgar:

> **Kennedy Once Keystone Cop.** Ed Kennedy Character actor whose most recent successes are Warner Brothers' 'Across the Pacific,' showing at the Uptown and that company's fun special 'The Better 'Ole,' soon to be shown here, was one of the eight original Keystone cops. The Mack Sennett Keystone cops in their heyday were as well known as Lloyd, Chaplin and Keaton are now. Kennedy's contract with the Sennett company in those days called for a guarantee of four days work a week at $3.00 a day. For that munificent wage Ed and his seven co-workers were supposed to do any and everything the director asked in the way of thrills, bumps and risks. Right now three companies are arguing for Kennedy's services, and the terms of the contract does not call for $3.00 a day.

Three days later, in the *Hollywood Citizen* newspaper, the following was printed:

> **Three Offers For Kennedy.** A New York producer has wired Ed Kennedy to come east and play the role of an Irish police sergeant in a big 'East Side West Side' comedy drama about to go in production. Another producer wants him to go to Texas and play the part of a top sergeant in a hard-boiled cavalry outfit in a big border story to be filmed around Fort Sam Houston. And a big independent concern in Hollywood is after the popular portrayer of character roles to do a political boss in an underworld drama. 'I never get a chance to be decent on the screen,' wails Big Ed. 'Why doesn't someone write a real prizefight story and let me be the hero once. I was one time amateur and professional heavy-weight of the Pacific Coast but I'll bet that if they do write that story they will send for me to play the big plug-ugly that tries to put cyanide in the champion's soup.'

The above quote perfectly reflects Edgar's later screen persona; frustrated and somewhat cynical, but with a comical overreaction. As a matter of fact, Edgar did play in a number of roles during his silent days in which he fought in the ring:

*The Wrong Mr. Wright* (1927) Universal
(Author's collection)

*The Knockout*
*Daredevil Jack*
*The Leather Pushers*
*The Battling Fool*
*Fight and Win (All's Swell on the Ocean)*
*My Old Dutch*
*Proud Heart*

In 1926, it was his character portrayal in the feature *Across the Pacific* that drew attention. Edgar portrayed a soldier killed in battle, with such convincing skill, he overshadowed the star, Monte Blue. An uncredited author at the time, related the following to his readers:

> Edgar L. Kennedy. Once in a while—not very often—something happens to make a fellow who writes such a column as this feel that the job's worth doing after all. Something like that happened this week. Tell you 'bout it. Writ-

ing about 'Across the Pacific' for the October 9 issue, I said, 'The cast also includes a fighting Irishman who pals with Blue until the natives get him. This actor is requested to submit his name so that a special item can be written.'

On October 22 a letter was received from Mr. Kennedy, just back from location with Universal's 'The Wrong Mr. Wright' company confirming the identity. From both letters I gained the information that Mr. Kennedy began his picture working in 1910 [sic] with Mack Sennett as one of the producer's famous Keystone Kops. He appeared in pictures for sixteen years without my finding out about it, so the fault must be mine. Anyway, the special item which would have been inserted in the original write-up of 'Across the Pacific' had Mr. Kennedy's name been known would have read like this:

> "Edgar L. Kennedy, a two-fisted Irishman with personality, punch and a very evident knowledge of what to do with them, epitomizes the spirit of Funston's heroic expedition and does the wide world a service by showing it how a real fighting man dies. There is nothing finer in any motion picture that the scene in which this hard-living, hard-dying trouper kicks off."
>
> But the thing that seems to make a job like this columnist's worth while is the fact that Monte Blue, who got no more than a passing mention in the write-up of the picture in which he starred, is man enough to write the letter at hand. While men like these are out there making pictures there is more than enough reason for running a column like this—or one a thousand times more worthy—for the purpose of recording their efforts. Thanks, both of you.

Myrna Loy and Edgar made a personal appearance at the Uptown Theatre for the premiere. The *Los Angeles Times* reported on 10-4-26: "Every seat in the theater was taken for the early presentation. A majority of the stars who played in 'Across the Pacific' were introduced by John T. Murray, as master of ceremonies.

"Among those who made personal appearances were Jane Winton, Myrna Loy and Ed Kennedy, who almost succeeded in stealing the picture at times through his performance as the corporal."

It also praised:

> Ed Kennedy, character actor, has just been signed by Warner Brothers for a role in Lloyd Bacon's production 'Fingerprints,' for the first co-starring vehicle for Louise Fazenda and John T. Murray which goes into production.
>
> The role assigned to Mr. Kennedy is that of a stuttering coroner's assistant and if you can think of anything lends itself better to comedy characterization, the director would like to know what it is so he can use the same.
>
> Ed accepted this role in preference to two offers he had for feature parts in productions just getting underway in New York and San Antonio because he saw the possibilities of this unusual character and hopes to make it a high light in the forthcoming comedy.

On June 8, 1927, the *Associated Press* printed this bit of information originating from Pasadena:

> STUNT ACTOR IN ACCIDENT—The filming of a screen comedy turned into a near tragedy today when Edgar L. Kennedy stunt actor for Universal Studios, accidentally failed to round a street corner on a motorcycle, and piled up against a telephone pole. Kennedy was playing the part of a motorcycle police officer pursuing Reginald Denny, who had turned the corner in his fleeing car.

Even the *Moving Picture World*, a trade paper for the filmmaking community printed a column regarding the above incident in their August 27, 1927 issue. It featured a photo of Edgar on crutches.

> Ed Kennedy—Injured while working on Reginald Denny's latest Universal production, is now up and around. Ed Kennedy had a tough break lately—it was one of his legs that was broken and, as a consequence, Ed has been limping around on a pair of crutches for the past

month or two. The damaged underpinning is coming along nicely, however, and he expects to throw away the supports and get down to the daily grind before the camera before long.

Kennedy was doing one of the featured supporting roles for Reginald Denny in 'Now I'll Tell One' at the Universal studio, when he was catapulted from a crazy motorcycle and took a hurried trip to the hospital. Tom O'Brien was called in to substitute for Kennedy and the picture went merrily on.

'Heavy' roles are Kennedy's specialties, but he is also recognized as a director of no mean ability. He has directed for several of the larger companies, including Fox, Sennett and Universal.

He started in pictures back in 1913 as a Keystone Kop in the Sennett custard pie operas. It was but a step from flashing the tin badge to directing. After leaving Sennett's he went to Fox for a year as a director and then moved his megaphone over to Universal where he transferred script to screen for another two years.

Recently he has been doing a little directing but mainly sticks to acting before the camera. He started his theatrical career as a stock actor, but later gave up the stage to enter the ring first as an amateur pugilist and later as a professional.

# 13.
# Hal Roach Studios

Edgar was indeed getting noticed. With his vast experience ranging from slapstick artist to support character, coupled with directorial credits, Edgar knew every trick in the book. The Hal Roach Studios beckoned.

There was a transition in progress since F. Richard Jones went from Sennett to Hal Roach in 1925. One of Jones' early major accomplishments was the luring of Stan Laurel from the Joe Rock studios. Jones hired Laurel primarily as a director. According to Randy Skretvedt's book, *Laurel and Hardy—The Magic Behind the Movies,* "Under the guidance of F. Richard 'Dick' Jones, Stan learned the craft of comedy film directing."

It was during filming of *Get 'em Young* (released 10-31-26) that Stan was enticed by Dick Jones to make an emergency appearance in the comedy. This directly led to the continuation of Stan Laurel acting in Hal Roach comedies, and ultimately to the matching of Laurel and Hardy onscreen.

As Laurel and Hardy slowly merged together with each Roach *All-Star Comedies*, one comedian, James Finlayson, suffered less screen time. After the smash hit *Hats Off*, Finlayson, in the words of Skredtvet, "knew that he was no longer being groomed for stardom at Hal Roach's, left the studios in September of 1927 to test the waters."

Finlayson may have forever been obscure had he not returned to the Roach lot a year and half later. With Fin's absence, a new comic foil was needed. F. Richard Jones, who had directed Edgar back in 1914 and was so pivotal to his directorial accomplishments, must have had his eye on Kennedy. The two comedians were not exactly interchangeable (though they both featured baldheads), they had completely different styles. If Edgar's anger was slow to ignite, Fin's anger could be described as a short fuse.

Edgar Kennedy most certainly was hired not so much to replace "Fin," but to add to the stock company used for comedies shot around the "Lot of

Fun." F. Richard Jones, who had directed Edgar back in 1914 and was so pivotal to his directorial accomplishments, must have had his eye on Kennedy. There were now many ex-Sennett veterans at Roach, including James Finlayson, Charley Chase and even Mabel Normand. Still, later, other Sennett veterans would join the lot: Mae Busch, Bobby Dunn, Tom Kennedy, and Harry Langdon. Billy Gilbert, however, was not an ex-Sennett player although there was a Keystone Kop with the same name. Edgar used to refer to the former as "Little Billy Gilbert" to make the distinction.

On November 3, 1927, filming began on Laurel and Hardy's *Leave 'em Laughing*. Edgar played the foil as a hard-boiled, agitated traffic cop. Even though Edgar's experience included Keystone Kop portrayals, there

*Leave 'em Laughing* (Roach) 1927
(Courtesy Kennedy Family)

Publicity shot (circa late 30's)
(Courtesy Kennedy Family)

was a difference in his characterization for Roach. Born was the victimized public servant, whose frustration slowly registered on his broad Irish pan. Completely void of hair by this time, Edgar emphasized it by pushing his uniform hat back to expose his shiny pate.

During the Roach years, Edgar accented his bald head like a comical prop. Up until the Roach period of his career, Edgar often wore wigs or toupees for various reasons. In existing photographs between 1913 and 1929, there are no two pictures in which Edgar's hair was similar. There has always been speculation that Edgar suddenly went bald starting with Roach. In actuality, Edgar's hairline was receding rapidly even in the early Mack Sennett days. In *The Knockout*, made during 1914, one can see Edgar's natural hair slicked back and thinning in the back and temple. By the time *A Game Old*

*Knight* was shot in late 1915, Edgar was almost completely bald. Edgar wore a toupee as late as 1927 for the feature film, *Finger Prints* for Warner Brothers.

The Roach comedies allowed Edgar's reactions to build to a crescendo of anguish and anger. There were sometimes close ups of his face to register the growing irritation. What better way to showcase his character than to place him into the uniform of a policeman directing traffic? Sprinkle the scene with a traffic jam, add liberal doses of Laurel & Hardy and the results are a comedy classic. An image forever frozen in time by photography is "Kennedy-the-Cop," whose pants had inadvertently fallen down to his ankles, with Laurel and Hardy laughing in pantomime, from the climax of *Leave 'em Laughing*.

Edgar played the stereotypical Irish cop of the day. Big, burley and with a name like Kennedy, he was a natural. Behind the scenes, Edgar was a jovial team player. Coming from the school of hard knocks, i.e., boxing, a stock player for Sennett, then a director, Edgar by this time knew the camera well and what would work in front of the lens. He was also crackerjack behind the lens.

Edgar received the opportunity to direct eight (not counting the foreign versions) Hal Roach comedies, two of them with Laurel and Hardy. Curiously, his director credits with Laurel & Hardy were as E Livingston Kennedy, the first initial of his name and whole middle name.

*The Los Angeles Times* reported on 6-17-28:

> The Hal Roach studios are staging a golf tournament at the Riviera Country Club this morning, starting at 9 o'clock. About thirty employees of the studio have entered, ranging all the way from the executive heads down to the prop men.
>
> Many beautiful trophies have been posted in the various divisions, as well as for low gross and low net scores. Particular interest centers about the play between Oliver Hardy and Ed Kennedy, both players of the Roach stock company. Hardy is looked upon as one of the champion golfers of the picture colony, having won sweepstakes in the motion-picture tournament last year, with a large collection of other titles and trophies to his credit. Kennedy, on the other hand, defeated all actors in that division of the same tournament this spring.

One of the most charming aspects of the Roach comedies is that, for the most part, the main characters were identified by their real names. The public embraced the screen images of Stan Laurel, Oliver Hardy, Charley Chase and Kennedy-the-Cop, among others. The name variation of E. Livingston Kennedy might have been an attempt to keep separate his screen character-acting persona from his directorial identity.

Nineteen Twenty-seven was a very good year. With a contract in hand, Edgar's future never looked brighter. The Kennedy family moved to 430 S. Crescent Dr. in Beverly Hills. The family phone number was listed as OX [Oxford] 6607.

Edgar directed *From Soup to Nuts*, starring Laurel and Hardy, shot between late December 1927 until January 5, 1928. The wonderful Anita Garvin was cast as Mrs. Culpepper, a high society dame. In one of the funniest scenes in the movie, she wore a tiara adornment that constantly

Serious business, this making of comedies. For every guffaw there's an hour of anguish! Observe above Roach-M-G-M buffoonery in the making. There's Director Edgar Kennedy (at left) with two of his stellar comedians, Stan Laurel (Center) and Oliver Hardy, struggling for a funny idea with which to banish sorrow. Such is the price of laughter.

Edgar, the Director w/ Laurel and Hardy
(Courtesy of Lois Laurel Hawes)

collapsed over her eyes as she impatiently chased a cherry around her saucer plate with a fork.

Anita made 11 films with Laurel and Hardy. In an interview later in life, Anita reflected on the films she made with the boys. She said that "no matter who the director was, it was really Stan that was directing the scenes. But he was so sweet about it, no one minded." Anita could very well be talking about *From Soup to Nuts*, among others. Edgar certainly collaborated with Stan Laurel for gags. There was a mutual respect between them, which developed into a lifelong friendship.

E. Livingston Kennedy helmed the megaphone immediately afterward for *You're Darn Tootin'*, shot between January 17 and 27 of 1928. This Laurel and Hardy short features the famous pants-tearing scene, inadvertently caused by Stan, of course. What starts as a careless tossing of a banana skin, resulting in a downed victim, develops into a slow tit-for-tat confrontation. An excellent example of "reciprocal destruction."[13] For every punch to the stomach, there is an immediate, equal response of a kick-to-the-shin by Laurel. Every peacekeeper that descends on the scene gets the same treatment until there is a gaggle of gentlemen all hopping up and down in pain. As the action gets

Anita Garvin & Edgar Kennedy in *A Pair of Tights* (Roach)
(Courtesy of Richard Finegan)

13. "Reciprocal Destruction" is a term coined by author John McCabe to describe Laurel and Hardy's tit-for-tat retaliation coupled with passive resistance.

quicker, Laurel and Hardy escalate the matters by tearing off the pants of anyone who approaches them. This, of course, leads to retaliation from the crowd of men who, at the film's climax, rip off Laurel and Hardy's pants. They in turn tear off the trousers of the policeman who had descended on the scene to keep the peace, or more accurately, to keep the pants!

The Laurel and Hardy short *Should Married Men Go Home?* featured Edgar supporting, or rather battling, the boys on the golf course. Edgar was an accomplished golfer, filming the comedy antics on the golf links seemed like a natural for the golf-minded Roach staff. A highlight of the film is a sight gag in which Stan hands Edgar what he thinks is his hairpiece, but it turns out to be a divot. During filming, Edgar was signed to a five-year contract, which also allowed him to freelance at the other studios.

Laurel and Hardy's *You're Darn Tootin'*, *Two Tars*, and *Big Business*, all had a similar theme to them. The slowly built tit-for-tat pace, with the Armageddon visual climax, thrilled audiences.

The "Lot of Fun" seemingly churned out these Laurel and Hardy classics effortlessly, but there was a lot of creative talent going into the mix. During this same time period, there was another short comedy of the same genre, only this time Laurel and Hardy weren't in it. It was called *A Pair of Tights,* and it featured Edgar Kennedy.

The similar theme has prompted film scholars to hypothesize that it was originally intended as a Laurel and Hardy short. Edgar, wearing a bowler hat, was cast as a grouchy, cheap boss. He was fixed up with Anita Garvin. It was hate at first sight. Edgar was uninterested in what he perceived as a "goldigger." She was annoyed at this ill mannered penny-pinching bore. It's a good thing that this is a silent movie because there was hardly any talking between them. Things were that icy.

Edgar's character brightens when he believes that buying the girls an ice cream cone will diminish their appetite for an expensive dinner. He willingly surrenders a nickel to buy his "date" an ice cream.

In a visual delight of flying and dropping scoops of various flavors of ice cream, one formula remained constant in this Hal Roach comedy combat scene: Misunderstandings + accidents = retaliation and revenge.

Laurel and Hardy couldn't have pulled this off better. Oliver Hardy's screen character was so chivalrous that it is impossible to imagine Ollie being anything but a southern gentleman to any lady. Stuart Erwin's character was similar to Stan in some respects, with the exception of courting

*Hurdy Gurdy* w/ Edgar & Gertrude Messinger
(Courtesy of Cole Johnson)

a girlfriend. The menacing cop who frustratingly tries to write a parking ticket, only to be thwarted over and over, could easily have been played by Edgar, but he played those roles before.

*A Pair of Tights* was later reedited and featured as part of *When Comedy Was King* (1960), a comedy compilation by producer Robert Youngson. Showing almost all of the second reel intact, this little comedy has been hailed by film critics, such as Leonard Maltin, as a minor film classic.

Edgar was again paired with Laurel and Hardy in the waning days of silent movies in *Bacon Grabbers*. Edgar's character was identified as Collis Kennedy. Stan and Ollie were unlikely Sheriff's process servers. Their ineptitude causes a stalemate to the repossession of Edgar's radio. Showing up in the last few seconds of the film is Edgar's wife, played by 19-year-old Jean Harlow. Edgar previously worked with Jean at the Hal Roach Studios in *Chasing Husbands*, *Why Is a Plumber?* and *Thundering Toupees*, shot in 1928. By 1930, Jean would become an international sex symbol for her starring role in Howard Hughes' *Hell's Angels*.

Something else was going on at Hal Roach during this time: A transition to talkies. The first "all dialogue" comedy released by the studio was entitled *Hurdy Gurdy* and starred Thelma Todd, Max Davidson, Eddie Dunn and, of course, Kennedy-the-Cop. With so much at stake, it was personally directed by Hal Roach.

*The Motion Picture News* reviewed this film on 6-29-29:

> The beautiful Thelma has had the iceman busy all day long bringing ice up to her top floor tenement and her neighbors, Irish, Jewish, German and Italian, are just dying to know why she should require so much ice. The iceman wonders too, but Thelma won't reveal a thing. Finally, one of the neighbors starts a rumor that a murder has been committed on the top floor and they compel Ed Kennedy, a tired out cop trying to procure a little rest amid the bedlam of the tenement's rear fire escapes, to investigate. After stretching your curiosity to a breaking point, it is revealed that Thelma has been keeping a trained seal and that's where all the ice has been going to.

Before filming began, Roach had sound tests done on all his contract players. Edgar's worst fears were realized; his voice was recorded and played back at a very high pitch. Obviously his voice did not match the burley Irish cop image. Edgar's very future was now in doubt. He wouldn't be the first person affected by sound. There were other bigger stars, like John Gilbert and Raymond Griffith, who couldn't make the transition to the talkies. Edgar knew this would be his first and only chance to continue film acting, so he did something about it.

It was May of 1929 and Edgar sought out a voice coach. He found one with her own drama studio in Los Angeles, a lady by the name of Josephine Dillion. At the time, she was the wife of an obscure stage actor by the name of Clark Gable. Dillion is the one that personally coached Gable's stage presence and, most important, his voice.

Even before Gable became famous, Dillion was very respected for her past acting talents. She ran her drama studio as a means of support to further her husband's career. Dillion abhorred movie acting and was convinced that only the legitimate stage was a respectful vocation.

It is unclear whether Edgar sought out Dillion on his own, or if Hal Roach was trying to protect his investment. Intense private lessons ensued. She instructed Edgar on proper breathing techniques and how to lower and project his voice. Edgar's natural Irish tenor voice went through a thorough metamorphosis. His voice could now emote in a gravely low voice that perfectly matched his character and, even more important, was perfectly recordable as such.

Edgar's daughter, Colleen, in reminiscing about her dad, always remembered that at home he was very soft spoken, "you had to listen." She also recalled that he had a beautiful melodious singing voice and sang a lot of Irish songs.

*Hurdy Gurdy* was successfully completed and paved the way for the next Laurel and Hardy short, *Unaccustomed As We Are*. In this tight little domestic setting (a precursor to their later feature film *Blockheads*), Edgar is again cast as Kennedy-the-Cop and married to the beautiful Thelma Todd. Their neighbors across the hall are Mr. and Mrs. Oliver Hardy.

*The Perfect Day* (1929) Roach
(Author's collection)

Ollie's wife was portrayed by Sennett veteran Mae Busch. She would later portray Hardy's wife in numerous Laurel and Hardy movies. *Unaccustomed As We Are* was actually released before *Hurdy Gurdy.*

The next Laurel and Hardy short that Edgar worked in was *Perfect Day*. Edgar was out of uniform for this one, creating a memorable character as "Uncle Edgar." Just turning age 39, Edgar could portray a man many years his senior.

For this short Edgar donned a straw hat, a cane and a ridiculous bandage encasing his gout-ridden foot. The cantankerous Uncle Edgar spoke in an authentic Irish accent, but his comic reactions of pain provide this film with some of its highlights. Laurel and Hardy, in a matter of moments, inadvertently steps on his defenseless foot, then slams a car door on it, dropped the car on it and unwittingly induced the dog to grab a mouth full of the bandaged extremity to play tug-of-war with it.

One thing was certain, the talkies were here to stay and Edgar had made the cut. He was already a veteran of films for more than sixteen years, many of which he made in obscurity. He was now a revered contract actor for the Hal Roach studios with a stable young family. The future looked rosy indeed.

*Girl Shock* w/ Charley Chase (1930) Roach
(Courtesy Rich Finegan)

*Moan & Groan, Inc.* (1929) Roach
(Courtesy Kennedy Family)

As the next Laurel and Hardy short, *Night Owls*, started production, the stock market crashed on the infamous date of October 29, 1929. Black Tuesday was just that for Edgar; he had lost his life savings in the stock market. Uncertainty was everywhere, and the ensuing Depression would have a profound effect in the direction of Edgar's career.

In *Night Owls*, Edgar's character again was Kennedy-the-Cop. Flat foot Kennedy walked his beat but was unsuccessful in preventing some forty-two burglaries in his assigned beat. In a desperate act, he coerced vagrants Laurel and Hardy to pretend to be burglarizing a house until he caught them red-handed. Simple. This, of course, was a little beyond Stan's comprehension, but the "wiser" Ollie, in an effort to please, was eventually convinced by the assurances of the nice policeman. "Don't worry, Kennedy will fix it."

Edgar was featured in the comedy climax, by not catching Laurel and Hardy (they escaped), leaving Kennedy-the-Cop inadvertently holding the bag (literally) of ill-gotten goods. As the lights flicked on catching Kennedy "in the act," Edgar held his pose with open mouth astonishment as he quickly realized how this was being perceived by the victimized Chief of Police.

This was the first Laurel and Hardy short that was made for the Spanish-speaking foreign market. The scenes were re-shot with Stan and Ollie, Fin and Edgar repeating their roles reading phonetic language cue cards.

*Night Owls* was the last short that Edgar worked with Laurel and Hardy. Edgar continued working in other Roach shorts starring Harry Langdon, Charley Chase, Our Gang and The Boy Friend series. He even directed several of them throughout the 1930 season.

Some of his best portrayals were in the "Our Gang" shorts. As Kennedy-the-Cop, Edgar had a chance to interact with the kids in sometimes a charming fashion. There he is with Jackie Cooper in *The First Seven Years* giving him some manly advice about winning the girl of his dreams.

Way before the term "Community Policing" was invented, uniformed Edgar walked the neighborhood beat looking to prevent trouble or apprehend the bad guy. Edgar compassionately warned the kids of danger of going into a deserted house in *Moan & Groan, Inc.,* and, presumably in the absence of a nearby dad, he changes a baby's diapers expertly while storing the safety pin in his lips for ready access. He does this while chortling in his Irish accent much to the amusement of his mom. "I've got to have fun on the job sometimes," Edgar remarks. If Edgar appeared like an expert diaper changer, he obviously was with his own children, Larry and Colleen, who were four and three years old respectively.

Another charming short, *Shivering Shakespeare,* featured Kennedy-the-Cop helping the kids as a prop man in the school play. The play is produced, allegedly, by Edgar's screen wife "Funston Evergreen Kennedy." The highlight is a pie throwing sequence complete with slow motion action following the path of a pie.

An interesting footnote to Edgar's "Our Gang" appearances is *When the Wind Blows.* One of the posed studio stills featured Kennedy-the-Cop, gun in hand, bumbling around a back alleyway. The Gang is posed smiling behind him. Despite the fact that Edgar is wearing a traditional eight-cornered uniform hat in the picture, when Edgar died, there was a lack of authentic Keystone Kop images of Edgar in photos. To substitute, newspapers used this still, cropping the kids out of it and replaced the hat with a tall-crowned comic cop hat of the Keystone era.

During 1930, Edgar also appeared in two Educational Pictures, teaming up with Arthur Houseman in *Help Wanted—Female* and *Next Door*

*Neighbors.* In the latter, Edgar played the comedy villain introducing himself and Houseman to Daphne Pollard (ex-Sennett and future Hal Roach comedian) saying, "we're a couple of boiglers." The latter title was directed by Harry Sweet, who would soon collaborate with Edgar for the future "Average Man" series. Harry was an experienced director with the Mack Sennett Studios as far back as 1924 when he directed (with Reggie Morris) *Romeo and Juliet,* with a cast of Ben Turpin, Billy Bevan and Dot Farley.

Edgar as Kennedy-the-Cop had his last screen appearance in *Love Fever* for "The Boyfriend" series. It was filmed between October 6 and 14 in 1930 and released on 4-11-31. Despite Edgar's talents as director and support comedian, he was being relegated to portraying Irish cops for the most part. Of the fifteen shorts in the "Boy Friends" series that were released, Edgar appeared in the first five of six. According to Hal Roach production records, the last filmed appearance of Edgar in a Hal Roach movie was actually for the ending of The Boy Friends' *High Gear* (filmed on November 7 and 22 of 1930). To end his career with Hal Roach, the final gag was filmed with Mickey Daniels inadvertently dropping a bathtub on Edgar's head from upstairs. There was an off camera crash, followed by a medium shot of Edgar in a daze, rubbing his bald head where contact was presumably made. It was a blueprint for later head-wiping finishes in his own film series in the years to come.

According to author Randy Skretvedt's *Laurel and Hardy, The Magic Behind the Movies,* Roach reported huge losses for his studio during the 1930-31 season and "Edgar Kennedy's contract was terminated." Edgar already anticipated changes and was preparing for his future.

Did the Roach studios let Edgar go because of their downsizing of expenses? Or was it because Edgar was negotiating for a series deal with RKO? It is interesting to ponder; despite the economic downturn of the Roach studio's profit margins, comedian Billy Gilbert (no relation to the former Sennett comic "Little Billy Gilbert") was hired as a stock comedian in the fall of 1931, just after Edgar left the lot. It was much like when Edgar was hired to replace James Finlayson in 1927.

America was in the depths of the Depression. There were cut backs and downsizing everywhere. These were scary times for all in the movie business, even the Laurel and Hardy series lost money at Hal Roach Studios. It seemed an unlikely time for anyone to entertain the thought of leaving a movie studio to star in their own series. Edgar had seen them come and go:

(Author's collection)

Fred Mace, Ford Sterling, Mabel Normand, Harry Langdon and, to an extent, Fatty Arbuckle. They all left the comfort of their home studios with the uncertain lure of being a star in their own series at another studio, just to fail. Some of them never made it back at all. There were a few success stories, of course; the most distinguished of this class was Charlie Chaplin. Besides the higher salary, there were the inevitable demands for script approval and high production budgets. Producers cringed at the risk. Hal Roach would call this "Chaplin Disease"; Roach would often accuse Stan Laurel of being so afflicted.

# 14.
# The Average Man Series

The little budgeted short comedy series for RKO made Edgar Kennedy a household name. He was not a glamorous star in prestigious feature films, but rather like a blue-collar worker in Hollywood, certainly a character for all moviegoers to identify with. Just the average Joe, or in this case, The Average Man.

For seventeen years Edgar churned out these two-reelers at the rate of six a year, often shot in a three-day shooting schedule. Plenty of time was left over for him to act in other RKO projects or freelance at the other studios. Edgar portrayed the "everyman," a victim in his own home. The beauty was watching Edgar's irritation mount until, inevitably, he couldn't stand it anymore. And it hardly took anything to irritate him. Anything of an inordinate object such as chipping ice from an ice block, repairing something, or trying to take a nap, the world seemingly conspired against him. He was, in a sense, just the opposite of the Harry Langdon character who, seemingly, God protected from the calamities of life.

Edgar's hypertension could always be triggered by just about any of life's annoyances. Throw in his chirpy wife, a meddling mother-in-law, a weasel brother-in-law and you have a slow building recipe for failure—in this case, a recipe for laughs!

Edgar's screen character isn't really that much of a departure from the roles he played at Roach. It would be easy to imagine that "Kennedy the Cop" off duty was "The Average Man" in a domestic setting. If Kennedy received no respect as a uniformed Officer-of-the-Law in the Roach comedies, he received even less in his own family.

Was Edgar's character an extension of the funny papers' *The Terrible Tempered Mr. Bangs?* The cartoon strip was established in 1910 by Fontaine Fox[14]

---

14. Fontaine Fox was also the creator of "The Captain and the Kids," also a long running cartoon strip in syndication.

and was printed in newspapers across the country until 1950.

Mr. Bangs was characterized as having little self-control and often over reacted in rage to the simplest situations. Mr. Bangs would throw things and yell to the point of exaggeration. It was simply drawn, but it was the character development, not necessarily the action, that amused readers.

No doubt children and adults alike could relate to Mr. Bangs' constant frustrations. They could be smug with assurances that they didn't quite act out like that.

Watching Edgar's screen persona slowly evolve from Kennedy-the-Cop at Roach to the slow to burn "Average Man" of RKO, it is highly unlikely there was any conscious borrowing of the little cartoon character. Still, it wouldn't be unprecedented. Oliver Hardy once shared that in his youth, he was influenced by a comic strip character named "Helpful Henry" as a forerunner to "Ollie." If it is any gauge at all, Edgar Kennedy's daughter said that she had never heard of the Mr. Bangs comic strip.

Louella Parsons once wrote in her syndicated column (5-1-31) that, of all people, author Sinclair Lewis claimed that the "Average Man" was based on the character he penned for his *Babbitt* novel. There are some parallels to Edgar's "Average Man" character and the George F. Babbitt written in the 1920s. Both are middle-aged, middle-class, and upstanding citizens. Lewis described Babbitt as "pink-skinned and baby-faced, with a slight tendency toward heaviness." Babbitt's dreams are threatened by the noises of milkmen, paper carriers, and automobiles. Such a scenario was depicted in the beginning images of Edgar's *Wrong Direction* (1934) of his "Average Man" series.

Lewis' Babbitt, however, is a "successful" businessman in Midwestern America. He relishes material possessions and is very money conscious. Babbitt is a conformist and is intolerant of different thinking. Edgar, in contrast, just wants his in-laws out of his house. George Babbitt was a man to be pitied, and is closer to Carroll O'Connor's "Archie Bunker" character on television's *All in the Family* series during the 1970s.

We empathize with Edgar's Average Man. Such was the basis of the humor, for who could tolerate such living conditions? Both "Mother" and "Brother" conspire against Edgar at every opportunity to make his life miserable. This, despite the fact that Edgar was the breadwinner and supported not only his wife, but also his in-laws. Florence naturally protected her blood family, not in a threatening manner, but by a disarming warning, "Now, Edgar!" And an incessant giggle.

Edgar was simply imposed on. One should not read too much into any of the episodes for social commentary or great messages, it was a simply a comedy formula with built in agitators to raise the wrath of Edgar. As Stan Laurel later said about the Laurel and Hardy comedies, "We did it for laughs, nothing more." Situations were built on gags, and a twenty-minute short was the perfect time frame to pull it off.

Whether Edgar's character onscreen was an evolution of his Roach persona or the brainchild of Harry Sweet, one fact is certain: Edgar's apprenticeship of twenty-three years served him well. Middle-aged now, his face and crowned baldhead easily mirrored various stages of frustration.

When the "Average Man" series debuted in 1931 for RKO, Edgar stole the whole show as the "head of the family." There were other situation comedy series during the silent era, but this all-talking entry inspired many zany radio (and later television) families in what eventually would be referred to as "sitcoms."

In retrospect, it was a wonder the series ever made it at all. The "Average Man" series was initiated during the Depression when some film studios were folding. If there was to be any success, they would have to be made as inexpensively as possible. This series was initiated after two successful releases under the "Whoopie Comedies" banner as part of the Masquer's comedies, supervised under Lou Brock. In what would now be termed a "pilot(s)" to the eventual Edgar Kennedy series, Harry Sweet wrote two scripts. The first one was completed on 2-6-31 and was entitled *Rough House Rhythm*. The script indicates it was adapted from another story, "A Prince of Good Fellows."

A reviewer of the short on 3-15-31 described it as "a very modern comedy showing a 'happy' honeymoon with the couple trying to keep house in one of these modern service-plan arrangements. The wife's brother camps with them, a sort of domestic racketeer. What with the cramped quarters and other troubles, poor hubby and his wife have a hectic time. Finally in desperation they go out to a restaurant to eat, and find it run by their landlord, who has been giving them so much trouble. Edgar Kennedy, Florence Lake and Franklin Pangborn make this a snappy number and nicely paced."

Harry Sweet's script described the opening as a wedding scene, possibly of the shotgun variety: "Before him is the unhappy Mr. Kennedy, his wife and brother-in-law. Lounging unconcernedly in the background, is the girl's father, while near him leans the shotgun. (The scene was actually a house being sold).

During the course of the two-reeler, Edgar battles the dishwasher, among other earthly demons. According to the script, Sweet describes Edgar's character in different scenes as "Seething unworldly," "Now on the verge of nervous prostration," "Clutches his throat in an attempt to choke back his rising exasperation." It is interesting to note that the "brother" character was played by Claude Allister.[15]

Harry Sweet started right in with another script, this time co-written by George Green, and it was completed on 3-18-31. Edgar's and Florence's characters were firmly established. However, the writers decided to add a dash-of-the-devil to the mix in order to have a constant antagonist, the dreaded mother-in-law. For this role, Louise Carver was hired. Carver was another Sennett veteran and worked with Edgar in *The Marriage Circus*. In the book *Smile When the Raindrops Fall* by Brian Anthony and Andy Edmonds, the authors describe Louise Carver as "a marvelous, bulldog-faced comedienne." William Eugene was cast as the bothersome "brother." The blueprints of what became the "Average Man" series were being laid.

According to the script: *All Gummed Up*

Scene 1
Fade in: Kitchen in Kennedy Home:
Mr. Kennedy (*gleefully—a boy at heart*):
                I got the afternoon off so I'm painting the room.
Mama:         He probably bought the wrong colored paint.
                Probably some red shade and uou know how I
                hate red, etc. etc. !!! Attacking pain can-undismayed,
                he tries again, a bit annoyed at this predicament.
Interruption:  Being a man of purpose, dislikes on something of
                his own choosing.
Mr. Kennedy:  "Howls of pain."
        His wife-all a-twitter flutters about suggesting all
        manners of relief.
Mama:         "The object is to smash the ice—not your finger."
        Mr. Kennedy is in no mood to be trifled with and if looks
        could kill, they would be ordering lilies for mama.

---

15. Claude Allister is better known as one of the British suitors to take Thelma Todd and Zasu Pitts on a date to the boardwalk in "On the Loose."

Known as the creator of the "slow-burn," bald Edgar Kennedy (*left*) was another Keystone graduate. Kennedy, who once went 14 rounds with Dempsey, was once hit in the face with 182 pies in a single day.

*Lemon Meringue*, 1ˢᵗ official short for the "Average Man" series (RKO) (Author's collection)

The last scene is described: His manner plainly shows the end of his patience. Mr. Kennedy lets out an agonizing scream and starts kicking and cries as we slowly, fade out.

On 5-17-31 a reviewer described *All Gummed Up*:

> The old domestic comedy triangle, with ma-in-law a visitor and making things rough for husband. The principals are Edgar Kennedy, Florence Lake and Louise Carver. The wife is preparing a party for the neighborhood kiddies, and puts hubby to work helping with the chores. Kennedy succeeds in squeezing a lot of comedy out of situations that are just fair to middling. One of the best gags is his business of chopping ice for the ice-cream freezer. It's a good takeoff on the husband who tries to be helpful around the kitchen.

With the success of the two shorts, RKO signed Kennedy to a series of film comedies now officially dubbed "The Average Man" comedies. To insure success, Harry

Sweet wrote a scenario called *Lemon Meringue.* Production started on 4-22-31 and was completed on 4-27-31.

Louise Carver was again written into the script as the mother-in-law. Although signed to a contract at $300 per week as a salary, she was replaced for some reason by another Sennett veteran, Dot Farley. Edgar, Harry Sweet and Dot crossed paths numerous times during their careers, so it must have been a comfort to have such a talent in the "family." Over the course of the series run, it came to be that Dot Farley was forever cemented in the minds of audiences as the prototype stereotypical ma-in-law.

On 5-1-31 Hollywood columnist Louella Parsons announced in her syndicated article:

> RKO-Pathe believes that daily happenings in the life of the ordinary citizen will furnish enough comedy for a series of short subjects. They have signed Edgar Kennedy, who has appeared in innumerable Laurel and Hardy comedies, to play the lead in Mr. Average Man, with Harry Sweet directing. The first of the series, "Lemon Meringue," starts this week and included in the cast with Mr. Kennedy are Dot Farley, Florence Lake and William Eugene.

On 6-7-31, from an unknown film exhibitor, this was written:

> A Mr. Average Man comedy, featuring Edgar Kennedy. His mother-in-law and brother-in-law with the aid of his wife, get him to open a restaurant and quit his regular salary job. The action takes place just before the opening of the hash house. The timing of the gags is pretty close to perfect, and it works up to a good old slapstick finish, with pies being thrown regardless. There is nothing new in the material, but a whole lot is new in the clever way in which the business has been directed. Harry Sweet gets credit for the latter. Florence Lake as the helpful wife is very good.

Studio shot w/Edgar & Florence
(Courtesy of Kennedy Family)

Edgar and Harry Sweet each received a salary of $1,000 per week during the filming of *Lemon Meringue*. The "Old Chicago" external street was used as part of the set. Also hired were (4) children, (8) extras, (1) welfare worker, (1) pie delivery man—at $25 a day, (1) "tough man" described in parenthesis as "very good bit," 2 days for $100, and (12) lunch meals were bought for the cast at 75 cents each for a whopping expense of $9. The whole production came in at only $17,235.75. It's too bad that the number of pies thrown was not recorded.

Edgar would later brag in interviews that he had once been hit in the face 164 times with pies in a single movie. Most people naturally think that claim was from Edgar's Sennett era, not so. It was from *Lemon Meringue*. Edgar capitalized on this "feat" by way of a *Ripley's Believe it or Not* column, illustrating Edgar being struck by a flying circular baked dessert.

This short was a great one to kick off the series, and it certainly got noticed. *Lemon Meringue* was not only a throwback, but the nostalgic feel for old-time pie-in-the-face comedy was well received. The sound of pies hitting their mark, with the exasperations of Edgar, enhanced the comedy greatly.

An interesting entry into the series was *Bon Voyage*, scripted on 7-8-31 and shot July 22, 1931. It wasn't released until September of 1931 brcause it was also being re-shot scene by scene in Spanish. According to existing records of the script, an interior ship scene had to be shot at the Hal Roach Studios.

Good old Charlie Hall (the Little Menace) plays a steward who has heard of the Kennedy family, but lets them on his cruise ship only when they promise not to fight. The script notes indicate that the internal ship's salon was shot at Stage #12 at Roach. Harry Sweet received $500 for the story in itself. By this time, Edgar was receiving a flat rate of $1,250 per week, "Mrs. K" a flat rate of $350 a week, "Dot" at $400 for 4 days, Billy Eugene received $200 for 4 day's work and Charlie Hall received $80.

In *Bon Voyage* we see Edgar's family packing to go to Havana. As Florence is chitchatting on the phone, Edgar can no longer stand it. While on board, there is an orchestra scene and a request is called out for a singer. Bashful Edgar is recruited, but the bandleader asks him what he would like to sing.

From the script: Ed: (*in a loud whisper*) Can they play 'When the Sands of the Desert Grow Cold?' (*Ed sings in tuxedo—minus stocking and shoes. Submarine begins to submerge*). It is unknown whether Edgar sang this song in his natural voice or the Kennedy gravelly voice. Regrettably we may never know the answer, because this film has allegedly been lost for some time.

Another singing opportunity for Edgar was in the Hal Roach short *Great Gobs*. This film was shot during the all-talkie transformation and also had a silent version. Unfortunately the sound version no longer exists so, again, we cannot evaluate Edgar's singing prowess.

Edgar's contract for RKO included the option of directing as well. By the end of August, Edgar started directing a comedy starring Louis John Bartels, *Blonde by Proxy*. It was the last film Edgar ever directed, he was now an established movie personality.

By the end of 1931 negotiations were underway to extend the fledging series. On 3-16-32, it was announced that Edgar was signed to make another series of six shorts. Jimmy Starr, an old publicist for Mack Sennett, was a syndicated Hollywood newspaper reporter when he wrote:

Dot Farley, Jack Rice, Florence Lake, Edgar from *Bric a Brac* (1935)
(Author's collection)

Edgar Kennedy, a former director who rose to histri-
onic heights in the comedy field when he starred in a series
of comedies for RKO Pathe called 'Mr. Average Man,' was
so successful in his funny antics that exhibitors throughout
the country have demanded more of the giggle-getters.
Naturally, RKO Radio wishes to please theater managers.
And so another group of the rib-ticklers will be made with
Mr. Kennedy. Louis Brock will supervise.

The ensuing episodes of this comedy series mostly revolved around the
tribulations of its star. There was rarely a scene without Edgar Kennedy present.
Even though the rest of the support cast fluctuated over the years, he was
almost always surrounded by a basic family of a wife with the seemingly always present mother-in-law, brother-in-law and sometimes pa-in-law.

Born Florence Silverlake, in Charleston South Carolina, in 1905, she
was the sister of Arthur Lake who starred as Dagwood Bumstead in the
"Blondie" film and radio series. Their parents were Arthur Silverlake and

the former Edith Goodwin, who were both in show business. Arthur and his twin brother were billed in an aerialist act called "The Flying Silverlakes." They performed their act in various circuses around the country. Edith, using her maiden name, was a stage actress.

Both Arthur, Jr. and Florence were educated by their mother in between shows. Florence once said, "I was raised in Vaudeville." At one point, both children and parents were featured in a vaudeville act called "Family Affairs." The act hit the skids during a run in southern California around 1917. Arthur was able to land a role as a juvenile in *Jack and the Beanstalk*, and shortened his last name to Lake. Florence followed suit.

While in her teens, Florence went to San Diego to play in stock. Arthur and Florence worked on the stage and in silents, whenever there were parts for adolescents.

In the early 1920s, Florence married Jack Good, a "song and dance man," and together they had a daughter named Joyce. The marriage was to end in divorce.

Florence had a role in MGM's *The Rogue Song* (1930), then was signed to a contract with Fox. While making *Through Different Eyes*, she became acquainted with Harry Sweet, who gave her the part of the wife in *Rough House Rhythm*. In a *Los Angeles Times* interview on 3-12-70, Florence described her role: "I was the dumb blonde talkative wife." When her part called for her to chatter, she said, "the lines were not written, the script just said 'Florence ad libs.'" In the same interview Florence offered, "I never 'decided' to go into acting, I've been acting my whole life."

On 10-19-33 Florence married John Graham Owens, who was a "Property Master" at RKO. Mr. Owens had two children from a prior marriage. He passed away in 1960.

During the time Florence was not working on the series, she toured with RKO at Loew's Circuts in a vaudeville act with her brother Arthur. For seventeen weeks she also played "Blondie" on the radio while Penny Singleton was pregnant.

Florence became best known for her comic portrayals as Edgar's incessantly chattering wife. In 1934 she had a reunion onscreen with her brother, Arthur, in a musical short for Vitaphone, *Glad to Beat You*. Florence had numerous appearances in pictures before and after the "Average Man," including many roles on television. She died on April 11, 1980 at the Motion Picture and Television Country House in Woodland Hills, California.

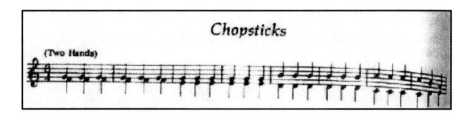

*Variety* ran an obituary on 4-23-80: "Florence Lake Owens, 75, was a child actress in films and on stage. Owens was under contract to RKO for seventeen years and performed frequently on the radio. Sister of Arthur Lake, she also wrote special material for her brother when he appeared as Dagwood Bumstead in the 'Blondie' film and T.V. series. There are no survivors [sic]."

Dorothy Farley was born in Chicago, Illinois on February 6, 1881. She was 5 feet, 5 inches tall with blonde hair and black eyes. Her parents were Eugene Farley and the former Alma Streeter. Her mother was a professional stage actress who prompted young Dorothy to start her show business career on stage at the age of three. The show, "an extravaganza," was entitled *Wedding Bells*, a production so successful that in show business circles she was referred to as "Little Dot." Dot was educated at the University of Valparaiso, allegedly by a private tutor. Dot continued her career by doing six years of stock, even traveling in the east and midwest with her own company in the melodrama *Lost in Egypt*. In the *Motion Picture Almanac of 1936*, her hobbies were listed as "music, writing, riding and all outdoor sports."

Some film references credit Dot with making her movie debut with the St. Louis Picture Company in 1910. The film was *Romantic Redskin*, a western short. However, in a document (Billy Leyser Publicity release) written on 10-20-26, the claim was that Dot started at Essaney in Chicago.

Dot allegedly wrote and sold more than 350 scenarios over the years. One of which was *Perils of the Plains*, which she sold for $1,800.

She died on May 21, 1971, at the age of 90, in Woodland Hills, Ca. She had never married.

Very little is known about the actor, sometimes billed as Billy Eugene, who was cast as Edgar's mooching, good-for-nothing brother-in-law. A small glimpse of his background was written by the *Los Angeles Times* on August 2, 1925. They discovered Billy as a juvenile and wrote that he had been born in San Francisco.

Not so many years ago that Billy stepped into the coveted and highly dignified shoes of head usher in one of the theaters of his hometown. With little to do except watch film after film as it unwound, he watched every gesture, comedy, emotional or otherwise until his repertoire equaled that of the average screen hero.

Then along came a small vaudeville team in which he unexpectedly had to 'sub' for someone else. He did it so well the manager offered to let him stay with the troupe, which later came to Los Angeles. Here, after another turn or two, Billy began to haunt the gates of the studios. It wasn't until he was given a small stock engagement in a local theater that he began to receive parts. Reginald Barker saw his performance one evening and shortly afterward gave him a small part in one of his pictures. Since that time, Billy has appeared in practically all of Barker's pictures and it is the leading juvenile role in the "The White Desert." Since making this picture, Eugene has been on the Lasky lot where he appeared in "A Son of His Father."

An article from the *Los Angeles Times* of 11-20-27 gives us just a tidbit on how Billy came to Hollywood:

Billy Eugene is the dashing Spaniard, Don Jose, in *Cradle Snatchers*, the frisky farce now being offered at the Majestic by P.E. Blackwell. Confidentially, Billy is not Spanish. And in spite of frequent bursts of suave villainy on the stage and screen, he is generally a very well behaved young juvenile. At a very early age, when he should have been in school, Billy wasn't. No sir. He hung around the theaters (in a very menial capacity, he frankly admits), and in a short time developed ambitions of one sort and another which finally ended in his going on tour in a vaudeville act. Then he came to Hollywood. Since his arrival here he has scored considerable success before the camera. In his most recently picture entitled *The Girl He Couldn't Buy* Bill played the villainous and unsuccessful 'He.'"

It is unknown how Eugene eventually received the part of "brother" once the "Average Man" series started. Even more mystifying is why he left the series after only a couple of years into it. Was it the pay? An urge to become a star some other place? Or did Edgar really tear him limb-from-limb out of frustration?

Part of the charm of this enduring series was the instantly recognizable "Chopsticks" musical theme song. The distinct piano notes introduced and ended each one of the Edgar Kennedy shorts. Often, especially in the early years, the opening scene would feature Florence emerging into the set while humming the tune.

Who came up with the suggestion to incorporate "Chopsticks" as the title tune? Unfortunately the answer to that question has never been revealed, probably because no one asked. Everyone associated with the original production of the "Mr. Average Man" series have long passed.

Edgar's daughter, Colleen, remembers hearing a story: "They were looking for a theme song and my dad said, 'This is the only one I know,' and played 'Chopsticks' on the set piano. He was just fooling around and they made it the theme song." Colleen said that his mother played the piano, but her dad never learned. However, "we always had a piano in the house. I learned to play."

An introductory theme song was an important ingredient to any comedy short subject during the talkie era. Undoubtedly part of the decision of what was used to musically introduce the shorts had to do with economics. For a budget-conscious fledging short series for RKO in 1931, there was no money to pay for the rights to a tune or commission one to be written. Renown author and film critic Leonard Maltin theorized that RKO used the theme simply because it was in public domain. A comparison in point, he offers that the Leon Errol series, also for RKO, had a theme song of "London Bridge." As Mr. Maltin says: "I believe we have a pattern there."

A highlight of the "Chopticks" theme was featured in *Bad Housekeeping* (3-5-37) when piano tuner Franklin Pangborn plays the engaging tune as part of the plot. While Pangborn tunes the piano by banging out "Chopsticks," Edgar enters the scene, and with a straight face says, "Hey, I know that one, I play it all the time." Both of them share the bench to bang out a version of "Chopsticks"; it is one of the most charming scenes of the whole series.

Edgar was now a commodity being utilized by RKO, and later other studios, to "save" a particular picture. When pre-released movies were received unenthusiastically, often a cameo of a well-known face could boost the star

(Courtesy Kennedy Family)

power or even add a comedy element. An example of this procedure was done in 1930 for MGM's *The Rogue Song*. Shot in color and featuring the singing talent of opera star Lawrence Tibbett, it was not enough to draw audiences. Edit in a few scenes with Laurel and Hardy and they had a movie for the mass market. In some venues Laurel and Hardy received star billing.

The Hollywood studios normally downplayed it when such movies needed "fixing." Throughout his career, Edgar was often cast in cameos to give some comedy relief. Such an occasion occurred for the RKO feature *Western Passage*. On 5-5-32 Jimmy Starr wrote:

> Ann Harding's latest production, *Westward Passage*, has gone back for repairs. Several comedy sequences will be added, according to orders from David Selznick, the headman of production. Florence Lake, clever comedienne; Edgar Kennedy, unusual comic; have been added to the long and impressive list of performers. They will be inserted, so to speak, to liven up various parts of the yarn. Miss Harding and her leading man, Laurence Olivier, have been recalled for the additional scenes, which Robert Milton is megaphoning.
>
> RKO Radio, as strange as it may seem, was not anxious to have the news leak out regarding the added scenes.

Personally (and I think everybody in the industry will agree with me), I think it is indeed a credit to Mr. Selznick to make a sincere effort to improve a film where it might appear to be a bit weak. MGM has followed the policy of 'added scenes,' or retakes for some time, and the product is the best in the business. I don't think anyone should be ashamed of doing his very best.

Edgar was now being sought out for interviews and publicity. On 9-19-32, Harry Mines of *The Los Angeles Illustrated Daily News* wrote a piece entitled: "Edgar Kennedy Grouchy?"

In the movies Edgar Kennedy is continually in a royal rage. Mr. Average Man in those RKO Comedies invariably becomes disturbed by members of his family begins to rant and rage and throw things about. Possibly Mr. Kennedy has done more to glorify a bad temper than any other actor in pictures. Anyway the more he yells and foams at the mouth, the more audiences love it. But over the luncheon table at the studio, Kennedy proved to be in calm disposition. He seldom loses his head: 'What about your bad temper?' asked the writer. 'How does your wife stand you?' 'Why don't you ask my wife?' returned Kennedy. 'We're still married and I haven't heard any complaints. Even my children aren't scared of me. I'm really very easy to get along with.' But for the sake of his art, our Mr. Kennedy goes along fooling the public into thinking he is a very vicious person. Edgar is very fond of Mr. Average Man as a person, he gets a big kick out of him and really finds work a pleasure these days. 'We try to make our comedies as natural as possible,' he explained. 'Sometimes they looked gagged. Of course we can't always help that. You've met families with such personalities as Florence Lake, Dot Farley, Billy Eugene and I typify. There's a million of 'em scattered throughout the world. Possibly they aren't as bad as we are—still we feel we're playing real people.

'For our stories we rely on Harry Sweet, the director. Of course, if some of us gets a swell idea, then we suggest it. But we generally take one or two incidents that will make good

laughs and then try to elaborate on them. We try to keep
from 'forcing' the gags, because that ruins the charm of these
series. I don't think the public is tired of us yet. It's pretty safe
to say we'll be able to make these comedies for a year or so.'

It was at Veratina, California 20 miles outside of Paso
Robles, that Kennedy first saw the light of day…He has
served apprenticeship at Century, Hal Roach and Sennett.
Until the advent of Mr. Average Man, he refused feature
billing. Now he has Mr. Average Man, a long-term contract and a reputation for a hectic disposition. So he is
happy. When not making comedies, Edgar works in feature length films for RKO and is now cast in *Penguin
Murder Case* with Mae Clarke and Donald Cook.

From a Los Angeles Times column by Grace Kingsley, May 26, 1934,
"Hobnobbing in Hollywood," came this entertaining ditty: "Edgar
Kennedy was telling how popular he is over on the Radio lot. 'Gosh, I'm
literally hounded by autograph seekers,' he said. 'Why, would you believe
it, when Tom Kennedy and I were returning from San Clemente, a fan
waved me down while we were making sixty and asked me for my autograph. Imagine that!' 'Yeah,' interrupted Tom, 'and he was the grouchiest
speed cop I've ever met.'"

For some reason, the publicists in Hollywood got the idea the the actor
Tom Kennedy and Edgar were brothers, even though it was extensively
denied every time it was brought up. Bylines like this one, from 7-5-33,
were often were printed. "Society in Filmland" by Jane Jackson: "Tom
Kennedy and his brother, Edgar, of the RKO lot, motored to the Peter Pan
Woodland Club, Big Bear for a holiday of golf, and horseback riding."

It is unknown how the rumor started that Edgar and Tom were bio-
logical brothers. Was it initiated from the above blurb or a misconception
from earlier in their careers? Maybe it was invented as a form of publicity
for RKO to promote their two contract players.

The confusion must have plagued them especially when they both
worked at RKO as contract players. An article, "THEY'LL FOOL YOU—
THESE BOYS," written by Scoop Conlan (a famous Hollywood celebrity columnist), on 6-30-34, in the *Los Angeles Evening Herald Express* did
not clear up the misconception. Conlan wrote how Tom was born July
15, 1885 in New York City and listed career parallels: Beside their com-

mon name, both had been professional boxers, both joined the Armed Forces during the Great War and they both started with Mack Sennett. In addition, both Edgar and Tom were of similar height, weight and reach. There was one physical characteristic that separated them; Tom had hair. For the rest of their lives, and even now, well-meaning biographers have identified the two as brothers, perpetuating the myth. Let it forever rest— Edgar and Tom were not brothers!

Colleen had this memory of Tom Kennedy, who often visited.

> I remember well our camping trips, because they were such a production. My dad loved his comforts, so we hired guides to take us way into the mountains. Often we would be on horseback all day, but when we arrived our tents were set up for us and our food was prepared. I hated the hunting and fishing part, but I nevertheless became proficient. Once we were visiting 'Uncle Tom and Aunt Fanny' in Course Gold. Everyone thought Tom was my dad's brother because his name was also Kennedy, but not so. Anyway,

Harpo with Edgar in *Duck Soup*
(Author's collection)

they were going out on an all-day cattle roundup, Larry and I begged to go. To my surprise we were allowed to participate if we kept out of the way. During the ride we were offered some chewing tobacco. My dad did not say no, he just advised against it. Well, the rest is history. Two very green kids returned to the ranch house that evening.

On 5-4-33, the *Hollywood Citizen News* reported: "George Stevens, director of 'Cohens and Kellys in Trouble,' just passed us skipping along…and the reason for his excess speed, he admits, is that he has just been signed to direct his favorite comedian, Edgar Kennedy, in his next 'Mr. Average Man' comedy for Radio…and is on his way out to celebrate it by arranging a game of golf with Kennedy."

Right after finishing *Good Housewrecking*, a tragic event occurred on June 18, 1933. On that fateful day, Harry Sweet, the person who developed the "Mr. Average Man" series for RKO died in an airplane crash. Sweet was an experienced flyer and that day took Hal Davitt, a screenwriter, and Vera Williams, a "movie extra," to his cabin at Big Bear Lake. Sweet owned the plane, which was flown from a Los Angeles airport the previous day. Witnesses said the plane failed to come out of a dive and plunged into the lake. Salvage crews found the bodies when the plane was raised from the bottom of the lake. The plane had fallen into the lake a quarter of a mile offshore. Fifty men aboard a barge, equipped with a crane, raised the craft.

The innovative Harry Sweet was only 32 years old. He had last acted with Edgar as a comedian in *Carnival Boat*. Prior to the accident, Sweet was in charge of all comedy short subjects at RKO. In addition, he wrote most of the "Mr. Average Man" scripts, as well as directing them. RKO expanded Lou Brock's duties overseeing the comedy shorts department.

It was fortunate that RKO had film veteran George Stevens on hand, just acquiring him from Universal. Stevens had also been let go by Roach in late 1931 and it must have been somewhat comforting to Edgar to turn over the directing reins to Stevens. They both enjoyed working together at Roach when Stevens was a cameraman, and later graduated to director of the "Boy Friends" series.

With Stevens at the helm, the series didn't look to skip a beat. Stevens' directorial debut in the series was *Quite Please*. Poor Edgar is hounded by his obtrusive in-laws while conducting big business on the train. Just when

Edgar is to score big with his boss, "Mother" and "Brother" ruin it for him. If there ever was an episode that exudes empathy for Edgar, it's this title. As Edgar's head crashes through the window, the frustration culminates with a close up of Edgar scowling while snow presumably sets and melts on his steaming head. Insert "Chopsticks" theme, Fade-out. Watching this entry of the series, in retrospect, the ending just screams for Edgar to perform his patented "slow-burn" ending that he incorporated a few years later.

On 1-20-34, *The Motion Picture Herald,* in their "What the Picture Did for Me" column, printed this response from one of their clients, The Star Theatre, Williamson, N.Y. Small Town Patronage: "Excellent comedy. Kennedy sure can make 'em laugh." A different viewpoint was noted from another small town, the Garlock Theatre, in Custer, South Dakota. "*Quiet Please*—To my mind this was poor and I surely got tired running it. Florence Lake is a pain in the neck to me, too, with all her yip, yip, yip. Despite my opinion, there were laughs."

With his recent success, George Stevens directed the next two "Mr. Average Man" in the series: *What Fur* and *Grin and Bear It.* Stevens graduated to features and became one of the premiere directors in Hollywood. Some of his later successes were the classics *Giant, The Diary of Anne Frank, Shane, A Place in the Sun* and *Gunga Din*, among others.

An interesting footnote in Hollywood occurred during the early 1930s when Edgar employed the Grant E. Doge Agency as his manager. Edgar had paid his contract up to the present time when Grant Doge suddenly died. Mrs. Doge sued Edgar claiming a $500 fee for services she rendered in line with her late husband's contract after his death. Mrs. Doge brought suit in municipal court and Judge A.E. Paonessa gave judgment in her favor.

Edgar felt the issue here was principal. Why should he pay the wife for services when it was intended for the husband? Edgar appealed the decision. On 1-4-33, in sustaining the contention of Attorney George Clark, Superior Judge Victor R. McLucas of the appellate division of the Superior Court, handed down a decision of wide importance to the theatrical world. Judge McLucas, upon reviewing the case and its merits, made a decision in favor of the defendant. Judge McLucas determined that "A contract between an actor and his employment agent is a 'personal relationship' and terminates with the agent's death." Edgar's appeal and its landmark reversal impacted the entire movie colony forever.

# 15.
# Duck Soup

During November of 1933, Edgar was recruited to appear in a few scenes in the newest Marx Brothers madcap feature, *Duck Soup*. The director, Leo McCarey, was another ex-Hal Roach employee. (The comedy director/supervisor, some claim, was the genius who actually teamed up Stan Laurel and Oliver Hardy.)

In *Duck Soup*, Edgar was the short-fused peanut vendor/lemonade stand merchant. Enter Harpo and Chico who at once peg him as a vulnerable victim to antagonize with their mischief. Poor Edgar didn't stand a chance. For all his bluff and threats ("I'll tear you limb from limb"), Harpo and Chico were about as intimidated as Laurel and Hardy were to his traffic cop in *Leave 'em Laughing*, which is to say, not at all. Instead of laughing at him, they ganged up on him. Building up to an exchange of comic actions and reactions to the taking of his hat, peanuts and pride, Edgar is soon left curbside to watch his bowler set ablaze.

The next scene is with Harpo only. This time, Edgar is prepared for him. As Edgar seeks his revenge by consuming Harpo's merchandise, Harpo retaliates, tit-for-tat, by splashing his feet in Edgar's lemonade vat.

The final sequence Edgar appears in is quite possibly the funniest. As Harpo gallops on his horse to warn the country *a la* Paul Revere, he sees an attractive female in the window (to the musical chords of "Ain't She Sweet") luring him up. His priorities now changed, Harpo parks his horse and investigates the lovely figure. Instead of chasing the female this time, Harpo finds this one almost accommodating, that is until her husband comes home. Naturally, it is Edgar Kennedy. Not suspecting a thing under the most suspicious of circumstances, even when his negligee-clad wife hands him his trusty rifle to defend the country, Edgar announces:

"Aahhh, I'm gonna take a bath." As the 6'2" Edgar slides into the small little tub to relax, a most surreal moment happens, we hear the distinct sounds of a bugle trumpeting. Then, like the mythical Pan himself, Harpo emerges from the same bathtub with his now soaked three-cornered hat, clothes and a devilish grin to exit.

The real beauty of Edgar's scenes in *Duck Soup* is, for the most part, that it was acted out in pantomime, a real throwback to the Leo McCarey silent film direction. Edgar certainly didn't need words to give the impression that he was slightly irritated; his whole body registered it. Playing off of Harpo, who never spoke in any of the films, was a perfect contrast. Out of all the 400-plus movies that Edgar appeared in, *Duck Soup* is probably the most recognized today, mostly because of the Marx Brothers legend.

With "talkies" firmly established in the movies, it sometimes frustrated Edgar to watch or be in films that were solely dependant on dialogue to advance the plot. In a 1938 interview for the British publication *World Film News* (July issue) by Russell Ferguson, Edgar offered these rare insights:

> You know, I think the men who were in the silent films have it over the newcomers who belong to the talkie time. Do you remember the old silent days? We had to act everything, and make the right faces and stand the right way and dope out actions and gestures for everything. That experience stays with you—many a time I forget my lines because I'm working inside on the business that goes with them, may be wrestling with a door handle or having a stand-up argument with a wardrobe door, and if it doesn't work out, I forget my lines because I haven't got the whole thing going smooth, from inside, while some guy standing by like a poker thinking of nothing but his lines comes out as smooth as silk and thinks he's an actor.
>
> That's what the talkies have done to the movies. In the old days, if you didn't act it, nobody knew what it was supposed to be. Nowadays, talk, talk, talk, talk, it's all on the sound track, and you can get by without acting at all. Did you know that there's a new school of acting taking place just now? They don't act.

The Evolution of a Burn' — by Hollywood's Prize Expert

"Slow-Burn" montage (circa 1936)
(Courtesy *Washington Post*)

I'll tell you a funny thing to show you what I mean. It was—well, he's a good guy, so I won't tell you his name. He was to get shot through the shoulder in a fight, and step forward when he heard 'Anybody hurt?' and say 'I'm shot through the shoulder.' Well, we play it, and he steps forward and says 'I'm shot through the shoulder,' like saying 'I'm all out of cigarettes' or something. The scene has to be taken again for some reason, right at the end of our stay on location, when we're all tired and wanting to get home, and I says to him 'Only another day now' and he says 'What for?' and I says 'For your shooting scene.'

He says 'Hell, that will take less than half an hour.' I says 'Yes, the way you did it. Have you ever been shot through the shoulder? It hurts like hell, and that bullet was supposed to go clean through you from the back, or else it was a pretty bum bullet. Look, hit me in the shoulder, never mind shooting me, and I'll let you know I've been hit, and I was a prize-fighter.' 'Ah,' he says, 'you're out-of-date. We don't act nowadays.' I couldn't resist it. I says 'Damn right. You don't act, but you call yourself an actor.'

During the making of *The Bride Comes Home* in 1935, Claudette Colbert told the *Los Angeles Times* her favorite movie stars were: Marlene Dietrich, Carole Lombard, W.C. Fields, Clark Gable, Charles Laughton, Gary Cooper, Joan Crawford, Fred MacMurray, Edward Everett Horton, and Edgar Kennedy.

On May 18, 1935, the *Los Angeles Herald Express* featured an article announcing that a movie entitled *Keystone Hotel* was going into production. There was a photo featuring Ford Sterling, Chester Conklin, Ben Turpin, Hank Mann and Marie Provost. The article announced a goal to present every Keystone comedian still living.

The list of guests included: Mack Sennett, Charlie and Syd Chaplin, Charlie Murray, Gloria Swanson, Phyllis Haver, Harry McCoy, Polly Moran, Al St. John, Slim Summerville, Mack Swain, Pathe Lehrman, Wallace Beery, Tom and Ed Kennedy, Harry Gribbon, Alice Davenport, Louise Fazenda, Mae Busch, Eddie Sutherland, James Finlayson, Bobbie Vernon, Harold Lloyd, William Seiter, Del Lord, Eddie Cline, Bobbie Dunn, Madeline Hurlock, Ray Griffith, and Blanche Payson.

The article even contained a listing of those Keystone alumni who had passed on: Fred Mace, Mabel Normand, Marie Dressler, Roscoe "Fatty" Arbuckle, F. Richard Jones and Charles Avery.

For unknown reasons Edgar did not make it into any of the filming. It is ironic that many of the photographs and filming of the Keystone Kops in action are passed off as original versions from 1913-1915.

# 16.
# Baldness

Edgar's firmly established screen character was as familiar to audiences as Jimmy Durante's nose, Jack Benny's cheapness or even Oliver Hardy's camera stare. The fun was watching him at first get irritated, then try and hold it in, all the while growing in his frustration until he exploded with rage like a human thermometer. Edgar registered his displeasure by various escalating body language expulsions. It culminated by Edgar pantomiming his defeat by raising his paw to his head and deliberately swiping down over his deadpanned face. It was like a squeegee wiping glass. The gesture was thus identified as a "Slow-Burn." While some people think Edgar always used his "Slow-Burn" as part of his comedy shtick, the truth is there was actually an evolution of what came to be his trademark. It didn't fully blossom until 1936, when it became a prominent inclusion of Edgar's movies.

There are some misconceptions that Edgar developed his "Slow-Burn" at Roach. While it is true that Edgar expressed slow-to-register irritation during the Hal Roach era, it would be more correct to describe his reactions in theatrical terms as a straight "burn," albeit a lingering one when compared to, say, James Finlayson who had a short fuse. Edgar's "burn" was so vividly portrayed, one could easily imagine that an egg could fry on his bald head.

Edgar did in fact run his hand across his face in many Hal Roach shorts and still photographs often captured the pose. Although the nucleus of the "slow-burn" was there, it is fair to say that Edgar's trademark did not fully blossom until his "Average Man" series. Hints of the later "Slow-Burn" were present in his many quick facial wipes, including one just before the fade out, in *Duck Soup*. He was even more on target during Eddie Cantor's *Kid Millions*; Edgar does a great slow hand-swiping down routine to register frustration in that one. The most developed "Slow-Burn" prior to his own series was in the feature *Tillie and Gus*, a vehicle for W.C. Fields. As a judge, Edgar does a full-blown "Slow-Burn" when the frustration mounts.

The first written mention of Edgar's hand-over-the-face deal was on 6-19-34 in a small column by Jimmy Starr of *The Los Angeles Evening Herald Express*, where the comic was first referred to as "Edgar (slow-burn) Kennedy." The term didn't stick at the time. However, in January of 1936, after ending *Gasoloons* with a close up of his greased hand wiping over his face for the ending, the term and action became synonymous. As though to market his distinct trademark, columnists started to refer to him as "The slow-burn guy," as opposed to how the press previously made reference to him, as "Edgar (Average Man) Kennedy."

As the series progressed, Edgar seemed to end just about every one of his shorts with his signature "Slow-Burn" at the final fadeout. The hand over the face reaction would be done in most of his later feature film appearances as well; it was a director's and audience favorite. The beauty of the "Slow-Burn" is that Edgar kept it fresh by never doing it the same way twice. Sometimes he would start at the top of his head by rubbing small little circles, then slowly swooping his hand down. Other times he would start his fingers at his forehead and, by keeping his right thumb stationary on his nose, would rotate his hand like a drafter's pencil to swipe above his eyebrows, right to left, and bring his fingers down in a half-circle until they passed his chin. Then, with one final emphatic gesture, he would reverse direction of his fingertips to swipe his nose with a back hand final wipe.

The "Slow-Burn" became part of America's consciousness. In *Hollywood Hotel*, during a musical number, Edgar is just about to do a "Slow-Burn" when a giant image of an 8-ball rolls in front of him. Instead, the camera pans to singing star Dick Powell who, along with Ted Healy, performs a "Slow-Burn" in timing with the musical number.

The routine was perfect for cartoons. Many an early Elmer Fudd registered such frustration by slapping his head and pulling his hand down (to an exaggerated rubber wringing sound effect). Donald Duck and Barney Bear both used the mannerism. Even Curly Howard of the Three Stooges used the effect, although his was much quicker and was accompanied with a high audible whine.

On January 22, 1938, the *Motion Picture Herald* printed a review of a Walt Disney/ Donald Duck cartoon entitled *Self Control*. The unnamed reviewer wrote, "Reminiscent of his equally famous explosive counterpart, Edgar Kennedy, Donald Duck's attempt to practice self control is even more funny."

As to the origin of the "Slow-Burn," Edgar was often asked about it. To this day there is no definitive answer, since no two stories were ever told that are the same. At one time Edgar remarked that he had been doing it for 20 years and that the public had just now caught on. Edgar's daughter, Colleen, remembers hearing a story that W.S. Van Dyke suggested that her dad should come up with "a gimmick." Another version entailed Edgar on the golf course and hitting an errant shot. In frustration, Edgar rubbed his head and pulled his hand down over his face. "That's it," his agent allegedly said, "use that in your next movie."

In an interview, on 2-14-36, in the *Los Angeles Illustrated Daily News*, columnist Eleanor Barnes wrote:

> Edgar Kennedy is a gentleman who goes into a 'Slow-Burn' often. With Edgar, it is a technique, inspired by thoughts about his friends, his country, his parking problems and his neighbors. 'And how do you achieve this art, Mr. Kennedy?' The great man was asked. 'Inverted glee,' said Mr. Kennedy, in a low voice, dropping his chin down on a broad and eloquent chest, 'is a display of futile exasperation that comes natural to easy-going men.'
>
> Of Irish lineage, and with a smile that contains some of the sly humor of the poet, Edgar Kennedy has that delightful comedy about him, in real life, best expressed in pantomime. It is all very simple, according to Kennedy. 'Take any average good-natured man and he does just as I do. He can get so irritated that he will work himself to the verge of apoplexy. In my screen 'mads' I do the same thing. The madder your Mr. Average gets, the funnier he looks. When he has reached the end of his rope and is just about to explode with irritation, then he starts to 'burn.'
>
> 'In my screen irritations I remember that Mr. Average Man does all that but I do not go through the build up. I start in with my irritation at the point where Mr. Average Man does all that, but I do not go through the build up. I start in with my irritation at the point where Mr. Average

Man is beginning to 'burn.' It saves footage. I can get as mad in 50 feet of negative as my real life examples who would probably use 200. Here's why; sometimes I really do get exasperated. The reason is my being continually discovered for the films. Do you know what it is to be discovered and rediscovered with sickening regularity? About every five years I am discovered. The last time I was discovered, I had given up hope and had become a director. By the time I was discovered as a director I had gone back to acting.'

Kennedy passed his hand wearily over his face like he does in films when he wants to show his exasperation, and settled back for more questioning. Then he suddenly jumped to his feet and started shouting in anger. His face expanded two times normal size. 'Every time I think of being discovered I get so mad I can't see,' he shouted. 'What do they think I am? Something to be discovered and rediscovered and given a new chance every few years? This has to stop! The next time anybody tries to discover me I'll make 'em think they've run into a tribe of wild indians!' 'But Mr. Kennedy...' 'Shut up! I got a creepin' suspicion that you're just about ready to discover me again!' 'But...' 'Please, do not 'but' me. You want to discover me?' 'But will you please let me say a word now and then? Well!' 'Thank you Mr. Kennedy.'

More insights are provided about Edgar's screen persona from a 10-15-37 interview for the *Los Angeles Examiner*'s "Behind the Makeup" column by Reine Davies:

Edgar Kennedy tells me that successful comedy is principally a matter of breaking the established rules for acting. 'When I left the stage and prize ring to enter silent pictures, there was a lot of don'ts for actors than do's. Persistently the director would warn, 'Never turn your back to the camera; keep your hands away from your face, and never raise your voice, but speak so clearly that the audience can read your lips.' Right from the start I began breaking the rules, and usually I was promptly jerked back and forcefully reminded. But these reprimands became less frequent as a new type of direction developed. I don't want to lead any kids astray by this rule-breaking advice, but my biggest laughs have invariably been achieved by going against instruction. In a 'slow-burn' (rising anger) I cover my face with my hand and it gets a laugh. Frequently I turn my back on the audience and somehow, the sight of a very bald pate again convulses the ticket buyers. I yell if I feel like it and at other times mumble so that even I don' know what I'm saying—if anything. Gosh, I'm talking like an actor and I'm only a comedian—maybe.'

*Los Angeles Examiner* columnist Harriet Parsons wrote on 12-19-37:

Edgar Kennedy's most lucrative talent is his ability to look more thoroughly mad than any other comic on the screen. The Kennedy 'Slow-Burn' came about by accident, twenty years ago he was making his first movie scene and muffed his business badly. In his exasperation rubbed his hand over his face so hard it flattened out his nose; everybody on the set laughed including the director. They put it in the picture and audiences thought it was funny too. They still do.

It is extremely doubtful that any of the above actually took place. It sure sounded good, and perpetuated Edgar's "Slow-Burn" legend. Furthermore, there are no known scenes from films that still exist that depict the scenario as described. Edgar himself seemed to contradict the "facts" this interview from 1942, "Looking Back with a Keystone Kop" by Roger Carroll: "Another thing. They didn't have close-ups then. They hadn't been invented [sic]. You had to figure out broad motions to attract attention to what you were doing. You played every scene as if you were playing to the last row in the balcony of a theatre the size of Radio City Music Hall. Those were the days when all the tricks of scene stealing were developed."

In a 1936 interview with Harry Morrison of the *Indianapolis Times,* Edgar offered this about the "Slow-Burn":

"About the 'Slow-Burn,' very few people really understand it." Edgar claimed that he was actually doing a slow-burn for about 11 years, but

"The country has caught on to it only the last few years. Most people think of it as the hand over the face deal. Even directors, when a scene is dragging, will stop everything and call: 'Edgar, we got to do something, give us a 'Slow-Burn.' And for what? A 'Slow- Burn' is slow. It has to be. It's a gradual growth of pen-up, inhibited emotions that break out. That's what audiences see. What they feel is the whole thing. It may take five minutes on the screen.

"I learned that from Charlie Chaplin, who, with Fred Mace, are the two greatest screen comedians. I was supposed to kick Charlie one time. In those days we did everything fast. It was bang, bang, bang. I kicked him once and nothing happened. I kicked again. The third time I kicked him he went flying.

"I thought he'd be sore. He wasn't. He just came back and explained to me what he was trying to do. He said: 'A kick is a laugh, but a kick that doesn't work for a couple of times is better. That's comedy. You've got to work up to it.' That, is the 'Slow-Burn.'"

In a *New York Times* interview in 1942, the writer A.H.Weiler wrote this entry, speaking of his "Mr. Average Man" series: "For thirteen years now he has made an art of hypertension. Since the customers don't complain, the plot never varies to any great degree. Mr. Kennedy as the nominal head of an average family is always genial and uncomplaining until driven to distraction and the eventual 'Slow-Burn' by numerous relatives headed by an omniscient mother-in-law and his wife. The gesture, he explained, was not a discovery of the comedies, but dated to the distant past."

Mr. Weiler quoted Edgar as saying that it was an RKO producer, Harry Joe Brown, who was "producing the subjects originally, first noted that piece of business and insisted on its being played up." Weiler observed, "The results apparently have paid dividends."

In a 1938 interview by Russell Ferguson, Edgar elaborates on comedy, timing and the "Slow-Burn":

> I guess that most of the movies start way up top, with no fundamentals, they don't get down to the things that get the belly-laughs.
>
> Just to show you what some guys know about acting, I'll tell you about the first musical I ever played in. The director has an idea and calls me into one scene, and says

'Ed, I want you in here, and I want a 'Slow-Burn,' and I want it in four beats of the music.'

Well, I ask you. Can you imagine what it feels like to be asked to do a quick 'slow-burn'? I'm a reasonable guy, so I practiced a minute or two, and then told him it was no use. He goes to the music director, and comes back with the great news that I can get six beats. This was just about as bad. Finally, I got eight beats from him and made it. But hell! What an idea! 'Slow-Burning' to a metronome. Timing isn't done with a clock. Timing is just thinking.

On July 26, 1940, Paramount Pictures came up with a new angle on Edgar's famous "Slow-Burn." The following press release takes advantage

A "Quick-Burn" for *The Quarterback* w/ Virginia Dale (1940) Paramount.
(Author's collection)

of mentioning the film in production to make it newsworthy.

> A wholly new comedy routine described as a "Swift-Burn" today took its place in the movie comic's bag of tricks. It is intended as a streamlined, speedier version of the time-honored "Slow-Burn" by which Edgar Kennedy in particular, and comedians in general, long have pantomimed the emotion of utter exasperation.
>
> It is the invention of Kennedy himself, for a scene in Paramount's *Touchdown* [released as *The Quarterback*] in which he plays comedy support to Wayne Morris, Virginia Dale and Lillian Cornell.

(Courtesy Kennedy Family)

It was Kennedy who, something more than a decade ago, evolved the since widely copied "Slow-Burn," through sheer accident. He put a spread-fingered hand before his face to "sneak" a look at another player during a scene for a picture. It made audiences guffaw with merriment. So the hand before his face as he pretended to grow livid with anger became his—and other comedians' stock in trade.

That's what bothered him. There are too many copyists who can do the "Slow-Burn" now as well as he can. And, try as he might, he never could do the "Slow-Burn" in quicker time than 36 seconds. That is too long for some scenes, and sometimes resulting in it being cut out entirely, or so chopped down as to lose its meaning.

So, to be a step ahead of his imitators and to get the same effect in less than half the time—14 seconds— Kennedy worked out the swift burn. Its chief point of contrast to his older routine is that he uses both hands in front of the face at the same time.

He feels that it is in keeping with the times, with the swiftened pace of motion pictures as with every other field of endeavor. And it will give plagiarists something new to worry about.

Needless to say, the "Swift-Burn" was merely a variation to his crowd-pleasing expression. Edgar was not about to abandon his most famous mannerism. It is interesting to note that the studio publicist who wrote the above came up with yet another version of how Edgar founded the "Slow-Burn." Checking with the original source apparently was not necessary.

An unofficial survey of Edgar Kennedy fans came up with the following most memorable "Slow-Burns" from his series:

1. *Gasoloons* (his first one at fade-out).
2. *Rough on Rents*
3. *I'll Build it Myself*
4. *Slightly at Sea*
5. *Wall Street Blues* (Florence burns too)
6. *Clock Wise*

(Courtesy of Lois Laurel Hawes)

7. *Mind Over Mouse* (five mousetraps on his fingers)
8. *Two for the Money*
9. *It Happened All Night*
10. *Contest Crazy* (Edgar's last burn, head encased in a fish bowl).

# 17.
# On Books and Films

Throughout the history of the movies, well-known novels were often transformed onto celluloid. With the establishment of a soundtrack, Hollywood produced movies from classic books throughout the 1930s. While some people thought that film made the story "come to life" on the silver screen, Edgar had a different perspective. From *World Film News*:

> Films should be films, not made out of books, at least not well-known books, because books are alive, and they are quite different for different people. A film of a book is never more than fifty percent successful for me, often a good deal less, at least as a film of the book.
>
> One film I read when I was a kid—no, I've never read it since, I'm afraid to, I might lose something of it—was "Les Miserables." Every time it's filmed, I go and see it. Every time, I feel, they've missed everything. But every time it's good as a film. Do I say it's a lousy film? No, I have no right to say that, because the man that made it has as much right to his "Les Miserables" as I have to mine, though I may go on thinking I know more about it than he does. Anyway, you should never say a film is lousy. It's not fair. It would be all right to lay into it if the guys weren't trying, but hell! I've never seen a film where the actors aren't trying all they know. Maybe not your way, but if you knew how much sweat goes into it, you would let it go by, even if you didn't like it much. Anyhow, that's my point of view, and I guess I know a little about films.

## KENNEDY TO AID SAFETY CAMPAIGN

The *Los Angeles Examiner* announced, on 11-19-36:

Edgar Kennedy, one of the screen's most popular comedians, will appear to aid a safety campaign of East Los
Angeles civic organizations tomorrow night. Kennedy will
inscribe a safety message to the children of that area in
concrete at a ceremony planned by the East Los Angeles
Chamber of Commerce.

He will add his message of warning to those of George
Jessel, Henry Armetta, Binnie Barnes and Buck Jones, all
New Universal players, J. Paul Swickard, Allan Martin and
Dick Pritchard, East Los Angeles civic leaders will direct
the placing of the inscription.

(Courtesy Kennedy Family)

The movement, which has been sponsored by this group for the past two years, has won recognition from national safety organizations. Judge E.P. Woods will officiate as chairman at the ceremony.

The following column was written by Erskine Johnson and printed on 8-31-37 in the *Hollywood Citizen News*:

Have you noticed how cooperative Paramount and Radio Pictures have become in exchanging talent? Their stars and featured players run out their back gates constantly for pictures on the neighboring lots. Latest to exit to Paramount is Edgar Kennedy. He starts work tomorrow as a dumb detective in "True Confession," co-starring Carole Lombard and Fred MacMurray. A big role was especially written into the picture for Kennedy. The script even calls for certain characteristic Kennedy gestures. At the rate he is progressing in features, he will soon be too busy to make his short comedies at Radio Pictures.

Edgar once recalled in an interview for the *Chicago American* newspaper (circa 1936), "Back in my Sennett days I could fall out of a second story window and always get a laugh ... all of a sudden along came Mickey Mouse, who can fall seven stories, peel bananas on the way down, land on his head without losing his hat, then get up and say 'Hyah folks!' I ask you, what chance has a ONE-story man got?" Wonder how ol' Edgar would feel about computer imaging?

On 4-1-36 there was a big opening of the softball season at Loyola Stadium, in which the female teams were sponsored by movie stars. The teams were: Edgar Kennedy's Cuties, Buck Jones' Cowboys, Joe Penner's Quackers, W.S. Van Dyke's Vagabonds, and Bing Crosby's Croonerettes.

The teams were members of the American Softball Association and were all amateurs. Some of the notables in attendance were Pat O'Brien, Jean Harlow, Jeanette MacDonald, Clark Gable and Ted Healy.

# 18.
# The Kennedy Home

Colleen reminisced about the house she grew up in at 273 S. Maple St. in Beverly Hills. They had moved there in 1930. Colleen emphasized that Beverly Hills "was a small town in the twenties and thirties. There were mostly working actors, directors and movie people living there. We all knew each other. It was a community of artists, where no one thought they were special. Everyone visited and had parties together.

"Our home was an old Moorish home on the corner of Maple and Charlie Ville. It was a three-story Mediterranean with a full basement that contained a maid's room, a bathroom, laundry room and one huge bar and playroom. The bar had a huge fireplace, with built-in benches on two sides of the room with a kitchen behind the bar. This is where my dad entertained his poker buddies for as long as three days at a time. His poker pals included all the greats and not-so-greats of Hollywood, but Charles Coburn, Lewis Stone, and W.S. Van Dyke were always among them. Sometimes Bing Crosby and Bob Hope would come. Those weekend poker parties would last 72 hours and no one would sleep. I hated cleaning up afterwards, all those cigars and cigarettes…

"The main floor had a huge well-equipped, but ugly kitchen. There was a charming glassed-in French breakfast room, a huge dining room that sat 20 with comfort and an equally large living room (where the Christmas tree would go) with a two-story ceiling. The next floor had three huge bedrooms. My room had a marvel of a bathroom, large enough to practice ballet in, my mother's room smelled of powder and my dad's room smelled of fine pipe tobacco. My brother lived in the turret room, where life became any adventure we chose to make it. The third floor was one large bedroom encased in glass. I remember once riding our St. Bernard as a pony and getting dumped in the fishpond. Our family dog was named 'Kong,' so named after the movie *King Kong*. My dad brought him home after not allowing me to go see the movie.

"I remember 'Uncle Bert' [Henderson], he was an old friend of my dad's. He sat with my dad's mom in the last days of her illness. Edgar never forgot his kindness. He was not a relative, but he was a family institution. When I knew Bert, he was a shriveled up, wisp of a man who always wore a wrinkled tweed suit, a crumpled tie, and a crushed gray felt hat of questionable vintage. Bert was never without a book in his hand and a flask in his pocket. He worked all year as a night watchman in Pittsburg, Ca. and then took two weeks off at Christmas to visit his girlfriend in Santa Ana and come by our house. He never called, just showed up. According to legend, when I was a baby, he decided to make gin in the downstairs bathroom (Prohibition was still the law). My mother threw him out and my father brought him back. He was persona-non-grate with my mother for quite awhile.

"We had a Christmas party every year. Holiday parties brought out the entire crowd: actors, grips, directors and producers. At our Christmas open house we would have as many as three hundred people filtering through our home, it was the who's who of Hollywood, but no one thought of it that way. Every year, Christmas was a very special occasion for the Kennedy household. Slim Summerville, we saw a lot of him, he was a nice man. He had a ranch in Coronado in the 1930s."

On 12-24-37 the *Los Angeles Examiner,* in their "Hollywood Parade" column, reported: Many years ago Edgar Kennedy's mother started the custom of entertaining each year at an old fashioned Christmas Eve open house. And for the past thirteen years the Edgar Kennedys have carried on in the traditional manner. About 150 friends have been in to drop by at any time during the long and very large evening. Edgar has got the largest Christmas tree he could buy, and each of the guests will be required to do his share of trimming. They will also find a huge buffet laden with Tom and Jerrys, turkey, plum pudding and other gastronomic accessories. Among the regular dropper-inners are Jimmy and Lucile Gleason, Ruth and Woody Van Dyke, Stan Laurel and Oliver Hardy, the Fred Stones, Glenda Farrell, the Lewis Stones, the Leo McCareys, Slim Summerville, the Guy Kibbees, etc.

Colleen also remembers Leo McCary, Jack LaRue, Leon Errol, Jack Rice, Florence Lake, William Frawley, Wallace Ford, Billy Gilbert, Alan Hale and, of course, Tom Kennedy. Colleen said that "I don't list names

X-mas at the Kennedys' w/ family (Circa early 30's)
(Courtesy Kennedy Family)

to name-drop, but to emphasize we were a community that worked and played together."

One of the highlights of each Christmas season was courtesy of W.S. Van Dyke. Being close to Edgar for many years, he had the self-proclaimed honor of placing an angel on the top of the tree. Every year there was W.S. Van Dyke, pleasantly sloshed, slowly climbing the ladder to the 20-foot-high tree. With each ascending step, there was a hush over the crowd as they watched, partly because of the drama, partly because of the danger. Unbeknownst to the celebrating elders, Colleen and Larry would stay up, sneak down and peer through the staircase rails to watch this traditional event. Colleen said, "W.S. Van Dyke thought it was his divine right to put the star on the tree, so we always reserved the star for him. Larry and I would make bets on his success every year. I always bet against him and lost. W. S. was totally drunk when he climbed the ladder to put the star on the top of the tree. It's a miracle he didn't fall."

Also on 12-24-37, the *Los Angeles Examiner*, in their "Behind the Makeup" column, printed: "There will be no surprise at the Edgar Kennedy household on Christmas. Mrs. Kennedy is giving him a wristwatch that he has already picked out. He is giving her a wristwatch she has already picked out and the two kids are getting wristwatches which they already picked out."

That preceding great piece of journalism obviously was meant to reinforce Edgar's image as everyone's Mr. Average Man. Regular visits to the Kennedy household, especially during Christmas, included the rest of the cast from Edgar's film series.

# 19.
# San Francisco Trips

On August 24, 1937, Edgar stopped over at the St. Francis Hotel. He and Patsy had made their way there after visiting Monterey at the Del Monte golf course during the California Amateur Golf Tournament, August 15-22. Afterwards, the couple continued their vacation on the Sacramento River. When they reached San Francisco, a local paper announced that the city was "chock-full" of additional film celebrities, including Randolph Scott, Adrienne Ames and a "14-year-old Judy Garland." The former Gumm sister was yet two years away from her triumphant *The Wizard of Oz*. Little Judy expressed disappointment to find the city sunny and bright. "I wanted to see some of San Francisco's divine fog and walk around in it."

The newspaper described Edgar Kennedy as "clawing his face impatiently waiting for a telegram to call him back to work. The movie 'mad' man is here to relax in the city he knew as a child."

In another of his frequent trips to San Francisco, one of the city's local newspapers, the *San Francisco Examiner,* caught up to him on November 8 in 1937. The headline of the column announced; "KENNEDY NOT HANDING OUT LOCKS OF HAIR"

> Edgar ('Me and Gable') Kennedy, the man with the most valuable bald head in the world, was in San Francisco yesterday, hiding out from Carole Lombard and a lot of other Hollywood beauties who are always after him for autographs, dates, and locks of his hair. More or less incognito at the St. Francis, the man who likes to think of himself as Clark Gable let it be known that back in the old days he was the nemesis of South of Market, sometimes called the 'Tar Flat Kid' and that was before he went into the movies where he was a heavy-

165

weight boxing champion, and has a gold watch to prove it. Skipping lightly over his roles of henpecked husband and harassed cop, Kennedy preferred to dwell on a recent role where he was Edgar Hamlet, a real tragedian. And on a picture he just made with Carole Lombard, Kennedy said, "Carole is the only girl my wife was ever jealous of. Carole feels the same way about me, too. Me and Gable that is."

The *Chronicle* also documented that he was staying in the City. Pictured in three different poses of trademark expressions, the captions are described.

> **Unhappy Mime is He:** Edgar Kennedy, portly mime of stage and screen, is a very unhappy guy. He made this confession yesterday at the Hotel St. Francis, and just to prove his great woe, tore his hair, mauled his face and gave vent to deep and wonderful moans.

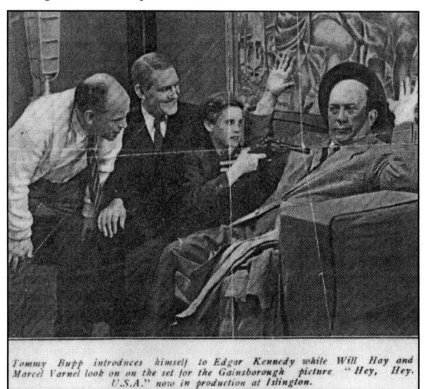

*Tommy Bupp introduces himself to Edgar Kennedy while Will Hay and Marcel Varnel look on on the set for the Gainsborough picture "Hey, Hey, U.S.A." now in production at Islington.*

*Hey Hey USA* (1938)
(Courtesy Tommy Bupp Jr.)

Kennedy has the soul of a poet. The trouble is no one gives him credit for the tenderness of his emotions. Least of all Carole Lombard, who is his idea of something very fine indeed.

Once Kennedy played 'Hamlet.' He recited the soliloquy as Shakespeare wrote it. Friends later took him to task for gagging the 'To be or not to be' lines. Kennedy still feels bitter about the whole business. Even Carole Lombard misunderstood.

For years, since February 22, 1913 [sic], Kennedy, a product of San Francisco's 'Tar Flats' and once a prizefighter, has been tearing his hair. As the result of his efforts he is almost nude on the top of his head and the sides are slowly thinning. Soon he says, he will be reduced to dehairing his chest. The prospect doesn't make him very happy. Carole Lombard might not like it. Kennedy, who comes to San Francisco every now and again because he can't help it, is in search of a little rest. Searching with him is Mrs. Kennedy, who also likes Carole Lombard.

# 20.
# Edgar Goes British

Elizabeth Yeaman reported, in an article entitled "**Edgar Kennedy goes British**," on 4-13-38:

> Since last November, Edgar has been waiting to play in 'Men With Wings,' current Wellman picture at Paramount. A choice comedy role was saved for him. But in the meantime Kennedy accepted a deal to go to England for a picture, and so he had to withdraw from 'Men With Wings.' And thereby hangs a tale.
>
> Edgar Kennedy was born on a farm in Monterey County and still owns the farm. He has traveled practically not at all. But in the last year he developed a yen to see the world. He got the travel bug when last year he went to New York to make personal appearances. It was his first visit to New York [sic] and on the trip he made his first airplane flight. He thought New York was pretty thrilling, and decided he'd like to see Europe. He's been thinking about it ever since, and so has his wife of 14 years.
>
> Finally Kennedy told his agent [Freddie Fralick] to get him a picture job in England. Edgar decided that would be a nice way to get his expenses paid. The agent got him an engagement. Title of the picture is 'Chicago Ben.' Gaumont-British will produce it and Edgar has been signed for five weeks work. He hasn't seen the script, doesn't know what the story is about, who will direct it, or who will be in the cast. Edgar doesn't care about that. His only interest is that he is going to Europe with his expenses paid! And he's giving up his choice part in 'Men With Wings' to do it.

Edgar wants to see England while he is making the picture, and since he is of Irish descent, he will take in Ireland. The only other place he wants to see is Paris. He leaves May 4.

On April 13, 1938, Louella Parsons wrote in her column:

Ireland, England and Wales are shortly to have a treat when Edgar 'Slow-Burn' Kennedy descends upon them in his comic rage. My friend, Edgar, who says the biggest thrill of his life is seeing his name in this column, merits additional recognition. He sails for London May 1 to be starred in a Gaumont-British picture, 'Chicago Ben,' [Also known as "Hey, Hey, USA]. This is his first trip abroad, and he will get in two weeks of sightseeing before the cameras start grinding. Of course, Edgar will make straight for the auld sod to visit the land of his people, and then he'll let the Beef Eaters take him through the Tower of London and do all the things that are so thrilling on that first trip abroad.

Child actor Tommy Bupp joined Edgar, Patsy and the film crew on a first-class cruise on the Queen Mary to Great Britain. Edgar and crew arrived in England on May 27 and checked into the Gainsborough hotel, near the Gainsborough Studios in Islington. Edgar wished that he could have stayed in the country. "Hotels are not my kind of life," Edgar said in the July 1938 interview for British magazine, *World Film News*. "I have to stay in a hotel, working till half-past seven with a call next morning at nine. I eat most of my meals in my room because I'm too tired to dress that time of night. Like a working man? Sure, that's what I am, a working man.

"During the making of the movie," wrote *World Film News*, "the script called for a group of Chicago policemen and it taxed the entire resources of the prop department to find uniforms. They managed to get hold of eight or so and everything was wrong, showing that what the research people knew about Chicago policemen, it knew only as hearsay."

While Edgar and Patsy were in England, they were looked up and joined by old pal Charlie Hall. Charlie, who was born in England, was back home during the time of the production. Charlie was summoned to have dinner, and Edgar even got Charlie into the movie playing an American gangster! In a letter originally written by Charlie Hall to George Stevens, Charlie raved about Edgar's generosity and good fellowship.

Edgar related his most embarrassing moment occurred when he went with a famous English actor to see a recently completed film. "Well, it looks good," thought Kennedy, noting the snappy beginning. Afterwards his opinion was asked and he said, "it's a good picture." The star looked worried and unhappy and said, "But didn't you think that hall sequence was a bit slow?" Kennedy thought a minute, trying to recall the hall sequence, then went into a slow-burn when he realized that he had slept through four reels of the sequence. "If they reedited that picture the way I slept through it they might have a good one."

While the Kennedys were in England, Will Hay, the star of the movie *Chicago Ben*, performed at the London Palladium. Edgar raved about Will Hay's school act to Russell Ferguson: "Remember the bit where he has that gag 'Moses was the daughter of Pharaoh's son,' and one of the kids asks him to write it on the board, and he writes 'Moses was the daughter of…' and then stops there with his back to the audience and his arm in the air ready to write and does nothing. It gets the biggest laugh in the whole act. The way Will does it, the audience gets its chance to use its own judgment, and that's why they think it's so good."

The Hollywood magazines of the era often featured fluff pieces of the stars. It is indeterminable if stories or quotes of the movie stars featured were authentic or the results of a studio publicity agent. One thing is for sure, Edgar elaborated with complete candor when he was interviewed by Russell Ferguson of the *World Film News*. Without the built-in "filtering" of explicit language, this English magazine captured Edgar in rare (or should I say raw) form:

"I'll tell you a good gag to try on some guy when he comes out of a movie with you, saying 'God, that stank.' It works every time. Start off with 'Well, I thought the bit about the shoes was kinda nice.' He says 'Yes, so it was.' Then go on with 'And the bit where the girl waived the handkerchief.' He says, 'Yes, quite nice.' Then you say 'And the bit where the dog ran out,' and he says 'Yes, it was quite well done.' Then when you've got him that far you say 'Why, you liked the main things in the film, and you have the cheek to say it's lousy. *You goddam son of a bitch, what do you expect for a quarter?*"

Upon the Kennedys return to Hollywood, naturally the columnists wrote a scenario featuring Edgar's famous impatience. On 7-17-38, in the *Los Angeles Examiner*, Edgar was quoted:

> After a week's steady grind at the Gaumont-British Studios, I more than welcomed a Sunday golf tournament. Well, there were three other actors and 72 agents. So you see the Hollywood actor-agent ratio holds true in England, too. We started at 10a.m. played one round and then adjourned to the clubhouse for tea! Then, what with periodic interludes for more tea, we finished another round at 9 o'clock that night.
>
> Our train trip to Edinburgh, Scotland, was another attempt at relaxation. But the two compartments we had engaged were expansive like a telephone booth, and after

With the family; Patsy, Colleen & Larry traveling (circa late 1930's)
(Courtesy Kennedy Family)

attempting to squeeze my 232 pounds of weight and six feet and three inches of length into one of the berths. I decided to sit up all night.

The next day we went to Glasgow, only to find the Scottish Industrial Exposition in full swing, and the hotel had graciously turned over our reservations to members of the Lord Mayor of London's party. That night we slept on two army cots in a linen closet, and that was the end of another relaxing weekend.

Three stall seats at the Epsom Downs Derby cost us $45.00 apiece! Then, quite naively, Mrs. Kennedy and her girl friend visited the paddock prior to the big race, got caught in a crowd, missed the race and got soaking wet in a sudden rain storm.

Oh, Europe is all right, I guess, if you don't happen to be a native Californian like myself and don't know the joys of owning a ranch in San Fernando Valley.

Colleen happily remembers that upon returning from the trip, her dad presented her with an outfit made from Scottish plaid. Edgar entertained her with stories that he was able to trace their family back to a Kennedy who was one of the men that helped Mary Queen of Scots escape.

# 21.
# Personal Appearance Tours

Some existing "biographies" and obituaries about Edgar Kennedy mention him performing in vaudeville. There needs to be some clearing up of the subject. According to Edgar's daughter, Colleen, her dad NEVER performed in any vaudeville act UNTIL he became popular in the movies.

The misconception started for two reasons: In Edgar's later personal appearances on the stage, starting in 1936, were often part of a musical revue in which Edgar did a skit. These were similar to old-fashioned vaudeville acts in lieu of showing his movies. Biographers assumed any vaudeville experience was in the beginning of his career, not after he was established. Even in the late 1930s live performances as a prelude to the films were being forced out with the coming of talkies and double features.

The other reason for the misconception that Edgar came from vaudeville to the movies came from Mack Sennett's autobiography. Speaking in a generic sense, he described that most of his actors were hired from a pool of out of work vaudevillians. Edgar Kennedy's name was never mentioned specifically, but assumptions by others became fact in printed form.

In 1936 Edgar was reaching a zenith of his career. Established now as a Hollywood star by way of his "Slow-Burn," even other studios promoted Edgar heavily in his film appearances. More and more inquiries were made about Edgar and if he was really like his screen character at home. Paramount wrote a "biography" about Edgar for distribution. The three pages of "facts" have a germ of truth to it, i.e., his boxing background, and Keystone Kop duties, etc., but in reality, it was written in a succinct and entertaining fashion. Perfect for Hollywood, but maddeningly inaccurate.

Fortunately when Edgar began making personal appearances, the local journalists always sought out a story of the great man. Depending on the question asked, Edgar elaborated on his life in his own way. His personality was such that it caused one scribe to remark, "That, as a rule, film funny-men in the flesh are the world's worst copy…half of them continuously knocking themselves out to be comic…the others being so sad and soulful about it all that we return to our typewriter in tears.

That one of the outstanding exceptions to the rule is Edgar Kennedy, trade-marked by the 'Slow-Burn' who is this week making a personal appearance at the Palace…and who knows how to talk in amusing and educational manner about the game in which he is a recognized player.

On June 26, 1936, Edgar began a personal appearance tour at the Roxy Theatre in New York City. One scribe had erroneously written that Edgar "had never been east of Chicago." Another journalist from the *Daily Mirror*, wrote that "Edgar Kennedy, celebrated Hollywood comedian who has been seen in more than 200 films, will appear in person as the headliner of the new variety stage show at the Roxy Theatre. This will be Kennedy's first personal appearance in the East in many years." Edgar did not reveal to anyone that in February 1909 he went to New York City to study opera singing. Most likely, Edgar thought it might ruin the screen persona he carefully crafted over the years.

Edgar & Patsy on stage (circa early 40's)
(Courtesy Kennedy Family)

An interesting aspect of the tour, and most of the ensuing ones, is that Edgar brought his wife Patsy to appear with as part of the act. It was an interesting time for Mr. and Mrs. Kennedy. Patricia had "retired" from show business when she married Edgar. She had no gumption to appear in movies or the stage prior to this. However, now that Edgar was a Star, all she would have to do was play it straight to set up the comedy for her husband. The Kennedys took advantage of the opportunity to go to all the top nightspots when they weren't working.

Edgar had prepared an especially written sketch with Herman Timberg that lasted 12 minutes. In the act, Edgar tries to sing. Mrs. Kennedy inadvertently "interrupts, baits and heckles him, until at the finish he mops his brow and almost expires with rage." Included in the sketch was a trick piano, specially designed for the show. At one point Edgar pulls the leg off the piano and is scolded off stage by the "stage manager" who says: "Do anything you like, but don't ruin that piano, it's the only one of its kind here." Naturally Edgar does just that, and before the act is through, he tears up the piano rolls, his hair and is thoroughly defeated as registered by his "slow-burn" at the conclusion.

One ad describes, "Edgar Kennedy, the popular Hollywood comedian, is this week's headliner of the Roxy's stage show and is repeating for the customers some of the most hilarious antics he has been up to in the celluloid; supporting him in the stage bill is Paul Ash, the veteran deluxe show master of ceremonies who attends to his duties informally throughout the program. Others in the Roxy bill include Hector and His Pals, Mickey Carol, Jimmy Barry, Betty Lee, the Roxy Rhythm Orchestra and the Gae Foster Dancing Girls." Across town at the Paramount, appearing the same evening, was Ozzie Nelson with Harriet Hilliard as his vocalist. Also performing at the Loew's State Theatre was Ed Sullivan and his "Dawn Patrol Revue."

One of the benefits of appearing at the New York stage was so Edgar could personally attend the Joe Louis/Max Schmeling fight in Yankee Stadium. It is easy to surmise that Edgar performed in New York City because of the Louis/Schmeling fight. This was being billed at the time as the "Fight of the Century." Edgar had long followed the sport and was an ardent fight fan. If he could make the arrangements through his manager just right, his trip would virtually be paid for.

Next stop on his personal tour was Washington, D.C. at the Earle Theatre on 13th Street. Columns announcing his appearance trumpeted the fact that Edgar "is aided by Mrs. Kennedy in an act designed to display his famous 'burning up technique.'" Preceding Edgar's performance at the Earle the week before was Ted Lewis.

This, from an unknown writer of the *Washington Post*:

> Edgar Kennedy, screen comedian headlining the vaudeville bill at the Earle, isn't having so much trouble working up his 'slow-burn' during the local engagement... It comes naturally...Ed, a former Pacific Coast heavyweight champion, was all primed to sit down front and watch the Schmeling-Louis leather-pusher last Thursday night when it was rained out and he had to take a train for his Earle engagement...Been on fire ever since...which may be why his act is going a lot better now...or was Sunday night, when I caught it...the whole stage show was a honey, as a matter of fact.

The Kennedys' act was followed by another musical revue featuring Loretta Lee, "deep-throated songstress from the South, whose rich contralto has become familiar to numerous listeners over the Columbia Broadcasting System during the past three years."

The next stop on the tour was Toronto, Canada. But first, Edgar made a planned stop in Connecticut. It was there that his very dear friend Joe Jackson's mother had a restaurant. She cooked Edgar's favorite game every time he showed up. Joe Jackson, Jr. was a clown, and his father before him was as well. Both father and son played before the crown heads of Europe, they both spoke fifteen languages and hundreds of dialects.

Edgar had met Joe Jackson, Jr. when they both worked for Sennett in the teens. Joe Jackson was typical in that Sennett often hired clowns for the screen. Clowns knew the art of pantomime, were action-fortified and were, well, funny. Both father and son had a famous act in which they did a breakaway bicycle act. Joe's home in Connecticut was filled with trophies of two wonderful careers. Joe, Jr. ended up doing his act on ice for the Ice Capades.

Edgar completed his personal appearance tour by August of 1936, where he received more money than his weekly movie salary. As a result, Edgar was in demand everywhere now: the stage, features, and personal appearances. Wisely, Edgar continued making his two-reel comedies for

*Robin Hood of El Dorado* (1936) MGM
(Courtesy Kennedy Family)

RKO. Edgar continued making these vaudeville-style personal appearances the next year for three weeks in Chicago, Detroit and Cleveland.

Colleen Deach remembers a story about traveling with her dad during these long car trips; it seems that ol' Edgar never liked to ask for directions. One time he drove 500 miles in the wrong direction before he realized it and had to turn around. It's not hard to imagine one long burn on the drive back.

From the *Los Angeles Express,* 5-22-40: "For the past 13 years one of filmtown's most brilliant annual events has been the midnight all-star charity show at the Hollywood Pantages Theater. It will include such stellar artists as Judy Garland, Jack Benny, Eddie 'Rochester' Anderson, Bill Robinson, Edgar Kennedy, The Three Stooges, Johnny Mack and dozens more."

Here's another personal appearance that makes one want for a time machine. On 3-22-39 there was a dinner dance at the Biltmore Hotel hosted by the Film Society (in which funds were raised for the film industry's needy families). The array of talent included Bob Hope as Master of Ceremonies, Fanny Brice, Rudy Vallee, Mickey Rooney, Jack Haley, Billy Gilbert, Ann Miller, Joe E. Brown, Scott Darling, Edgar Kennedy, John Wayne, Ward Bond and W.S. Van Dyke.

Another little ditty from *The Los Angeles Times,* 3-20-42:

> HOLLYWOOD CELEBRITIES WILL APPEAR TONIGHT—When the curtain goes up promptly at 8:30 p.m. today at Shrine Auditorium, the capacity audience gathered to witness the All-Star Show of '42 will settle back to enjoy three full hours of fun.
>
> Jack Benny and Mary Livingstone will offer fresh new material especially prepared for this show. Red Skelton will show how to take care of a baby in a blackout. Milton Berle will trip the light fantastic in competition with beautiful dancers of Aida Broadbent's ballet.
>
> Bob Hope, Jerry Colonna, Don Ameche, Cesar Romero, Ann Sheridan, Veronica Lake, Rudy Vallee, Billy Gilbert, Betty Hutton, Henry Armetta, Maxie Rosenbloom, Edgar Kennedy...

# 22.
# Character Acting

While Edgar was known mostly for being a film comedian, he certainly had the repertoire as an actor to portray character roles. One such example was when he was cast as the Sheriff in *Robin Hood of El Dorado*. The following is from a column emanating from the *Washington Post* in June of 1936, written to coincide with Edgar's personal appearance there:

> Hollywood wanted to try something, so, as usual, the victim was Edgar Kennedy, famous movie comedian, who is coming in person to the stage of the Earle Theatre to-morrow. Hollywood wanted to prove if a comedian was placed in a dramatic role, his disguise changed a little, his lines built along serious situations, would the public recognize him and burst out laughing?
>
> The test case was Kennedy's part in the novelette "Robin Hood of El Dorado." He was cast as a sheriff and for the part he had to grow a mustache. The same baldhead was projected on the screen, but a different Kennedy was introduced. A poll was taken after the preview and the audience asked what they thought of the new ' heavy,' and 92 per cent raved about the new strong-arm character and did not recognize the favorite comedy character in a new role. The others saw behind the makeup and every time Kennedy spoke his serious lines they shrieked with laughter.
>
> This proved to ambitious Hollywood that no matter what you do there will always be a few who can see behind the movie tricks. Kennedy is very unusual, but, being wise, he is perfectly satisfied to stay as he is as long as the movie cashier

gives him his weekly stipend. He is probably the only actor in Hollywood who does not want to play Hamlet, which is enough to put Kennedy in the movie hall of fame.

The reality was, Edgar had been playing various character roles for years, even bad guys.

*Hitler's Madman* in 1943 is a good example. It was made mostly for the low budget studio PRC, but bought by and released by MGM, who shot a few extra scenes. It remains a rather obscure little film. Made during the height of World War II, this saga was based on a true story of a

*Hitler's Madman* as Nepomuk the Hermit (1943) MGM
(Courtesy Kennedy Family)

*In Old California* w/John Wayne (1942) Republic

*Heaven Only Knows*, as Judd
the town drunk. (1947) United
Artists
(Courtesy Kennedy Family)

small Czech village wiped out by the Nazis. John Carradine played Commander Heydrich with relish in his most sadistic way. Edgar plays the cave dweller hermit named "Nepomuk."

In retaliation for Carradine's character being gunned down, the Nazis seek revenge by lining up and executing every adult male in the village. Edgar stands defiant and leads his fellow countrymen into a nationalistic song (dubbed in baritone!), as the men are mowed down. Edgar is the last one standing holding up an elderly man, arm over shoulder. The women are seen carted away to the Russian front to "entertain" the Nazi soldiers, while the children are seen being separated from their mothers and rounded up for Hitler's schools. The grim ending to the film was even more intense when ghostly images of the main Czech characters reappear reciting the poem the film was based on. It was capped off with a plea to the audience not to be complacent, but to fight for liberty.

Powerful stuff in 1943. Edgar's daughter, Colleen, cannot watch this movie without being driven to tears at seeing her father's character being shot and killed. Colleen said, "More than any film role, that was my father."

Also in 1943 Edgar really strayed far away from his screen persona by playing a puppeteer bent on revenge in *The Falcon Strikes Back*. In this entry in the detective mystery series, Edgar's character, of course, is the least expected by the audience as the murderer, but Edgar fooled his fans by portraying a sinister no-nonsense killer. As with any true villain in the movies back then, Edgar's character meets his fate (off camera) by falling off a roof to his death. One anonymous reviewer hypothesized, "So this is how Edgar Kennedy really is. After all those years of being picked on and cheated, he resorts to murdering his victims." It was almost like the coyote finally capturing the roadrunner.

Edgar even played John Wayne's sidekick for the feature film, *In Old California* (1942). Edgar steals the show, starting in his first frame. Suffering from a toothache, Edgar is mad with pain like a wounded animal, as he tears up the bar and throws anyone he can through the window. John Wayne portrays a gentleman pharmacist and soothes Edgar's character (Kegs McKeever) by giving him pain medicine. Like the Aesops' fable, in which a thorn is removed from the lion's paw, Kegs is so grateful for the pain relief, he becomes Wayne's loyal sidekick for the duration of the movie.

In 1947 Edgar played another memorable role in *Heaven Only Knows*. By donning a wig and a mustache, Edgar was almost unrecognizable playing Judd, the town drunk. Edgar had a very touching death scene, again proving that he could have made a living playing character types.

By now the major studios were including incidental publicity about Edgar when announcing their releases. One outlandish example was from Warner Bros. for *Three Men on a Horse*. Their publicity department released that "Edgar Kennedy is playing his 500th role in *Three Men and a Horse*, for Warners."

Columnist Lloyd Pantages announced the above "fact" in his Hollywood column for the *Los Angeles Examiner* on 9-3-36. The number "500" was purely an arbitrary figure, for no one, including Edgar, at that time had any idea how many movies he was in. In a 1942 interview with the *New York Times*, Edgar estimated he was in more than 200 movies up to that point. Edgar had been active in the trade for 24 years by then. Many of them were produced in the first few years with Sennett. There was no active filmography kept on screen actors then, unless they were big stars acting in features. The number 500 was to stay with him through the rest of his life, and beyond.

> Colleen said that when her dad returned from Europe after making *Chicago Ben*, he knew that war was inevitable. The whole family moved to the San Fernando Valley, in a comfortable ranch house, in 1941. It was on 40 acres near "Ivan Parker's Stock Farm" in Pacoima. Tom Mix had a house nearby. Life on the ranch was self-supporting; they raised chickens, turkeys, cows, etc.
>
> For Edgar, it provided a reconnecting to his growing up days in Monterey County. For Colleen, it represented getting up at dawn to milk the cows and do other farming chores.
>
> My mother designed our ranch house; it was a Spanish Hacienda at 13208 Wentworth Ave. It had covered porches in the front and rear that ran the length of the house. The house had a 40-foot-long and 20-foot-wide living room with beamed ceilings. One wall contained a huge fireplace and windows enclosed by a floor to ceiling bookcases. The other wall was all glass. The room was large enough to hold a full-size grand piano in one corner. There were four very large bedrooms with three large bathrooms. The dining room was 15 feet by 20 feet and so was

the kitchen. The kitchen floor was green concrete with a drain in the center. My dad's shower had eight spouts in it. There was a guesthouse in back that had three bedrooms, a living room and kitchen. It was a large comfortable home and everyone who came felt that comfort.

The ranch stood on 40 acres. My dad was one of the original survivalists. When war came to us, we were ready and almost totally self- sufficient. The ranch was stocked with all types of livestock, we had every farm animal, including three horses, and we grew all our own vegetables. We even had a gas pump and tank, which the government allowed because my father donated all his spare time to entertaining the troops. My mother donated all our extra milk and butter to the USO. We all worked on behalf of the USO in those years. I believe we logged over 100,000 miles in military aircraft.

The Kennedys also had a maid named Ruby. Colleen remembers that once, while her parents were gone, Ruby taught the kids how to "Boogie." One particular night, character actor Lewis Stone (then playing Judge Hardy in the "Andy Hardy" series), came over unannounced and rang the doorbell. Between the music and teachings, Ruby neglected to answer the door, so Larry did. Mr. Stone was taken aback. When hearing about the incident, "mother was perturbed!"

On 4-12-39 the *Hollywood Citizen News* printed:
**Actor and Wife Enjoy Family Party on Ranch in Pacoima Quiet.** Rustic spots on their San Fernando Valley ranch at Pacoima were the settings for an informal entertainment which Mr. and Mrs. Edgar Kennedy gave Easter Sunday for a large number of friends. Activities ran the gamut from bridge, baseball and croquet in the morning to an egg hunt and races in the afternoon for the 'younger fry,' chums of the Kennedy children, Larry and Colleen. Interlarding the games was a buffet luncheon served outdoors on long tables set in the shade of friendly oak and acacia trees. At dusk, many of the guests were still present, reluctant to leave the delightful spot.

Among those who enjoyed the day were Messrs. and Mmes. Freddie Fralick, Vivian Oakland, Mrs. Scott Darling, Walter McCormick and Walter McCormick Jr. [Edgar's cousin and his son]. Also present were John and Bud Kennedy who are sons of Tom Kennedy, who is a comedian, like the host. The actors are good friends, but not relatives.

Just before Edgar's 49th birthday, Patsy took her husband to the Kentucky Derby. When they returned on his actual birth date, April 26, there was a small family costume party held in his honor. Larry and Colleen were dressed as a pirate and a Dutch girl. The table decorations had a toy soldier theme. The big surprise of the evening was that Edgar's old boyhood pal, Stanley Kelly, arrived, wearing a Robin Hood costume. At the time, Robin Hood was a hot property due to the release of the color spectacle *The Adventures of Robin Hood* (1938) starring Errol Flynn and Olivia de Havilland. The newspapers identified Stanley Kelly as "Judge Stanley Kelly of San Francisco." In actuality, during that time, Stanley Kelly was a former Police Judge for the city of Burlingame (just south of San Francisco).

Colleen said that "visiting 'Uncle Stan' and 'Aunt Polly' was a place we all loved to visit. Dad was always ready for one of Polly's dinners. Aunty Belinda, Polly's aunt, was my dad's favorite partner for an Irish jig."

Colleen continued, "Aunt Margaret was Uncle Stan's sister and married to Dr. Brindamore, a San Francisco surgeon. They lived in a twenty-four-room house on Clay St. They had four unruly kids. Aunt Margaret held court in her bedroom with her dogs and chocolates, distributing big juicy kisses on everyone who paid attendance. She was always out of bed at eight o'clock, dressed and ready to go to dinner. If you were staying there, you had better be ready and dressed too, since that was the only meal of the day. When my dad was in town, and had time aside from Polly's dinners, he would have dinner with the Brinamores. He tried, like all of us, to avoid the kisses, but he did love those people."

# 23.
# Ring Protégé

In a syndicated column entitled "Behind the Makeup," Harry Crocker wrote on May 15, 1943:

> Natives of the town of Pacoima, which is in the San Fernando Valley, have approached their newest resident, Edgar 'Slow-Burn' Kennedy, to become Mayor. But he's turning it down. While he has a twenty-acre estate in Pacoima, Kennedy points out that he pays his taxes in Los Angeles, his telephone bill in Burbank, his telephone has a Roscoe prefix, he gets his water from Van Nuys, his daughter, Colleen, 14, goes to school in Westwood, and his son, Larry, 15, attends classes in North Hollywood. To top it all, his wife shops in Reseda. 'I'm just too cosmopolitan' claims Edgar, 'to confine myself to one town.'

An interview by Edwin Martin occurred during this time:

> When Edgar Kennedy invited us to visit his new ranch out Pacoima way, we welcomed the opportunity. The big, jovial screen comedian is living on a ranch for the first time since he left the old homestead many years ago. Ed was born on a farm in northern California, not far from San Jose.
>
> The urge to go back to the soil got in his blood, so he put his Beverly Hills home up for sale and completely remodeled the ranch house. 'You can take the boy out of the country,' chuckled Edgar, 'but you can't take the country out of the boy.
>
> 'I'm 46 and I'm in better physical condition today than I have been in many a year.' All this sounded surprising to us,

as we have always regarded Edgar Kennedy as one of screenland's best athletes despite the fact that he has reached the middle 40's. It wasn't surprising after we reached the ranch, however, because on of the first things to strike our eye was a real prize ring, erected out in the open on the back ranch.

'See that?' said the comic, gesturing. 'I'm in training.' At this moment up stepped a tall, stalwart young man, one of the finest physical specimens we have ever seen. Very broad shoulders, amazing reach, slender waist, long but sturdy legs, rugged but handsome features. 'This is Doug Coleman, maybe the next heavyweight champion.' The comedian has young Coleman on the ranch all the time. Ranch work is the greatest conditioner in the world for a fighter. They work out in the ring together every day. Young Doug may turn out to be quite a fighter. Despite the fact that the big comedian is long past fighting age, we saw him jump into the ring with the boy and put on two of the fastest rounds a fight fan could hope to see.

'This ring was a birthday present from Patsy, and I've had more fun with it than I did with a new toy.' In his spare time he alternates between the ranch and Lakeside Golf Club and is regarded as one of the best golfers in Hollywood. He shoots in the 70's. The Kennedys have two splendid children; a boy, Larry, and a girl, Colleen. They are real folks and they get the utmost of happiness out of life. This back-to-the farm movement is a grand idea.

Edgar once told the *Los Angeles Times'* Bill Henry (8-15-37) that he "discovered" Doug Coleman, who lived as a hillbilly in Truckee, Ca. The *Los Angeles Times* also printed on 4-25-37 that Doug Coleman "was a 21-year-old ex-footballer from Oregon State College." In actuality, Edgar met him while "the Kid" was looking for a job about a year earlier. Up until that point he had been working as a chauffeur for Max and Buddy Baer when they were touring the west. Coleman doubled as a preliminary fighter and had a lot of fights in the ring, allegedly.

Edgar took Coleman under his wing and polished up his footwork and boxing skills. He did this by personally scrapping with the young man and then supervising him with match-ups at his ranch.

By early 1938 Edgar had taught Coleman everything he knew. He invited Joe Herman, a respected fight manager in San Francisco, to come down and take a look at his protege. Longtime boxing journalist for the *San Francisco Examiner*, Eddie Mueller, wrote about Coleman in his "Shadow Boxing" column. On April 7, 1938, Mueller quoted Herman as saying; "Too many guys are trying to grab him in Los Angeles, that's why Kennedy wants to get him started up in this part of the State. I don't know how good he is, but from what Kennedy told me he must have something on the ball."

Mueller wrote:

> For one year the motion picture star, a fighter himself twenty-five years ago, has been tutoring his protege on his ranch. When it got to a point where he showed him all he knew, he hired Eddie Bradley to work with and train the fighter. Coleman is 6 feet 3 and weighs 204 pounds. Kennedy thinks the lad has the ability.

Studio shot w/ Florence Lake
(Courtesy Kennedy Family)

His connection with the fighter isn't a publicity stunt. As a matter of fact Kennedy won't be present when the lad makes his debut here. Herman said 'The fighter is on his own, he makes good with his own ability.'

Never having had a fight, Coleman must be taken along slowly. He needs experience and Herman believes by starting at the smaller clubs he can improve by degrees.

Herman arranged with Benny Ford to show the young prospect at National Hall on April 25. The venue was on 16th Street in the Mission District of San Francisco. According to Eddie Mueller, Jr., "National Hall was a small little 'Cracker Box' with weekly fight cards. Its nickname was 'Bucket of Blood.'"

It seems very relevant that Coleman was to make his ring debut two days before the 26th anniversary of Edgar's big fight. A coincidence or a calculated effort to schedule a lucky date?

# 24.
# The Average Man Series Continues

Every other month Edgar's screen family played at the cinemas around the country. By now the unofficial name of the "Average Man Series" was "The Edgar Kennedy Series." This, at a time when two-reelers at the movies had all been fazed out, double features had taken their place on the bill.

It was the heartland of America that demanded these short comedies most. For Edgar, his series was the "bread and butter" of his career. They would continue making them as long as the public turned out for them. For RKO, it was profitable for the studios to produce. Generally it only took three to four days to shoot each episode.

Each of the Hollywood studios that were producing two-reelers during that era had distinctly different production values: The Roach Studios had their charming incidental music to enhance the scenes. Columbia Studios (who were still churning out The 3 Stooges, Andy Clyde, Charley Chase, et al) featured exaggerated sound effects. The "Average Man" series remained real because it relied on the comedy of situations, with one constant: Edgar Kennedy blowing his top. One knew it was coming, but the fun was watching how much he could tolerate before he finally succumbed to his implosion.

In the course of the seventeen-year series run, there actually were many changes to the cast and characters, except for Edgar, of course, he was the glue to the whole show. For some inexplicable reason, the brother-

*In-laws are Out* (1934) RKO
(Courtesy Sam White)

Jack Rice, studio shot (RKO)
(Courtesy Kennedy Family)

in-law part played by William Eugene was replaced in 1934, after 19 episodes had been released.

Eugene added a unique touch to the character. At times he would talk tough and stand up to Edgar, only to be reduced to an audible whimper when Edgar looked at him in a threatening manner (sometimes as subtle as lifting a menacing eyebrow). He would literally hide behind his mother's apron strings and seek her protection. Edgar had no use for him.

William Eugene's last film in the series was *In-Laws Are Out*, released 6-29-34. The director of that short was Sam White. He was the youngest of the famed "White Brothers," Jules and Jack. All three got their starts at the Sennett Studios and went on to direct at Educational and Columbia Studios.

94-year-old Sam White is one of the only contemporaries still alive to have worked with Edgar. He directed three of the "Average Man" comedies and was the last one to direct William Eugene in his brother role. Sam White also directed William Eugene in *Love on a Ladder* (3-2-34).

I was hoping Mr. White could provide me with a profile of Eugene

W/ Billy Franey & Vivian Oakland. RKO
(Courtesy Kennedy Family)

and, more important, tell me why he was replaced. His answer? "William who? No, no, no, Jack Rice was the brother-in-law!" He had no recollection of Billy Eugene or William Eugene. It perfectly sums up Mr. Eugene's career, who exited from the series almost without notice.

Jack Rice first appeared as the brother-in-law for *A Blasted Event* (9-7-34). Rice added a different element to the role; he was a bit of a weasel. Rice portrayed a "mama's boy" and never seemed to be inspired to get a job unless he was conniving Edgar for money to start a business. Dot Farley uttered these lines in the 1936 *Gasoloons*: "I didn't raise my son to be a soldier!" Nothing could define a character so succinctly in those prewar years.

With Jack Rice inserted into the "Brother" role, the series went on as though nothing had happened. You can bet the small town moviegoers noticed. The "Average Man" was in their eyes a real family, warts and all. When *In Love at 40* was released in August of 1935, one theatre proprietor commented in the *Moving Picture Herald*: "Who is the new ' brother' in these shorts? He isn't as good as the former 'brother' but not many squawks." (Capital Theatre, Harrisburg, N.Y.)

During 1937 there were continuing changes to the series. Florence Lake was less available, so film veteran Vivien Oakland often portrayed Edgar's wife. She did not play this role as Lake did, a chirping bird brain. Instead, she was more stately mannered. Her character was almost a melding of the mother-in-law and wife. As a result, Dot Farley was not used until 1942 when the series evolved again.

It was almost as though Edgar married into another family. Gone was Jack Rice, for the most part, and instead a new character was introduced: Edgar's father-in-law, Billy Franey.

Little Billy Franey was allegedly born in 1882, making him a mere eight years Edgar Kennedy's senior. Franey actually looked about twenty years older.

Franey's death certificate indicates that he was born June 23, 1889, making him a mere fifty-one years old at the time of his death. He was a tiny, frail man, who added much to the series in the short three years he was associated with it.

Franey was born in Chicago and at one time was a circus clown doing a tumbling act. In his *New York Times* obituary (12-11-40), it stated that Franey fought in the Spanish-American War. (If his listed birth date of 1882 is correct, it would have made him only 15 years old at the time.)

According to an RKO publicity department mini-biography of 8-18-37, Franey also served in the First World War and received a serious wound while in France. The same biography indicated that Franey remembered the first dollar he made, "it was from sweeping out the floors of a tobacco shop," while he was only eight years old.

Billy Franey broke into the movies by way of vaudeville, landing at Universal for the Joker Comedies in 1913. He also produced twenty-six comedies for O'Connor Productions. His favorite hobby was fishing.

Edgar supported Franey in some early Fox Sunshine Comedies, most notably in *The Roaming Bathtub*, 2-21-18.

By the late 1920s Billy was starring at the Reelcraft Film Corporation, an independent company. In the book *Clown Princes and Court Jesters* by Kalton C. Lahue and Sam Gill (1970), they described Franey's persona in these long forgotten silent shorts:

> Much of Franey's material was clever, and as such was a refreshing change from the average comedy offerings of the twenties. Billy seems to have been at his best when the script

"W/Vivian Oakland" RKO
(Courtesy Kennedy Family)

called for a bunko artist or confidence man. He came on the screen as one who could con a little old lady out of her life savings or part a youngster from his all-day sucker with equal success. His air of self-assurance that he was more than capable of the task at hand came across very well on the screen.

By 1937 Billy was no longer a physical comedian, but brought with him an added comedy element in his screen character, an old con artist. Edgar was often swindled by Billy, who often turned up just as often as a bystander with bad advice. The fun was watching this defenseless little man often get the best of Edgar. When Billy was invariably confronted, his subtle, pleading facial expressions contrasted nicely with Edgar's rages.

On December 9, 1940, Billy Franey suddenly died of a heart ailment complicated by influenza. His last short in the "Average Man" series was *It Happened All Night* and actually released on 4-14-41. In this short, Edgar was back in a cop uniform (as the Constable) in the fictional town of Fairview. "Aw nothing ever happens here," says Edgar as he performs his monotonous foot patrol of the small town. During the next twenty minutes, "Moocher and Danny the Dip" have broken jail from somewhere and descend on Fairview to recover a fortune in gems they buried in a vacant lot five years before.

As the crooks hide from Kennedy, the FBI arrives and captures four crooks. Edgar hasn't the slightest idea of what's been happening, to him it's been a quiet night.

Originally named Vivian Anderson when she was born in 1885, the petite blonde was allegedly part of the *Ziegfield Follies* in the early days. She graduated to silent films with work at the Hal Roach Studios. Laurel and Hardy fans remember her in *Scram* and *Way Out West*. The former featured Vivian as the hangman Judge's wife. L&H inadvertently get her roaring drunk until she wants to party and dance with the reluctant house guests. She shares one of the greatest gags ever with the boys in a laughing fit clad in nightclothes. A mature woman by the mid-thirties, she played various wife roles at Columbia and RKO. Vivian at times played Leon Errol's wife, as well as Edgar's, in the late 1930s and into the '40s.

The Vivian character, as Edgar's wife was, to her credit, played differently than Florence. Vivian was bored with Edgar and had no patience with him, she was a bit of a nag but couldn't hold a candle to Dot Farley's mother-in-law antagonisms. Most of the time when Vivian was the wife, Billy Franey played the pa-in-law.

Of course there were exceptions throughout the series. During the time Vivian was unavailable, the wife was sometimes played by Sally Payne who did her best to impersonate Florence Lake. An interesting exception was in 1943 when Irene Ryan played Edgar's wife in *Hold Your Temper* and *Indian Signs*. Irene Ryan became better known to America twenty years later as "Granny" in the *Beverly Hillbillies* television comedy.

Irene Noblette was born on October 17, 1902 in El Paso, Texas. Irene was living in San Francisco by age eleven when she entered an amateur contest. Reportedly her singing of "Pretty Baby" at the Valencia Theatre launched her into a career as a vaudeville headliner, and she toured the country while still a teenager.

By the time she was 30 the medium of radio called for her talents. She was on the Jack Carson and Rudy Vallee shows, but most notably on the Bob Hope radio show.

Irene's role in her two films as Edgar's wife was fairly brief. It didn't showcase her own talents, so it wouldn't draw attention that Florence was not playing the wife. It was noticed.

Sally Payne was born on September 5, 1912 in Chicago, Illinois. She died of a stroke on May 8, 1999. According to her *Los Angles Times* obituary, written on May 13, 1999, Sally Payne was "originally known as the 'Sunshine Girl' of artists' models and came to Hollywood under contract to Republic Studios. There she appeared in a number of westerns with such cowboy stars as Roy Rogers and Gene Autry.

"When studio executives requested that she have her nose altered through plastic surgery, the model-turned-actress dutifully went to what was then Cedars of Lebanon Hospital to have it reshaped, telling reporters: 'I've always found it a pretty good nose, but if they want to change it, I guess I'll have to let 'em do it. Things are that way in Hollywood.'"

She made her debut in a bit part as a tourist in the 1934 short *Hollywood Hobbies*. By 1940, before moving into a series of westerns, she appeared as a maid in *No, No, Nanette* and as the character Lucy Endover in *La Conga Nights*.

Sally Payne divorced her husband, radio gag writer William Telaak, in 1941. On May 8, 1942, Sally married Arthur F. Kelly, who in the 1970s was president of Western Airlines. For six films Sally was cast as Edgar's wife, starting with *Westward Ho-Hum* (9-15-41) and ending in *Crooks and Cooks* (6-5-42). According to Leonard Maltin's *The Great Movie Shorts*: "Sally Payne was obviously shown a bunch of Miss [Florence] Lake's comedies, for she mimicked her to the letter, with only fair results."

Semi-retired after marriage, Sally enjoyed painting in oil for her home and friends. In 1974, Sally's son, Jim Kelly, authored three children's books that Sally illustrated: "The Little Neighbor," "The Secret Hole," and "Star Flower."

Sally Payne for many years ran a small bookstore "The Bookworm" with her son in Brentwood, Ca. In later years, Sally volunteered with the "Reading is Fundamental" program and earned a degree in nutrition and a pilot's license.

There were a number of directors who worked on the series over the years. Arthur Ripley was one. Colleen said that Ripley was "another old timer and favorite of my dad. He was a fine director and person. A rugged face. He wore tweed jackets with leather patches and always smelled of great pipe tobacco. My dad loved to have long discussions with him and they were great chess mates."

By the early 1940s hardly anyone was making two-reel comedies (*sans* Columbia and MGM). The "Average Man" series got its last wind once the original cast was reunited in *Two for the Money* (8-14-42), and really finished strongly when Hal Yates became the permanent director in *The Kitchen Cynic* (6-25-44). For the next twenty-four episodes, Hal Yates instilled the continuity the series sometimes lacked.

Hal Yates was another Roach veteran director who started in the silent era. Yates was the director of numerous classic titles including: *A Pair of Tights*, and Laurel and Hardy's now missing classic *Hats Off*, where the boys deliver a washing machine up and down a long flight of stairs. It was the predecessor of Laurel and Hardy's *The Music Box*, in which the boys deliver a piano up a long flight of stairs in the Silver Lake district of Los Angeles. This talkie short garnered them the Best Short Subject award of 1932 at the Academy Awards.

One of the Hal Yates-directed episodes for the Edgar series during this time was *It's Your Move* (8-10-45). A short synopsis in Leonard Maltin's

*Bric-a-Brac* (1935) RKO
w/ Walter Brennan

*The Great Movie Shorts* is as follows: "Ed has two weeks to buy his house before the landlord sells it out from under him." Those notes, probably written on the film's release, don't begin to explain this short.

The highlight of *It's Your Move* is when Edgar and brother have to deliver…an old-fashioned washing machine tub, complete with ringer, up to the resident at the end of a seemingly never-ending ascending flight of stairs. If some of this sounds familiar, it should. Hal Yates wrote the script for *It's Your Move* and uses some of the very same gags *Hats Off* had. An example: Anita Garvin was in the original and was featured summoning Laurel and Hardy up the stairs. Thinking she is a ready customer, they arrived huffing and puffing with the washing machine. Instead of buying the damn thing, Anita hands them a postcard to deliver. Gentlemen as they are, there are no complaints, and the boys dutifully take the letter down the flight of stairs with the metal tub.

The scenario was probably fresh in Hal Yates' memory when shot a mere eighteen years prior with Laurel and Hardy. Is it any wonder that the same gags on the stairway were recycled? Yates even positioned an Anita Garvin look-alike at the top of the stairs to reenact the postcard scene.

Unfortunately, the team of Kennedy and Rice pales in comparison with Laurel and Hardy's version in the *Music Box*. The comic sequence of the washing machine carried up the stairs fails because Rice's whiny character is just plain irritating. Were the stairs the same as in the original version? Regrettably, no. It's possible they couldn't find the original steps with all the development in the area.

Part of the fun in watching this series during contemporary times is seeing, who were then, little known players in supporting roles. Such examples include Betty Grable (*A Quiet Fourth*), Walter Brennan (*Bric-a-Brac*), Hugh Beaumont (*Prunes and Politics*), and Lucille Ball (*Dummy Ache*), to name a few.

The series was also sprinkled with Hal Roach alumni players from the old two-reeler days. It's a pleasure to see James Finlayson in *False Roomers*, Tiny Sandford in *Trailer Tragedy* and *A Clean Sweep*, Anita Garvin in *Sunk by the Census*, Eddie Dunn in *Mind Over Mouse*, Walter Long in *No More Relatives*, Iris Adrian in *How to Clean House*, Tom Kennedy in *Sock Me to Sleep, Fish Feather* and *Love Your Landlord*. The Little Menace—Charlie Hall appeared in seven of the Edgars: *Wall Street Blues, Radio Rampage, A Quiet Fourth, I'll Build It Myself, Rough on Rents, Trailor Tragedy,* and *Bon Voyage*.

Edgar, Patsy, & Colleen welcoming Larry home after the war.

One of the most charming entries in the series, *Vocalizing*, was also the most unusual. The premise of the original story, "Seeing Nellie Home" by Elisabeth Sanxay Holding, was originally published in *Women's Home Companion* in August 1935. The story featured the husband, wife and adoring son and daughter. It seemed so perfect for Edgar, that the rights were purchased for the "Average Man." Les Goodwins and Monty Collins wrote the screenplay. In the original script, the daughter was written out, but a son made it into the script. Thus, this new character was introduced into the series, "Sonny" Kennedy, an 18-year-old offspring.

*Vocalizing* featured Edgar, who was escorting "Nellie Bristead," an opera singer, home after performing on the piano at the Kennedys' house. After one mishap after another, including a near arrest, Edgar is picked up by a kind soul and returned home. Along the way the driver, "Willie," encourages Edgar to sing. Will Edgar sing in his Irish tenor voice? No. Edgar harmonizes with Willie by singing in deep tones; "…and 'twas for Aunt Dinah's Quilting party I was seeing Nellie home, I was seeing Nellie home…"

A good example of this series' situation comedy development is in *Edgar Hamlet* (1935). Only interior sets are used at the Kennedy household. Mother and Edgar have a raging debate over Shakespeare. In real life, both Dot and Edgar loved their Shakespeare and it is not hard to imagine some of the script emanating from this interest. At the climax of the short, Edgar recites *Hamlet* for a full two minutes (uncut), in eloquent fashion. It was such a sincere scene, that even mother's raspy disposition melts into a smile and, of all things, an apology! A rare moment for the series, indeed.

# 25.
# Baseball

One of the most engaging and entertaining fund raisers was initiated in the 1930s, pitting film comedians against the leading men of the day, playing baseball! Edgar Kennedy was involved in many of them. Unfortunately, these games were not well-documented in the sports pages, or anywhere else for that matter. It was treated at the time as just another fund raiser in which the various film studios would assign their "stars" for publicity. The difference in these games as opposed to say, film premieres, is that it was terrifically interactive for the movie stars. Usually the men involved had some skills and/or interest in the sport. The result was a visual crowd sensation and it was anything goes for a laugh.

On July 15, 1939, one such baseball game was played to benefit Mt. Sinai Free Hospital Clinic. On a Saturday afternoon, at Los Angeles' Wrigley Field (so named after the Chicago Cubs and chewing gum magnate), the national pastime was mugged, mangled and mutilated by the celebrity "baseball players."

On this day Ken Murray emceed the event on the loudspeakers. Jean Hersholt was the Parade Master, a parade that included "two hundred film celebrities riding in open cars preceded by 100 drum majorettes, and 10 bands will play."

35,000 people attended this event and heard little Shirley Temple read the lineups which included:

| LEADING MEN: | COMEDIANS: |
|---|---|
| Gene Raymond (Captain) | Buster Keaton (Captain) |
| Leo Carrillo | Jimmy Durante |
| Buck Jones | Edgar Kennedy |
| Allan Jones | Stan Laurel |
| Ken Maynard | Oliver Hardy |

BASEBALL: "Comedians vs. Leading Men"
(Author's collection)

| | |
|---|---|
| Preston Foster | Andy Devine |
| Tony Martin | Billy Gilbert |
| Frank McGrath | George Burns |
| Jackie Coogan | Jackie Cooper |
| Porter Hall | Mickey Rooney |

And just to make sure the game didn't get out of hand, the Umpire in Chief was Hugh Herbert. The other base umpires? The Ritz Brothers, naturally. There are no accounts on how many people died laughing or broke their funny bones, but Mt. Sinai Medical Clinic must have been busy.

Edgar played in the above titled fund raiser in San Francisco on September 17, 1939. Some 100 movie stars made the trip north in a special Hollywood train. They included, in part: Jane Withers, Billy Gilbert, Preston Foster, Allan Jones, Wally Ford, Roscoe Ates, Buster Keaton, Keye Luke, Lucien Littlefield, Roy Rogers, Hugh Herbert, Dick Purcell, Eddie Quillan, Buster Crabbe, Arthur Treacher, Guy Kibbee, Pat O'Brien, Lee Tracy, Sidney Blackmer, Jimmy Gleason, Buck Jones, Edgar Kennedy, Nat Pendleton, Ray Milland, Dick Powell, Bob Hope, Jerry Colonna, Tom Keene, Jean Hersholt, Claire Trevor, Jean Parker, Chick Chandler, Chico Marx, Morey

Amsterdam and Leo Carillo, among others. The celebrities stayed at the St. Francis Hotel, where plenty of merriment was served.

The *San Francisco Chronicle* published a photograph taken at the hotel for pre-publicity. The posed picture featured Edgar Kennedy as the catcher and Buster Keaton sliding into home plate, in this case, a sofa cushion. Jane Withers signals "safe." Edgar was wearing a catcher's mitt for a prop and had his ever-present pipe in his mouth.

The big day came with some 20,000 people at Seals Stadium. Tickets were ranged from 50 cents to $2.50. The Leading Men wore the uniform of the Seals while the Comedians wore uniforms of the hated cross bay rivals, The Oakland Oaks. The starting lineups were:

| LEADING MEN | Pos. | COMEDIANS |
|---|---|---|
| Richard Arlen | 1b | Allen Jenkins |
| Ray Milland | 2b | Buster Keaton |
| Dick Purcell | SS | Mischa Auer |
| Keye Luke | 3b | Eddie Quillan |
| Wally Ford | CF | Hugh Herbert |
| Brian Donlevy | RF | Andy Devine |
| John Howard | LF | Edgar Kennedy |
| Preston Foster | C | Nat Pendleton |
| Wayne Morris | P | Bob Hope/Jerry Colonna |

At 2:00 p.m. the game began with Bob Hope sweating on the mound. Andy Devine strode to left field in specially-made big pants. At one point, Andy and Allen Jenkins pitched a pup tent in left field and roasted wienies.

In the bottom of the first, Buster Keaton got a hit, then as he was approaching second base promptly "shot" Dennis Morgan. The ballgame was more of a circus than anything resembling the national past time. Other highlights included Lucien Littlefield pitching "an invisible ball," Buster Crabbe falling into a tub of water on the way to first base and Chico Marx hitting golf balls.

The *San Francisco Chronicle* said "the game broke up in a riot of flour balls and custard pie throwing, leaving the score in confusion." Official scorers, "after a long and debatable consultation by three score keepers and representatives of both nines, favored the Leading Men by a score of 58 to 38." Buster Keaton claimed victory and vowed to appeal the score to the U.S. Supreme Court.

SCREEN SNAPSHOTS

During the annual Leading Men vs. Comedians charity baseball game in 1942, Columbia sent a film crew to record the action. The game would be released to the theatres as part of the series "Screen Snapshots" (Series #21, No. 6). The ten-minute short film is unavailable for viewing, but fortunately a picture continuity script still survives.

The picture opens up at the "Mayflower Do-Nut Shoppe," with customers Frank Morgan, Fanny Brice, Don Wilson and others all dunking donuts. The scene dissolves to "Slapsy Maxie's" where Forrest Tucker, Slapsie Maxie, Victor Mature, Artie Shaw and Betty Grable are seated.

The above two scenes are connected by "telephone conversations" and dissolves to a sign: "To-night at 8:30, Hollywood's Comedians vs. Hollywood's Leading Men—Baseball game for charity." Down on the field soldiers are seen carrying flags and drum majorettes are featured.

Then the celebrities are driven onto the field: Arthur Lake, Baby Dumpling and Daisy the dog, from the "Blondie" series, are all featured in one car. Cesar Romero and Martha Raye are in another car. "Wild Bill" Elliott and Roy Rogers rode in on horseback. Nat Pendleton is shown carrying a "dumb-bell." Comedians Billy Gilbert and Edgar Kennedy were in a wagon being pulled by four horses. Throwing out the first pitch was Joan Blondell. Adolphe Menjou appeared with an apron on.

The players went to their respective positions to start the game, and the leading men were up first. The following is an excerpt from the original script:

> Jack LaRue at bat, people bg.—CAMERA PANS with him as he runs by basemen back to home and slides on base (shoots gun on the way).
> Edgar Kennedy, player and people bg.
> Billy Gilbert at bat, CAMERA PANS right with him as he skips to first base.
> Edgar Kennedy, player and people bg.
> Allan Jones at bat, by catcher—CAMERA PANS right with Allan.
> Edgar pitching, fielder and people bg.
> Ronald Reagan and catcher—crowd bg., CAMERA PANS right with Ronald past men fg.
> Andy Devine, running to base, crowd bg.
> Players and crowd.
> Edgar, crowd bg.
> Keye Luke at bat by catcher, Keye Luke exits, crowd bg.
> Stubby Krueger at bat, standing in tub of water, catcher— crowd bg.—Stubby steps out of tub, gets back in, sits, starts splashing water.
> People around Lucien Littlefield, nurse and player help him up.
> Edgar, crowd bg.
> Lucien at bat, nurse and people, crowd bg.
> Lucien, starts to exit, catcher enters, crowd bg.
> Lucien, CAMERA PANS left with him past people.
> Leon Errol at bat by catcher—crowd bg. CAMERA PANS right with Errol as he runs to first base, crowd bg.
> Allan seated, talking on phone, reporter bg., exits, girl enters.
> Girl and Allan; he rises, girl opens fur coat revealing bathing suit—address hung over each arm—Allan sits— FADE OUT
> Columbia the end emblem—FADE OUT
> (Reel footage...799 ft...10 Fr.

FOOTBALL?

Also in 1942, during the fall, Edgar participated in the "Comedians vs. the Leading Men" in a football game! The game was played on October 18 at the Los Angeles Coliseum.

The Lineup:

Betty Grable and Rita Hayworth were the two Captains. John Wayne served as the official coach. Film director William Seiter was in charge of directing the contest.

| *Comedians:* | *Leading Men:* |
| --- | --- |
| Billy Gilbert | Broderick Crawford |
| Edgar Kennedy | Randolph Scott |
| Buster Keaton | John Wayne |
| Milton Berle | Anthony Quinn |
| Jack Oakie | Allan Jones |
| Jimmy Durante | Edward Arnold |
| George Tobias | Lon Chaney, Jr. |
| Phil Harris | Cesar Romero |
| | Dennis Morgan |

One of the cheers that was allegedly used for the game:
    Ha Ha Ha, who are we?
    Movie comics full of glee.
    Watch us run and pass and kick.
    Watch us make those heroes sick.
    Can we beat them? Wait and see.
    What a slaughter it will be.
    Ho ho ho, he he he.
    We'll laugh our way to victory.

Described by Jane Walsh 10-19-42 *Hollywood Citizen News*:

**LEADING MEN WIN GAG GRID BATTLE:** Hollywood gagmen staged the world's most stupendous football game yesterday at the Coliseum when the Leading Men brought the Comedians to their knees with a 94 to 79 score for the combined benefit of the USO and Mount Sinai Hospital.

Unfortunately, the game got off to a bad start when one of the players was injured by the oversized toss-up disc, which fell on his toe. When a bevy of beautiful nurses was rushed by jeep to the scene, all of the players took sick in need of the comforting of the gorgeous nurses.

In the first play of the game, the score was brought to a 66-66 tie. The way it was done was simple—everyone had a ball. Things were going along fine until the screen lovers refused to come out of a huddle. The reason was discovered when a curvaceous starlet came skipping out of their midst.

Both teams displayed unusual playing. Noticeable were the swing-shift plays, the leapfrog breaks over the line, and the spectacular flip-flop runs up and down the field. The game was called to a halt at one point when an uniformed messenger from the local selective service board "drafted" comic Dewey Robinson. But it took Joe Lewis to break up the free-for-all that broke out on the field when one of the players was penalized five yards for shooting a member of the opposing team.

Most stupendous play of the day was the 100-yard 'creep' made by Lon Chaney Jr. (alias Frankenstein) [sic] when he paralyzed everybody on the gridiron, including the refs, and then chased the whole screwy game to the showers.

By 1943 the "Comics vs. the Leading Men" were celebrating their 9th annual baseball game on 10-11-43. Edgar was promoted to umpiring the ballgame. Among the participants was an "invisible character," Claude Rains. The Comics featured Buster Keaton and Lucien Littlefield, among others. George Jessel was the emcee, while Spike Jones and Harry James, with their respective orchestras, provided the music. Edgar was reportedly a real hit as the umpire, slow-burning when engaged in arguments by batters, managers and fans alike.

The Leading Men vs. Comedians baseball game continued into the 1950s, alas without Edgar. It was a very successful venture for the charities, as well as the spectators and celebrities.

The crude beginning of the concept of film stars playing a baseball game for charitable purposes goes all the way back to 1915. Sure enough, Edgar was there. On 10-25-15 *The Los Angeles Evening Express* reported:

**Filmdom BALL STARS TO CLASH WITH COUN-CILMEN.** The dignified members of the city council in regulation baseball uniforms made their debut as members of the municipal team which will join in fray with the movie actors' nine at Washington Park next Saturday.

*The Los Angeles Times* 10-28-15 reported:

**Three runs and they're out**—that's the slogan for the ball game to be played at Washington Park Saturday afternoon between members of the City Council and prominent moving-picture actors for the benefit of the police band fund and the work of the city mother's bureau. Councilmen Foster Wright—who is shortstop on the Council team, will be matched against Roscoe Arbuckle of the movie team. Wright weighs just one hundred and twenty pounds, while Arbuckle beats him by just one hundred pounds. Arbuckle is some sprinter, holding a record of a hundred-yard dash in thirteen seconds.

Messrs. Kolb and Dill will also have a little game of their own on the side and De Wolf Hopper will recite "Casey at the Bat" when he isn't competing with Fred Mace as umpire.

A parade starting from Washington and Hill streets promptly at noon will be composed of the police band, city officials, firemen, police, movie stars and society girls in automobiles. The society girls and movie actresses will distribute programs, peanuts and pink lemonade.

Unfortunately there are no written accounts of the game, but for the record, the line-up of the Mack Sennett stars were as follows:

| | | | |
|---|---|---|---|
| 1b | Charles Murray | RF | Edgar Kennedy |
| 3b | Mack Swain | LF | Harry Gribbon |
| SS | Roscoe (Fatty) Arbuckle | CF | Chester Conklin |
| P | Slim Summerville | Umpire: | Fred Mace |
| C | Hank Mann | | |

The question begs to be asked: Where were the Mack Sennett cameras?

# 26.
# World War II

When the United States declared war on Japan and Germany, the old army veteran Edgar Kennedy did his part to support the war effort. Colleen adds, "Our ranch provided us with more than the necessities so we shared them with our neighbors, friends and the U.S.O." They raised enough beef and mutton to invite numerous servicemen over for wonderful home cooked meals. Says Colleen, "Our home was always open to GIs. We had as many as 5 or 6 of them staying each weekend."

Larry Kennedy, like the rest of his schoolmates, was anxious to join the war effort. As soon as he was 18 Larry enlisted into the Navy. Edgar and his wife felt the same pride and fear for their only son that millions of other American families experienced at the time.

Edgar volunteered to be an "Air Raid Warden," as did neighbor Clark Gable when the war broke out. They both were in charge of their rural neighborhoods, covering it on horseback. Colleen said, "It was a serious job then, we were actually afraid of being attacked by the Japanese. The sad thing was our good friends and neighbors, who were Japanese and good people, were spirited away one day and we never heard from them again."

Colleen was also growing up. She was 15 years old in 1941 and Edgar took Colleen with him everywhere by then. "Whatever my dad wanted to do, I wanted to do," she said. Edgar brought her golfing, and on the bond tours and the other personal appearances to benefit the armed forces.

Colleen described herself as feeling awkward growing up. "I was tall and gangly." She remembers a special moment during her adolescence when her dad bought her "my first long dress. It was accordion-pleated blue chiffon, a dream dress for a ten-year-old. I wore it to a grownup dance at a special occasion at Catalina Island. I was all dressed up, and escorted my father to a dinner dance at the huge ballroom. We danced together with the wonderful orchestra, and all of dad's friends cut in wanting to dance with me." Colleen was developing into a charming young lady with social graces.

"Another Catalina trip that was a total disaster was a deep sea fishing trip. I was so seasick I never even saw the ocean much less the fish. Although my father was very athletic, he was never into winter sports. We went to Big Bear and rented a cabin because Dad belonged to the Peter Pan Club up there. He played golf, and in the winter we did sledding and tobogganing. That did not deter the fan magazines, they wrote a huge article about how Edgar Kennedy broke his leg skiing."

Colleen remembers the time when they had a "shotgun wedding" at the ranch.

My dad's dear friend, Josephine Cohen (who was often our piano player on the road), had a daughter named Ardis. Now Ardis was Jewish and she fell in love with an Irish Catholic. No one wanted to handle that one in those days. So we had the wedding at our house. The wedding cake was covered with red roses, the minister was a Protestant, the ceremony was half & half, while my dad held the shotgun. Everybody had a ball. Their eventual baby became a Protestant.

Dad loved fast cars, and if you check the records, he never got a ticket. Of course the cops loved him. I remember one story about a drive to Elko, Nevada with several friends. They drove nonstop at a constant speed of ninety miles an hour. They were in a hurry so they didn't stop to change drivers. One would slip under the driver and the driver slopped into the back seat. According to the story they didn't miss a beat. I wonder, considering my dad's size, how they managed that one.

When traveling we had little time to sightsee because in the early years my parents were working on the road, but one trip stands out. It was to Arizona and the Grand Canyon. We stopped in Phoenix to drop off my dollhouse to a friend, and afterward we visited with Del Webb and Barry Goldwater, two dear friends of my dad's. Then we went to Cameron to witness an Indian rain dance. That was before there were too many tourists. Dad had a friend who ran a motor court, store

At Galveston, Texas Army Airfield during the war
(Courtesy Kennedy Family)

and soda fountain near the reservation. We had to wrap wet
rags around our noses to breathe. It was a great history lesson,
but I didn't realize it at the time. Then we went to the canyon,
it took my breath away. With all the work trips I took with my
dad, this was the most fun because it wasn't work. We did the
Petrified Forest on that trip too. They gave my father a huge
piece of petrified wood just because he was there.

I remember one act my parents did about Romeo and
Juliet. My mother was standing on a stepladder pretend-
ing it was a balcony over the stage (house lights low) and
she inadvertently breaks the pearls she is wearing. They
scatter all over the stage and, trying to keep her cool, she
ignores it and goes on with her call: 'Romeo, Romeo where
for art thou Romeo?' My dad answered right on cue in an

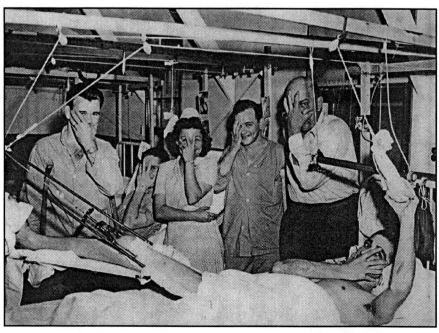

An unknown military hospital during the war. Everyone knew the "Slow-Burn"

agitated voice, 'Down here picking up your lousy beads…'
A roar would invariably erupt from the appreciative audience and the skit would be off and running.

Colleen often went with her parents during these vaudeville stage acts. "They
just loved my dad," Colleen says. One day in 1937, while performing in San
Francisco, Colleen's mom suddenly became ill. "Even though I was only 11
years old, I took my mom's place because I knew the routine. It would have
been scary but I knew they were there to see Dad, not me. It was the Romeo and
Juliet gig. Mom and Dad did lots of those personal appearances. At one time
they did a breakaway piano on a baby grand. He'd sit down to play and a piece
would go. Eventually the top would come down and the piano would collapse."

Often, when Edgar performed at service shows, Colleen would sometimes substitute for her mother. "Once World War II broke out, my dad
gave all his extra time to the USO. I was a quick study and good at
improvisation so I got to do a lot of those gigs. Flying side-saddle in
army bombers was not my dad's favorite sport! We both lost five pounds
doing one army show in Galveston in July. Another Texas memory was
an army camp in Longview. My dad wasn't a big drinker but he liked his

Scotch. Longview was dry. If you didn't have a bottle at the local pub, you were out of business. A local general supplied the bottle and Dad was happy."

"My dad loved doing this work and the GIs loved him. We both loved working the wards in military hospitals; it was one-on-one. Guys who had lost their faces were happy you could look at them without flinching.

"I remember the day dad met Joseph Kennedy in Woonsocket, RI. It was another history lesson I failed to recognize since I didn't know who he was or what he did. The elder Kennedy wanted me to meet his son, John, who was attending Annapolis, but I wasn't going to be in town that day. Another missed opportunity!"

Colleen had this observation about show business: "Many people have the notion that show business is very glamorous and not too taxing an occupation, that couldn't be further from the truth. My dad rarely stopped moving. As we got older, Larry and I were introduced to the rigors of acting and, believe me, I would never choose it as a profession."

Once during the war, Patsy and Edgar were invited to entertain dignitaries in Camp…in New Mexico. Unbeknownst to them, the military was in the progress of harnessing the atom to be used in a bomb. It was a top-secret project known only within restricted military circles as "The Manhattan Project."

This entertainment starved base received Edgar and Patsy in a non-typical fashion. Once they arrived at the base, they were transported by jeep by a team of military police. In later years Patsy told her grandson, Mark Kennedy, "we were told to keep our eyes straight ahead or we would be shot." Terrified, the couple complied but it did reinforce a concern that there was something "big" going on at the base.

Later in the evening, when Edgar and Patsy were preparing the skit for their military audience, Patsy addressed the high-security-cleared audience by saying: "I know what's so secret on this base." A concerned hush fell over the crowd. Patsy continued by saying, "you're inventing a synthetic replacement for nylon stockings." A sigh of relief, followed by an eruption of spontaneous laughter, resulted.

On August 23, 1944, Edgar and Patsy made another trip to San Francisco to star in a comedy show at the Warfield Theatre. Hortense Morton wrote this column for the *San Francisco Examiner*.

*Air-Raid Wardens* MGM (1943)

Edgar 'Slow-Burn' Kennedy whose ability to bring a gradual boil to his facial distortions are well known wherever comedy holds forth on the screen, headlines the new stage show at the Warfield.

Assisted by his comely wife, Kennedy produces all of his popular gags; gets entangled in his coat and vest; romps with the boys in the orchestra; is heckled by a stooge in a box, and generally disports himself in zany fashion, even to stretching out flat on the stage in a true Kennedy tantrum. It's all wacky and amusing.

Lee Havens and the Warfield musical contingent start the show with a sparkling medley trio of popular airs, introducing the Helene Hughes Dancers in a gay, brisk killer routine, followed by Ray Vaughn and his attractive partner who also give out on the musical side with xylophone piano and a rack of liquor bottles, in several tuneful arrangements.

Val Seitz, juggler and comedian, just returned from the European war front where he entertained servicemen, presents a good act featuring mirth and dexterity. Sinclair and Leroy, are two sepia steppers of speed. Don and Beverly, a ballroom dance team of charm and grace close the show with the help of baritone, Loren Welch, and the H.H. Dancers, in a colorfully costumed and brilliantly staged miniature revue. On the screen is 'Melody in the Sky,' Technicolor hit of the late thirties.

Colleen remembers that many times while the family traveled to different cities, she and her dad were interviewed on the air by the local radio stations.

Stan Laurel and Oliver Hardy were in real life very dear friends with Edgar. They lived fairly close by and would visit often during the year for parties and holiday celebrations. Stan's daughter, Lois Laurel Hawes, remembers Edgar coming over for social reasons, sometimes retreating to the den. Colleen recalls that Stan Laurel "only lived two blocks away and was over all the time." Unfortunately, both Lois and Colleen, despite being only one year apart in age, never recalls meeting each other until later in life.

It is likely that Stan and Edgar collaborated on gags and scenarios that would never be used, or possibly they were waxing nostalgia about their early days together. One thing is clear: That they all had the utmost respect for each other, professionally and personally. For some inexplicable reason during the war years, Laurel and Hardy were treated as B comics. Though Edgar never thought of himself as a "star," he held Stan Laurel and Oliver Hardy with the highest regards. According to Leo Brooks, "Edgar Kennedy's star was rising and Laurel and Hardy's star was starting to drop." It seems hard to imagine in 2005, but at least during the late 1930s and 1940s, they were truly peers.

During Laurel and Hardy's post-Hal Roach period in film they had lost some of their magic. In *Air-Raid Wardens* for M-G-M in 1943, there was an obvious attempt to generate old fashioned "tit-for-tat" confrontations with their old nemesis, Edgar Kennedy. By this time, Edgar was used all over Hollywood to put a little spark in each scene he was in. Edgar played his character to the hilt, complete with slow burning hand wipes. The smoke discharged from the pipe in his mouth created an allusion that Edgar was indeed burning up. Working with "the masters" again would automatically make each scene they shared hysterically funny. At least on paper it did.

Randy Skretvedt's excellent book, *Laurel and Hardy-The Magic Behind the Movies,* accurately articulates how each scene the three shared failed to provoke laughs (and, for that matter, the entire film). Mr. Skretvedt suggests that it wasn't the comedians who failed, it was the directing, pacing and editing. Even Edgar's performance looked about as wooden as the cigar store Indian standing in front of the store.

The three comics performed together one last time, this time in a different medium all together: Radio. Laurel and Hardy, Edgar and, ex-Sennett and Roach comedian, Patsy Moran were recorded in a sketch called "The Wedding." According to Scott MacGillivray's book, *Laurel and Hardy—From the Forties Forward,* it was aired on November 25, 1943 for Armed Forces Radio's *Mail Call* series.

Stan is credited as writing the play, involving Patsy and Stan eloping with best man Ollie summoning the Justice of the Peace, Edgar Kennedy. Dr. John McCabe reproduced the entire script in his book *The Comedy World of Stan Laurel* in 1974.

The running gag is that every time they wake up irritated Edgar to perform the wedding, something goes wrong. The running punch line is expressed first by Stan to his bride, "I've taken a dislike to her." Later in the sketch Patsy interrupts the marriage ceremony by explaining, "I've taken a dislike to him." When everything is finally worked out, Edgar refused to follow through because, "I've taken a dislike to the whole bunch of you."

The "Wedding Sketch" was delightfully worked for the spoken word, but we know all three characters (Stan, Ollie and Edgar) so well we can actually visualize them as they speak their words. Stan included necessary "sound effect gags" to help the comedy along.

The "Wedding Sketch" is an example of a comic idea that was used before, but freshened up by Stan.

For the above radio sketch, Lucille Ball introduced the audience to the players. It is intriguing to hear Lucy's zesty introduction of Edgar Kennedy. One can't help but wonder about the comic possibilities if Lucy had been able to play Patsy's part in the skit, but in all fairness, Lucille Ball was then considered a dramatic actress. During the early 1940s, she was appearing in movies, and even radio, as sophisticated dames or gun molls. This was way before she took off with her *I Love Lucy* television series and even her preceding radio show, *My Favorite Husband,* in the late 1940s.

In 1936 Lucy and Edgar made a brief appearance in an obscure musical short, *A Night at the Biltmore Hotel.* That same year, Lucy was in the

"Average Man" short, *Dummy Ache*. Unfortunately, Lucille plays it straight (as a blonde) and doesn't get to display any of her comedy talent that later became her staple. Despite this, *Dummy Ache* was nominated for an Academy Award for the Best Short category for what was listed as "The Edgar Kennedy Series." It lost out to Our Gang's *Bored of Education*. It was the only time an entry from the series was nominated.

On June 15, 1943, Edgar and fellow Hollywood stars took off for a cross-country tour of forty-three Army camps in twelve states. Carole Landis entertained troops in Mississippi, Grace MacDonald covered the Midwest while Marjorie Main, Donald Meek, that "Slow-Burn" guy and George Tobias followed routes set by the war department.

Edgar continued making personal appearances at civilian venues during this time. November 6, 1944 was just such an occasion when he took to the stage in his vaudeville-style act at the Palomar. Instead of Patsy, Florence Lake appeared with Edgar, recreated her film role as Edgar's spouse.

In a review by Willard Elsey, he states:

> Big bluff and bald-headed Edgar Kennedy lived up to all advance notices yesterday when he opened his personal appearance visit on the Palomar theater stage.
>
> Kennedy is an expert showman who has a definite stock in trade and knows how to use it. He is not pretentious, but sticks to the routine that has made him one of the best-known comedians on the screen.
>
> With the assistance of Florence Lake, seen with him in numerous motion picture shorts, and Frankie Roth's band, he turned on his "Slow-Burn" in a way that had the large audience in an uproar.
>
> His 'mad' during the coat gag was as funny as they come. Harry Dunn was the emcee. Richard Hayman, a whirlwind on the harmonica, was well received. "I'll Walk Alone," "Chinatown," and "Holiday for Strings," as an encore, were expertly done.
>
> The Singing Barries, a personable girl's trio, who have made a number of recordings, whipped up some nice harmony on "I'll Be Seeing You," "San Fernando Valley," and the wild hotcha number, "Why Don't You Straighten Up and Fly Right, Jack." Renee Villon filled out the bill with

This unique photo from the Kennedy family includes: Lucille Ball, Judy Canova, Dennis Morgan, Dinah Shore, amongst others.

some dances that wanted to go into the exotic but apparently was frightened by the 'This is a Family Theater' sign in the dressing room.

## CELEBRITIES AT WASHINGTON, D.C.

July 4, 1945 marked a special day in the nation's capital. An estimated crowd of 300,000 people attended the day's events. The nighttime was a twin celebration—the end of the Seventh War Loan drive and the 165th birthday of America.

During the twilight, a police-escorted Hollywood cavalcade came onto the grounds. The stars made their entrance in a parade of jeeps in front of the stage as sirens wailed and people cheered. A 90-minute show featured the talents of Mr. and Mrs. Edgar Kennedy (in what was most likely the largest crowd he ever performed to), Lucille Ball, Judy Canova, Roddy

This photo w/ Patsy, Edgar & Edgar presumably was shot during their visit to
Washington, D.C. during July 1945.
(Courtesy of the Kennedy Family)

McDowall, Edward Everett Horton, Dennis Morgan, Dinah Shore,
Henny Youngman and the Nicholas Brothers. Emceeing the event was
Edward Arnold.

Everyone had fun with the crowd, a mix of civilians, military and dip-
lomats. They were in a mood to celebrate the Allies' dominance in the war
effort, but not ready to celebrate an all-out victory. That would come later.

Of all people to keep a proper somber perspective during the evening was Lucille Ball. *The Washington Post* reported; "Miss Ball was the only serious performer, making a brief address on the war loan drive."

Two heroes made famous for their part in placing the flag on top of Mount Suribachi in Iwo Jima were introduced (Rene A. Gagnon and John H. Bradley). That part of the program was climaxed with a stirring "American Cavalcade of the Armed Forces," an overture composed especially for the occasion.

The ending signaled the launching of fireworks, which, at the highlight, showed the outline of the American flag with President Truman's image. It was purportedly described "as the most spectacular ever." The White House reported that the President, in keeping with the war time edict, "No holiday except Christmas," kept busy at his desk.

Sometime during the trip Edgar and Patsy were invited socially to meet with J. Edgar Hoover at his headquarters. On the back of the above photo is this inscription: "To Edgar Kennedy, who has contributed so many hours of refreshing entertainment to another Edgar. Your friend, J. Edgar Hoover."

After the war the Kennedys realized that their children were growing up. Larry continued service in the Navy and Colleen was pursuing mod-

Generic picture of Edgar at Unk. golf course w/ unidentified partner
(Courtesy of Kennedy Family)

eling jobs. In 1946 Edgar and Patricia moved back to Beverly Hills at 360 S. Doheny Drive. It was an apartment complex that kept Patricia busy.

During peace-time, Edgar kept up his hectic pace. He appeared in a special *Truth or Consequences* radio broadcast aired on October 11, 1945. This *Command Performance* was recorded and played over the Armed Forces Radio Service. It was hosted by Ralph Edwards and Bob Hope. Appearing on the program was Connie Haines, William Frawley, Edgar Kennedy and Ken Carpenter.

Edgar was in demand in every medium, to include early television. In addition, Edgar starred in a stage production of *Charley's Aunt* in 1946, on a personal tour in the east.

Nineteen-forty-six was also memorable in that it was the fifteen-year anniversary of the "Average Man" series. RKO decided to surprise Edgar with a huge celebration to commemorate the event. According to Sam White, who attended, "every director and actor he ever worked with was invited." Lou Brock, who supervised the unit, acted as the Master of Ceremonies. Sam added, "Kennedy was in pretty good shape then."

# 27.
# Golf

The gentleman's game of golf was a passion for Edgar Kennedy. No one knows exactly when Edgar first picked the game up, but a good guess would be The Olympic Club in San Francisco during his youth.

Edgar was in many a comic movie in which golf was the theme: *Should Married Men Go Home?*, *All Teed Up* and *The Golf Chump*. Even in those conditions, it is obvious by his mannerisms and finesse that he was quite skilled in the game.

Edgar was associated with many golf-related charity events, often walking away with a trophy. Lake Arrowhead was one of his favorite venues.

Edgar belonged to the famed Lakeside Golf Club and it was, according to Colleen, another actor's hangout. "It was a club for golfers and their families so we could all do our thing. They had a wonderful pool, and they served lunch and dinner. They even had dinner dances that the kids were welcome to attend. Some of the members I remember well were Charles Coburn, John Wayne, John Carroll, Bing Crosby, Bob Hope, Mickey Rooney, Bonita Granville, and the Mauch Twins. The latter three I remember well because we swam together. The others kindly danced with me at parties and allowed me to play in their foursomes with my father. I do remember one day when Mickey Rooney missed a great shot and broke his club, being sure it was the culprit."

Colleen said that her father was always on the go. He arose early every day and was just burning with energy whether he was working or not. "When he wasn't on the set at 5 a.m., he was on the golf course at 7 a.m. If he had a week or two off, he was off hunting and fishing. My mother was never enamored with sports so my brother and I learned about all of them quite early in life. He was a patient, but demanding teacher, and we learned our lessons well."

Throughout his Hollywood years, Edgar participated in many golf fund-raising events. One such example was at the Frank Borzage's invitational golf tournament at the Rolling Hills Country Club on 8-4-45. How's this for a lineup? Bing Crosby, Randolph Scott, Forrest Tucker, Bill Frawley, Adolphe Menjou, Ed Kennedy, and Andy Clyde. The "one dollar admission" went to the Ann Lehr's Hollywood Guild Canteen.

This golf outing made Louella Parsons's column on 5-11-40: "Lloyd Nolan, Edgar Kennedy and Henry Rogers in San Francisco for the union label exhibition, stopped at Carmel for golf. They telegraphed me Lloyd won enough to pay for the baby."

During mid-January of 1939, Edgar was invited by Bing Crosby to play in his first pro-amateur event at Rancho Santa Fe in San Diego. It was the start of a tradition that eventually relocated to Pebble Beach, California.

Edgar was a very dear friend of Bing and it was an honor to participate in any golf tournament that Bing hosted. Starting in 1939, Edgar participated in every Bing Crosby Pro-Am. In 1947 Bing Crosby wanted to bring his pals to golf on the beautiful Monterey Peninsula at Pebble Beach in northern California. By doing so he established a new tradition for the golfing world on the Monterey peninsula. All local charities would benefit.

Bing and his family owned a home off the famous 17-mile Drive. His backyard led to a fairway on the 14th hole. Even from the first layout of the course, by S.F.B. Morris in 1922, Pebble Beach has been hailed ever since for being the most spectacular and challenging golf course in the world.

After years of playing in San Diego, Bing brought the same concept of golf play to Pebble Beach. The professional golfers would be partnered with amateur golfers, most of whom would be Bing's Hollywood pals. On each succeeding day the golfers would play at the Del Monte golf course in Monterey (with claims as California's first golf course), Cypress Point (a very private and exclusive course in Pebble Beach), and ending the tournament at the famed Pebble Beach course. The winner would receive $10,000, courtesy of Bing Crosby.

The special hand-picked participants were limited to 150 players. Among those were documented in the *San Francisco Chronicle* in January of 1947 by Art Rosenbaum: "The Crosby tournament at Del Monte will be filled with movie golfers, including Bing himself and friend Bob Hope. Others from movieland and environs are Johnny Tarzan Weissmuller, Edgar slow-burn Kennedy, Director Frank Borzage, former welterweight champ Jimmy McLarnin, Orchestra Leader Bob Crosby, Actor Richard Arlen and ex-Trojan gridder Marshall Duffield.

"Other well-knowns, aside from the professional golfers are Lewis Lapham, son of the Mayor, Del Webb owner of the Yankees…etc., etc., etc."

For the record, Edgar's pro partner was Toney Penna who had finished as runner-up to Hogan in the just-completed Los Angeles Open.

During the actual tournament from Friday, January 10-12, 1947, this event was hardly even mentioned in the local Monterey papers. Unfortunately there was no "local boy makes good" article about the return of Edgar Kennedy to Monterey County. Maybe no one knew. Maybe no one cared. It probably never occurred to Edgar to make a big deal about it; he was there just to have fun. The old homestead in southern Monterey County was certainly nothing like the dramatic ocean and land of Pebble Beach. As Edgar said once in an interview, "the land I grew up on costs me

Montage of photos from the *San Francisco Call Bulletin* (1948)
(Courtesy Kennedy Family)

more in taxes than it's worth. I just keep it for sentimental reasons."

Bing Crosby again invited Edgar to play at his pro-am on January 9, 10 and 11 in 1948. This time there was more attention given the event. *Golf World* wrote a story on it, as did the *San Francisco Chronicle*. The latter captured Edgar slow-burning after an errant shot.

Preceding the tourney was a "clinic" put on by the professionals. It attracted a gallery numbered around 1,000 who paid one dollar to watch. The final day gallery was estimated about 7,500 who each paid two dollars for the day. A pass for the whole 3-day event cost $5. Parking was free. *Golf World* said in reference to the tournament of 1948:

> Last week Mr. Crosby gave his annual $10,000 golfers party at Pebble Beach. This is one party the golfers love to attend. They are as eager for invitations as debutants to the top masquerade balls of New Orleans' Mardi Gras.
>
> The tournament will feature by Bing's invitation most of the prominent professionals who played in the Los Angeles Open. Each pro will pair with an amateur partner and these amateurs have been selected (1) because Bing likes them and (2) because they sometimes swing a golf stick.
>
> Since the crooner is putting up the money for prizes, and since every cent at the gates goes to Sister Kenny's charity it would seem to be Bing's privilege to invite whomever he chooses. Probably the best-known left out is Bob Hope, Bing's buddy. This wasn't intentional, Bob was invited, never fear, but although he tried to be present other things like making pictures and money interfered.

Art Rosenbaum, of the *San Francisco Chronicle*, wrote:

> Harold Lloyd sat under a cypress tree wearing dark glasses last week at Pebble Beach, a guest and spectator. The girls sighed when bright faced Dennis O'Keefe and manly Randolph Scott strove desperately to tame the little white ball. The kids giggled when Edgar (Slowburn) Kennedy took his swipes under a tree. The crowd trudged after der Bingle loving every moment of his casual com-

petence while turning in a score of about 80 in his first round. Bing's professional partner was Cam Puget, Cypress Point. They scored 74-70-72—216, which was not far from the bottom of the listing in the amateur-pro, but they had fun. The winners were John Dawson (amateur) and Professional Ben Hogan.

Edgar was partnered with professional Lloyd Wadkins who finished 70-69-74-213. *Golf World* informed their readers, "All of the simon-pures received radios from host Bing; they were not Zeniths—they were Philcos." Charles Rice from *Golf World* wrote:

> Any resemblance between Bing Crosby's National Pro-Amateur Championship and a golf tournament is purely unintentional. This annual party on the spectacular Monterey Peninsula of the California coast is the likeable Crooner's gift to his golfing friends, both amateur and professional. He calls it a 'fiesta,' which in most respects is apt; last year it might be dubbed a 'rat-race.' In any event, the purpose of the whole thing is for everyone to have a good time; no one yet has denied having one. The actors, the millionaires, the journeymen pros all place golf secondary to laughs and, in general, to raising merry hell.
>
> From the standpoint of the pros this is one of the toughest of all tourneys to win, not only because of the resistance one has to put up towards the night-life but also because it stands as an extra-ordinary test of golf, being played on three of the most difficult courses in this country. The initial round goes to the pictorial Cypress Point, the second is played on the tree-packed Monterey Peninsula, and the final at disaster-filled Pebble Beach. Picking the most difficult of the three is haphazard at best, but the general opinion among this field ran towards Pebble Beach, with Cypress Point running a close second.
>
> All proceeds from the program and ticket sales were donated to charity while Crosby picked up the tab for everything else. His bill was estimated at $22,500, which

is not exaggeration. As a host he is unparalleled, not only for the money he spends, but for the little things that he makes sure all the contestants and the press have.

Colleen accompanied her dad to the 1948 Crosby and remembers having a ball. It really was a party back then. Bing would rent the Golden State Theatre in downtown Monterey for his Clambakes in the early days. The liquor would flow, and so would the entertainment. Just getting this bunch together up in Monterey marked the start of a tradition that lasted until Bing Crosby died in 1977. The concept continues annually in Pebble

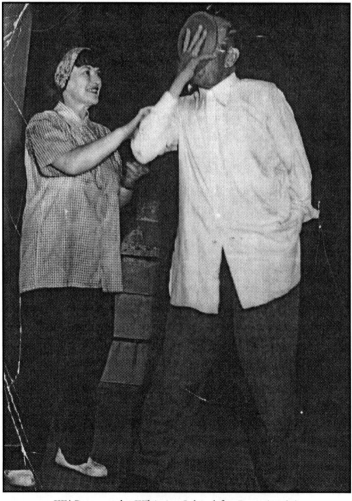

W/ Patsy at the Whittier School for Boys (1948)
(Courtesy of the Kennedy Family)

Beach as the corporately sponsored AT&T Pro-Am. There isn't an Edgar Kennedy amongst them.

The 1948 Crosby Pro-Am was the last one that Edgar participated in. Although only 57 years old during the tournament, photographs of Edgar made him appear gaunt. If there were health problems, Edgar didn't let on.

Colleen noticed that sometime after the war, her dad just didn't seem to have the same bounce that he used to. "That man never slowed down," Colleen said. "He'd be up early and out the door when they were shooting and when he wasn't filming, he would be up at the crack of dawn to go golfing."

Over his lifetime, Edgar performed in front of countless numbers of people. Edgar's last stage appearance was not on a grand scale, he chose to bring his family to perform in front of the Nellus School for Boys in Whittier, California. Colleen remembers being in a silly little skit, but the conclusion of the show included Edgar being hit in the face with a pie. On March 30, 1948, a young student, Toribio Valverde, hand wrote a letter to Edgar on behalf of his schoolmates:

*For Lincoln Cottage.* Edgar's last stage appearance (May 1948)
(Courtesy Kennedy Family)

Dear Mr. Kennedy,

I am one of the boys from Lincoln Cottage at the Nellus School for Boys in Whitter. I am very proud that I have been selected to tell you how much we enjoyed your program last Sunday.

We all know how busy people in your position must be and it makes us double happy that you would take time to come out to share your talent with us. We have all been talking and chuckling over the funny situations in the play. We thought the one about the lamp couldn't be funnier. It must be great to have such a talented family.

We hope you will come again and come often. We boys will always be waiting to welcome you.

Cordially yours,
Toribio Valverde

In May of 1948, Edgar went into production for *Contest Crazy.* Although no one knew it at the time, it was to mark the last short of his

*My Dream is Yours* w/Doris Day (1948) Warner Bros.
(Courtesy British Film Institute)

"Average Man" series; it wouldn't be released until 10-1-48. Even though Edgar looked rather emaciated, his comic timing was still sharp.

It is interesting to note that the scripted ending detailed Edgar inadvertently eating dog food that he had won, and letting out a dubbed-in bark. Fortunately cooler heads prevailed at this freak ending. Edgar ultimately ended his long running series by somehow getting a fish bowl stuck over his head. The resigned Edgar, just prior to the "Chopstick" theme and fade out, ended it with a memorable "Slow-Burn" over the glass contours that contained his defeated face. It was the perfect showcasing of the gesture he was internationally loved for.

Edgar's last feature film was for Warner Bros., *My Dream is Yours*. It starred a young up-and-comer named Doris Day. Edgar played her uncle. Colleen accompanied her father sometimes on the set while shooting the picture. "My dad was just smitten with Doris Day, he thought she had so much charm and talent that she was a can't miss for future stardom. He couldn't stop talking about her."

For purposes of an earlier article about Edgar, this author interviewed Doris Day who graciously cooperated at her Cypress Inn hotel in Carmel. When I first asked if she remembered working with Edgar in *My Dream is Yours*, her response was immediate, she said, "Wait a minute…wait a minute," a pause, then she slapped her hand on her forehead and pulled it slowly down over her face and protruding, pouty lower lip. A splendid impression of the "Slow-Burn," Doris Day style!

Edgar apparently made a big positive impression on Doris. She said, "You can imagine how I felt working with him, he played with everyone and this was just my second movie. He was so kind, sweet and everything dear. Everyone in the business knew he was a genius. Tell Colleen that I really loved her dad."

The *Los Angeles Times* printed this from their "Studio Briefs" on 4-17-48: "Edgar Kennedy, now the uncle of Doris Day in 'My Dream is Yours' will play the straw-hat circuit with his 21-year-old daughter Colleen. Incidentally, his son Larry is studying camera work at the Geller Workshop, but is more likely in the long run to be in front of the camera than behind it."

I asked Doris if she or anyone else on the set knew that Edgar was sick at the time of production. She, of course, had no idea. It was a shock when Edgar died just after completing the film. The film would be released posthumously.

# 28.
# The Slow Burn Extinguishes

Colleen had been working in New York (as a Harry Conover model) when, in August of 1948, she received a phone call from a girlfriend. The message was urgent: "Your father is ill and can't get out of bed." Colleen made immediate plans to fly home.

Colleen was in shock since none of her family, including her father, had mentioned it. She couldn't understand at the time why her mother or father didn't tell her. In retrospect, Colleen said that no one really knew that much about cancer back then. Edgar went to several doctors, none of which knew what was wrong. Colleen's mom didn't want to needlessly make anyone alarmed, hoping that the illness would be brief, with a full recovery.

Edgar never did recover; he got worse by the day. All those years of smoking had caught up with him. "My dad smoked anything he could get his hands on; cigarettes, cigars, his pipe…" Indeed, Edgar was rarely without his pipe, even in the movies. Edgar's image was once featured in the "Seeing Stars" syndicated publication (6-1-41) illustrating the fact he "smoked over 6,000 pounds of tobacco over the last few years."

Even though Edgar was very sick his last three months of life, Colleen's mom, Patsy, made sure that the media and gossip columns were at arm's length. No one printed how ill Edgar was until he was on his deathbed.

On 9-17-48 old pal Louella Parsons announced in her column, "Edgar 'Slow-Burn' Kennedy is very ill, his many friends and admirers will be sad to hear."

As Edgar's condition worsened, his Lakeside Country Club and Hollywood buddies hurried to put together a stag dinner testimonial for him. It was hoped that if Edgar could come, it would boost his spirits and give everyone the opportunity to show their appreciation.

A date had been set for November 10. Some eighteen hours prior to the planned event, Edgar Kennedy passed away at the Motion Picture Hospital in the San Fernando Valley. The official cause of the death was cancer of the throat. As Edgar would have wanted it, the testimonial dinner went on, minus a symbolic empty chair, which occupied the place of honor at the head table. Edgar was toasted, praised and eulogized by his friends.

Seated with the empty chair at the speaker's table was T.C. Luxford, Chairman of the event; Charles Coburn and Harry Von Zell, Masters of Ceremony; President Charles Kemper of the Masquers' Club and Father Victor J. Follen. Other Hollywood notables attending were Tom Kennedy, Rudy Vallee, William Frawley, Forrest Tucker, George Murphy, Leon Errol, Roddy McDowall, Leo Carillo, John Carroll, Wallace Ford, and Henry O'Neill.

Leo Carillo had this to say: "Any man who did so much for happiness is truly a great man in Hollywood or any other place in the world." Coburn said: "Ed was a great contributor to the welfare of the nation with his ability to make people laugh or cry, and bring out the best emotions in them." The guests reportedly both laughed and cried as Father Follen spoke of Edgar's idealistic spirit and family life. George T. Davis, sports editor of the *Herald-Express*, traced Kennedy's early struggles as a heavyweight boxer.

On Friday morning November 13, 1948 friends and family of Edgar gathered at St. Gregory's Church on 910 S. Norton Avenue in Los Angeles. According to the *Los Angeles Times*:

Tribute to Edgar by members of Lakeside Golf Country Club (11-10-48)
(Courtesy Kennedy Family)

[Reverend Victor Follen] began the solemn requiem mass. The Keystoners who had cavorted with Mr. Kennedy—grayed somewhat now but bright with nostalgia—talked of Ed in fond whispers. Tom Kennedy was

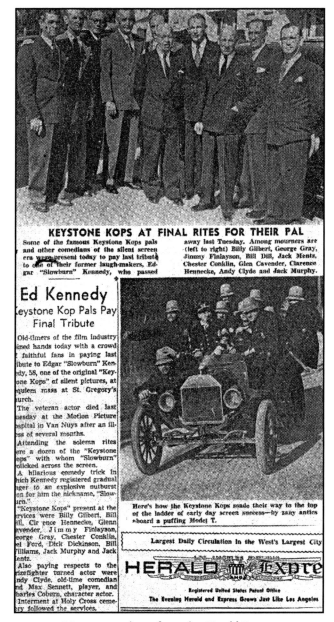

**KEYSTONE KOPS AT FINAL RITES FOR THEIR PAL**

Some of the famous Keystone Kops pals and other comedians of the silent screen era were present today to pay last tribute to one of their former laugh-makers, Edgar "Slowburn" Kennedy, who passed away last Tuesday. Among mourners are (left to right) Billy Gilbert, George Gray, Jimmy Finlayson, Bill Dill, Jack Mentz, Chester Conklin, Glen Cavender, Clarence Hennecke, Andy Clyde and Jack Murphy.

## Ed Kennedy
### Keystone Kop Pals Pay Final Tribute

Old-timers of the film industry lined hands today with a crowd of faithful fans in paying last tribute to Edgar "Slowburn" Kennedy, 58, one of the original "Keystone Kops" of silent pictures, at requiem mass at St. Gregory's church.

The veteran actor died last Tuesday at the Motion Picture Hospital in Van Nuys after an illness of several months.

Attending the solemn rites were a dozen of the "Keystone Kops" with whom "Slowburn" clicked across the screen.

A hilarious comedy trick in which Kennedy registered gradual anger to an explosive outburst won for him the nickname, "Slowburn."

"Keystone Kops" present at the services were Billy Gilbert, Bill Dill, Clarence Hennecke, Glenn Cavender, Jimmy Finlayson, George Gray, Chester Conklin, Mel Ford, Dick Dickinson, Bill Williams, Jack Murphy and Jack Mentz.

Also paying respects to the prizefighter turned actor were Andy Clyde, old-time comedian and Mack Sennett, player, and Charles Coburn, character actor. Interment at Holy Cross cemetery followed the services.

Here's how the Keystone Kops made their way to the top of the ladder of early day screen success—by zany antics aboard a puffing Model T.

**Largest Daily Circulation in the West's Largest City**

**HERALD Express**

Registered United States Patent Office
The Evening Herald and Express Grows Just Like Los Angeles

Newspaper photo from the *Herald Express*
(Courtesy of the Kennedy Family)

Edgar caricature by Tony Hawes
(Courtesy of Lois Laurel Hawes)

one. No relation to Ed, the cauliflowered comedian was
Mr. Kennedy's friend for 35 years [sic]. He had the eastern amateur heavyweight boxing championship when Mr.
Kennedy was western amateur champion and they almost
met in the ring [sic]. Instead they went into motion pictures together and became fast friends.

Monocled Charles Coburn recalled Mr. Kennedy as
the one man in films who welcomed him to Hollywood
warmly when he traded footlights for the kliegs.

Chester Conklin, Del Lord (he drove the patrol wagon
for the Kops), Jimmy Finlayson, Bill Dill, Billy Gilbert,
Glen Cavender, Clarence Hennecke, George Gray, Dick

Dickinson, Bill Williams, Jack Murphy and Jack Mintz—among others—were there.

Father Follen echoed their thoughts when he said: 'We have lost a friend, a gentle, happy, generous man, an honorable and upright husband and father...'

For the *Daily Mirror* newspaper, Editor Virgil Pinkley wrote this in his editorial:

> Movie industry old-timers are holding a testimonial dinner for Edgar Kennedy tonight at the California Country Club. Their guest of honor died yesterday. They planned this party weeks ago. Death won't halt it. The men who knew him best say Kennedy would have wanted it that way. That's quite a lot of testimonial by itself.
>
> Kennedy played for 18 straight years at R-K-O in the "Mr. Average Man" two-reelers. Nothing pretentious. Just common, husband-wife, mother-in-law stuff. Big, bald Ed was the guy next door defeated by lawnmowers, outflanked by can-openers, puzzled by a leaky faucet. He made the small confusions and frustrations of every man's life hilariously funny—and somehow easier to endure.
>
> The average man is going to miss Edgar Kennedy. His famous 'Slow-Burn' when things got just too tough released the tensions in a lot of us. We'll remember, and things won't seem too tough. It's a good way to be missed, and remembered.

Colleen said she remembered three things about her father's funeral: "The three-day wake we held in our apartment for all his Irish cronies. We were so tired when it was over—who had time to cry? Another was the glorious turkey dinner that was brought to our house Christmas Eve by Horace Love, one of my father's poker cronies. The most surprising was an infamous racketeer that wrote my mother offering financial assistance if ever needed!"

Colleen said that Edgar "was an extremely good father, he worked hard and played hard, but always had time to talk. He was extraordinarily intelligent and very witty, so his actions around home gave no hint of the slapstick comedian he portrayed on the movies. That wild man on the screen wasn't my father.

My dad was very soft spoken at home and my greatest memories were the talks we had. He never stopped being a student, so our nighttime talks were not fairy tales, but discourses. We talked about world religions, Greek mythology, art, music, history, you name it, and we must have covered it. He rarely talked about his work. At home he was a gentle giant with a witty sense of humor and an insatiable thirst for knowledge. In public he was a clown, a superb golfer, a high-stakes poker player and a good friend. As a father he taught me to think, and be true to my friends and beliefs. The day he died he was telling jokes to all the nurses and he left this world a happier place." Edgar Kennedy was only 58 years old when death arrived; *the Slow-Burn would ignite no more.*

# Epilogue

To the moviegoing public of 1948, Edgar Kennedy's face was familiar to millions. However, because of his modest background and humbling beginning experiences in Hollywood, Edgar never considered himself a star.

"I guess I'm one of the guys that never let himself get too big—like Jean Hersholt for instance. Just moving along and doing his work without wanting to be a star. Stars get too much money, and they get into bad pictures, and that's one of the ways they go out. You see, when a star gets popular the company gets to rely on him to sell pictures whether they're good or bad, and anyway, if the star is real big they can't afford to pay for good support.

"If you're a good-featured player, now, it pays you in a lot of ways. You get good money, and you get into good pictures, because if the company has to pay a good figure for you, they want to put you in something worthwhile so as to get their money's worth out of you. When a featured player gets well known, he gets into better and better pictures; when a star gets well known, there's the danger he gets into worse and worse pictures."

In other words, Edgar was most comfortable at representing the average guy. He considered it his responsibility. His legacy continues to that degree today, for even if the "baby-boomers" and their children don't know him by name, there is a likelihood that they've seen his face. If not in old movies, then on commercials. Many of Edgar's films lapsed into public domain years ago. Ironically because of that, Edgar's images sometimes pop up at tax time when a stock footage film clip is needed of a man enraged or who tears his hair from frustration.

Edgar's mad character was unique, we knew he was never really out of control like, say, the Ralph Kramden character in *The Honeymooners*. The Ricky Ricardo character in *I Love Lucy* sometimes lost his "Latin" temper, (John Cleese's Basil Fawlty character deserves an honorable mention here),

"FOR THE LAST TIME, TOM KENNEDY IS NOT MY BROTHER!"
(Courtesy of the Kennedy Family)

but there has been no one since Edgar who entertains us so much at being angry, with the possible exception of Donald Duck! It is interesting to ponder that Donald was born in ink in 1934 just when Edgar was nearing the heights of his screen mad. Donald often slaps his hand to his face in exasperation and blows his top in outrage. A coincidence?

Edgar Kennedy was a true pioneer in the movies for more than 37 years. He played support to all the major comics of the era, became a comedy director, made the transition into talking films, and found his niche starring in his own short comedy series.It is intriguing to ponder what impact Edgar would have had in television. All of the other cast members of the "Average Man" lived long lives and conceivably could have gone on at least for a few seasons. If Edgar didn't want to keep up with the riggers of a star in a regular series, he

Author w/Stan Laurel's and Edgar Kennedy's daughters @ the Edgar Kennedy
Celebration (Courtesy Marcia Opal)

would have been great in support or as a special guest.

Edgar was admired by his fans, family and peers in the industry. In summing up his film career, Edgar Kennedy may have portrayed the everyman, but the description of him as an "average man" is not very apt. He was a unique individual and a gifted clown. The world has never seen his likes again.

It was in 1924 when the publicity department of Pathe (Sennett's film distributor) asked young Edgar to write down his professional goals. His reply was simple and succinct, "*to make good comedies.*" To that end, Edgar Livingston Kennedy has fulfilled his destiny.

From July 3-6, 1997 the international Laurel and Hardy appreciation society known as the Sons of the Desert had a fitting tribute for Edgar Kennedy. The local chapter (tent) named "The Midnight Patrol" (after a Laurel and Hardy title) hosted a celebration in Monterey. Over 200 people from America, Canada, England, France and Germany attended. It included Stan Laurel's daughter (Lois Laurel Hawes) and an Edgar Kennedy family reunion, hosted by his daughter Colleen.

A city resolution was drawn up making July 3rd "Edgar Kennedy Day." His honor, Mayor Albert delivered it in person to the assembly. After some encouragement, the follicly challenged Mayor completed the task with his

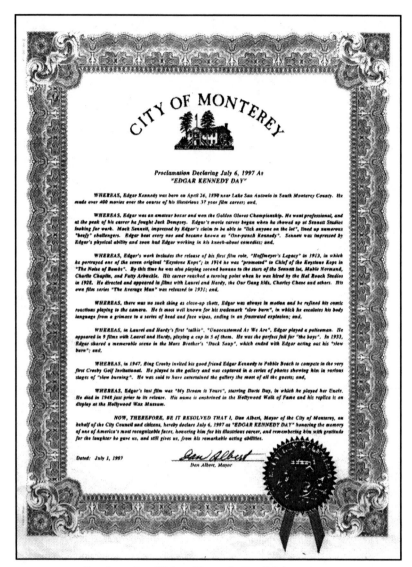

Proclamation "Edgar Kennedy Day" July 3, 1997

own "slow-burn." After watching fireworks launched over the Pacific Ocean, celebrants convened to a film screening room. The event was dubbed the "Midnighty Patrol," for to enter one had to be dressed in nightclothes. Imaginative Sons came with oversized nightgowns, nightcaps, curlers in hair, cold creme on their faces, and shared an evening of rare Edgar Kennedy films such as *The Knockout, It's Your Move,* and *Limousine Love.*

The events continued the next day and featured *A Pair of Tights* ice cream drop in which contestants had to catch a scoop of ice cream in their cones from a second-story overhang. There were vaudeville acts at the California First Theatre (built in 1850) where Henry Brandon (who portrayed evil Silas Barnaby in Laurel and Hardy's *Babes in Toyland*) once performed on stage.

The Perfect Day picnic was featured at Dennis the Menace Park. Billed as the "Battle of the Century," a softball game pitted the Laurel's vs. the Hardy's (skinniest vs. the Portliest) with a straw-hatted Edgar Kennedy look-alike umpire (Phil McCoy), behind the plate. The two Kennedy grandsons, Mark and Glenn, were named Captains of the two teams. Mark helmed the task for the portliest and Glenn led the way to victory with his skinniest teammates. Glenn is a chiseled specimen of an athlete reminiscent of his grandfather in his boxing prime. Mark took every opportunity to clown around, bumping into people while they were making plays and pratfalling on the ground.

The first night, Sons of the Desert dressed for the cold weather at Carmel's "Theatre in the Forest." Projected on the outdoor screen was *The Perfect Day*, followed by a question and answer period with both Stan Laurel's and Edgar Kennedy's daughters on stage.

*When Comedy Was King* (1960)
(Author's collection)

The feature movie was *In Old California*, with John Wayne, Edgar and, two Roach alumni, Patsy Kelly and James C. Morton.

Another film event featured a live piano accompaniment to the silent short classic *Two Tars* at the now defunct Dream Theatre. The last night was celebrated by another banquet with a "Policeman's Ball" theme. Sons went all out dressed as Keystone Kops, jailbirds, gun molls, etc.

The highlight of the evening was a live radio reenactment of "The Wedding Sketch." On stage, the play featured Phyllis Coates (in the Patsy Moran role), Bevis Faversham as Oliver Hardy, and Jeffrey Weissman as Stan Laurel. Bart Williams was the director and sound effects engineer. Edgar Kennedy's grandson, Mark Kennedy, recreated the role that his grandfather portrayed, with a recent barber-shaved crown to look authentic.

Only a few miles from the birthplace of Edgar Kennedy, the Monterey County Parks Department has a visitor's center on the south shore. This manmade lake was constructed in the mid-1960s to make a recreational area. Of the original 160 acres of the Kennedy homestead, only about 40 acres remain. Specimens from animal life of the still open area are on exhibit, as well as historical references. The exhibits include artifacts from the local Indians, settlers and homesteaders. The Veratina School and Edgar Kennedy are well represented by photos and maps displayed.

### ACCESS MONTEREY PENINSULA

A.M.P., a public-access television station for the greater Monterey Peninsula, celebrates the legacy of Edgar's film and local connection on an annual basis. Since 2002, the station honors the county's top filmmakers by bestowing the **Edgar Kennedy Award** to deserving recipients during a live broadcast. It's a fitting tribute to the man who has made so many people laugh.

In 1960 Edgar was one of the first celebrities honored for the "Hollywood Walk of Fame," located on Block One, 6901 Hollywood Blvd. In addition, his image is alongside Laurel and Hardy as wax figures at the "Hollywood Wax Museum" in Buena Vista, California. This great clown is buried at the Holy Cross Cemetery, Section D, Grave 7, Lot 193, in Culver City, California.

# The Films of Edgar Kennedy

## 1911

**Brown of Harvard** (12/11/11) **D:** Colin Campbell (IV). **C:** Edgar A. Wynn, Charles Clary, George L. Cox, Edgar Kennedy. **L:** ½-reel **P:** Selig Polyscope Company, Chicago *(As Claxton Madden)*

## 1913

**Rural Third Degree, A** (3/6/13) **D:** George O. Nicholls **C:** Charles Avery, Nick Cogley, Dot Farley, Fred Mace, Edgar Kennedy. **L:** ½-reel **P:** Keystone/Mutual **(One of the detectives)**

**Man Next Door, The** (3/17/13) **D:** __ **C:** Nick Cogley, Dot Farley, Ford Sterling, Edgar Kennedy. **L:** ½-reel **P:** Keystone/Mutual *(Cop)*

**Chief's Predicament, The** (3/24/13) **D:** George O. Nicholls **C:** Nick Cogley, Ford Sterling, Edgar Kennedy **L:** ½-reel **P:** Keystone/Mutual

**Toplitsky and Company** (5/26/13) **D:** Henry "Pathe" Lehrman **C:** Nick Cogley, Alice Davenport, Ford Sterling, Edgar Kennedy, Hank Mann **L:** 1-reel **P:** Keystone/ Mutual *(Masseur)*

**Bangville Police, The** (4/24/13) **D:** Henry "Pathe" Lehrman **C:** Ford Sterling, Fred Mace, Nick Cogley, Edgar Kennedy, Dot Farley **L:** ½-reel **P:** Keystone/Mutual *(A farmer holding a pitchfork)*

**That Ragtime Band** (5/1/13) **D:** Mack Sennett **C:** Nick Cogley, Ed Kennedy, Ford Sterling, Hank Mann. **L:** 1-reel **P:** Keystone/ Mutual *(Stage Manager)*

**Algy on the Force** (5/5/13) **D:** Henry "Pathe" Lehrman **C:** Nick Cogley, Dot Farley, Ed Kennedy, Fred Mace, Mack Sennett **L:** ½- reel **P:** Keystone/Mutual *(Cop)*

**Mabel's Awful Mistake** (5/12/13) **D:** Mack Sennett **C:** Mabel Normand, Mack Sennett, Ford Sterling, Edgar Kennedy. **L:** 1-reel **P:** Keystone/Mutual. **Note:** Working title: *The Saw Mill.*

**Their First Execution** (5/15/13)  **D:** Mack Sennett **C:** Charles Avery, Nick Cogley, Raymond Hatton, Ed Kennedy, Mack Sennett, Ford Sterling. **L:** 1-reel **P:** Keystone/Mutual  *(Cop)*

**Twixt Love and Fire** (5/19/13)  **D:** Henry "Pathe" Lehrman **C:** Charles Avery, Edgar Kennedy **L:** ½-reel **P:** Keystone/Mutual  *(Jealous husband)*

**Gangsters, The** (5/29/13)  **D:** Henry "Pathe" Lehrman  **C:** Fred Mace, Roscoe "Fatty" Arbuckle, Nick Cogley, Edgar Kennedy **L:** 1-reel **P:** Keystone/Mutual *(Man pulling rope)*

**Out and In** (6/19/13)  **D:** Mack Sennett **C:** Phyllis Allen, Hank Mann, Harry Bernard, Ed Kennedy, Ford Sterling **L:** ½-reel **P:** Keystone/Mutual  *(prison guard)*

**Peeping Pete** (6/23/13)  **D:** Mack Sennett **C:** Mack Sennett, Ford Sterling, "Fatty" Arbuckle, Nick Cogley, Edgar Kennedy  **L:** ½ reel **P:** Keystone/Mutual  *(Cop)*

**Rastus and the Game Cock** (7/3/13) **D:** Mack Sennett **C:** Ford Sterling, Nick Cogley **L:** 1-reel.  **P:** Keystone/Mutual

**Safe in Jail** (7/7/13)  **D:** Mack Sennett **C:** "Fatty" Arbuckle, Charles Avery, Ed Kennedy, Ford Sterling **L:** 1-reel **P:** Keystone/Mutual  *(A crook)*

**Love and Rubbish** (7/14/13)  **D:** Henry "Pathe" Lehrman **C:** Ford Sterling, Charles Avery, "Fatty" Arbuckle, Edgar Kennedy  **L:** 1-reel **P:** Keystone/Mutual  *(Cop)*

**Get Rich Quick** (7/24/13)  **D:** Wilfred Lucas **C:** Ed Kennedy, Fred Mace  **L:** 1-reel **P:** Keystone/Mutual  *(A Henchman)*

**Game of Pool, A** (8/7/13)  **D:** Wilfred Lucas **C:** Ford Sterling, Fred Mace, Ed Kennedy **L:** 1-reel.  **P:** Keystone/Mutual  *(Man in pool hall)*

**Riot, The** (8/11/13)  **D:** Mack Sennett **C:** "Fatty" Arbuckle, Mabel Normand, Edgar Kennedy  **L:** 1-reel **P:** Keystone/Mutual  *(Cop)*

**Fire Bug, The** (8/21/13)  **D:** Mack Sennett **C:** Nick Cogley, Ford Sterling, Mack Sennett, Alice Davenport, Ed Kennedy **L:** 2-reels **P:** Keystone/Mutual  *(Cop)*

**Mabel's New Hero** (8/28/13)  **D:** Mack Sennett **C:** "Fatty" Arbuckle, Mabel Normand, Edgar Kennedy  **L:** 1-reel  **P:** Keystone/ Mutual  *(Cop)*

**Mother's Boy** (9/25/13)  **D:** Henry "Pathe" Lehrman **C:** "Fatty" Arbuckle, Nick Cogley, Alice Davenport, Billy Gilbert, Edgar Kennedy **L:** 1-reel  **P:** Keystone/Mutual  *(A mug)*

**What Father Saw** (9/15/13)  **D:** George O. Nicholls **C:** Charles Murray, Edgar Kennedy, Betty Schade **L:** ½-reel  **P:** Keystone/Mutual

**Bowling Match, A**  (9/27/13)  **D:** Mack Sennett  **C:** Ford Sterling, Mabel Normand, Edgar Kennedy **L:** 1-reel **P:** Keystone/Mutual  (**Bowling alley operator**)

**Their Husbands**  (10/13/13)  **D:** Wilfred Lucas  **C:** Cecile Arnold, Ed Kennedy, Dot Farley, Harry McCoy, Hank Mann, Al St. John, Peggy Pearce **L:** 1-reel **P:** Keystone/ Mutual  *(Deputy)*

**Quiet Little Wedding, A**  (10/23/13)  **D:** Wilfred Lucas  **C:** Mabel Normand, "Fatty" Arbuckle, Charles Avery, Minta Durfee, Little Billy Gilbert, Alice Davenport, Al St. John, Edgar Kennedy **L:** 1-reel **P:** Keystone/Mutual

**Janitor, The**  (10/27/13)  **D:** Wilfred Lucas  **C:** Nick Cogley, Edgar Kennedy, Betty Schade **L:** 1-reel **P:** Keystone/Mutual  *(Cop)*

**Speed Kings, The** (10/30/13)  **D:** Wilfred Lucas  **C:** Ford Sterling, Mabel Normand, "Fatty" Arbuckle, Barney Oldfield, Edgar Kennedy **L:** 1-reel **P:** Keystone/Mutual

**Our Children** (11/17/13) **D:** _ **C:** Thelma Slatter, Billy Jacobs, Edgar Kennedy. **L:** 1-reel **P:** Keystone/Mutual

**Muddy Romance, A**  (11/20/13)  **D:** Mack Sennett  **C:** Mabel Normand, Ford Sterling, Minta Durfee, Mack Swain, Edgar Kennedy  **L:** 1-reel  **P:** Keystone/Mutual *(Water cop)*

**Fatty Joins the Force**  (11/24/13)  **D:** George Nichols  **C:** "Fatty" Arbuckle, Minta Durfee, Edgar Kennedy, Mack Swain, Hank Mann **L:** 1-reel **P:** Keystone/Mutual *(Cop)*

**Ride for a Bride**  (12/8/13)  **D:** George Nichols  **C:** "Fatty" Arbuckle, Charles Avery, Edgar Kennedy. **L:** 1-reel **P:** Keystone/ Mutual. **Note:** Working title: *The Golf Ball (Man in mustache)*

**Bad Game, A**  (12/22/13)  **D:** Mack Sennett  **C:** Ford Sterling, Edgar Kennedy, Hank Mann **L:** 1-reel **P:** Keystone/Mutual

**Some Nerve**  (12/25/13)  **D:** Mack Sennett  **C:** "Fatty" Arbuckle, Cecile Arnold, Dot Farley, Ford Sterling, Edgar Kennedy **L:** 1-reel **P:** Keystone/Mutual

**Gusher, The** (12/15/13)  **D:** Mack Sennett  **C:** Ford Sterling, Mabel Normand, Edgar Kennedy  **L:** 1-reel  **P:** Keystone/Mutual *(Cop)*

# 1914

**Mabel's Stormy Love Affair** (1/5/14)  **D:** Mabel Normand **C:** Mabel Normand, Alice Davenport, Nick Cogley, Hank Mann, Edgar Kennedy. **L:** 2-reels **P:** Keystone/ Mutual. **Note:** Working title: *Servant Hero*

**Flirt's Mistake, A** (1/12/14) **D:** George Nichols **C:** "Fatty" Arbuckle, Minta Durfee, Virginia Kirtley, Edgar Kennedy **L:** 1-reel **P:** Keystone/Mutual. *(Cop)*

**In the Clutches of a Gang** (1/17/14) **D:** George Nichols **C:** "Fatty" Arbuckle, Mabel Normand, Ford Sterling, Hank Mann, Al St. John, Nick Cogley, Harry McCoy, George O. Nicholls [George Nichols], Edgar Kennedy. **L:** 2-reels **P:** Keystone/Mutual. **Note:** Working title: *The Disguised Mayor. (Cop)*

**Won in a Closet** (2/2/14) **D:** Mabel Normand **C:** Mabel Normand, Harry McCoy, Alice Davenport, Hank Mann, Nick Cogley, Edgar Kennedy. **L:** 2-reels **P:** Keystone/Mutual. **Note:** Working title: *The Rube*

**Jealous Waiter, The** (2/10/14) **D:** Mack Sennett **C:** Fred Mace, Harry McCoy, Betty Schade, Al St. John, Edgar Kennedy **L:** ½-reel **P:** Keystone/Mutual.

**Thief Catcher, A** (2/19/14) **D:** Henry Lehrman **C:** Harry McCoy, Al St. John, Hank Mann, Edgar Kennedy. **L:** 1-reel **P:** Keystone/Mutual.

**Film Johnnie, A** (3/2/14) **D:** George Nichols **C:** Charlie Chaplin, "Fatty" Arbuckle, Minta Durfee, Edgar Kennedy. **L:** 1-reel **P:** Keystone/Mutual *(As the director)*

**His Favorite Pastime** (3/16/14) **D:** George Nichols **C:** "Fatty" Arbuckle, Charlie Chaplin, Hank Mann, Peggy Pearce, Edgar Kennedy. **L:** 1-reel **P:** Keystone Film Company. **Note:** Reissued as *The Bonehead* and *Charlie Is Thirsty.*

**Tango Tangles** (3/9/14) **D:** Mack Sennett **C:** Charlie Chaplin, Ford Sterling, "Fatty" Arbuckle, Chester Conklin, Edgar Kennedy **L:** ¾-reel **P:** Keystone/Mutual *(Dance hall manager)*

**Hide and Seek** (3/20/14) **D:** Mack Sennett **C:** Ford Sterling, Betty Schade, Edgar Kennedy **L:** 1-reel **P:** Keystone/Mutual.

**Cruel, Cruel Love** (3/26/14) **D:** George Nichols **C:** Charlie Chaplin, Minta Durfee, Alice Davenport, Chester Conklin, Edgar Kennedy. **L:** 1-reel **P:** Keystone/Mutual. **Note:** *A.K.A.: Lord Help Us.*

**Chicken Chaser** (4/2/14) **D:** Roscoe Arbuckle **C:** "Fatty" Arbuckle, Edgar Kennedy **L:** 1-reel **P:** Keystone/Mutual *(Cop)*

**Star Boarder, The** (4/4/14) **D:** George Nichols **C:** Charlie Chaplin, Minta Durfee, Alice Davenport, Gordon Griffith, Edgar Kennedy. **L:** 1-reel **P:** Keystone/Mutual *(As the landlady's husband)*

**Mabel at the Wheel** (4/18/14) **D:** Mack Sennett/Mabel Normand **C:** Mabel Normand, Charlie Chaplin, Fred Mace, Joe Bordeaux, Harry McCoy, Mack Sennett, Al St. John, William Seiter, Minta Durfee, Alice Davenport, Chester Conklin, Edgar Kennedy. **L:**

2-reels **P:** Keystone/Mutual. **Note:** Working title: *Racing Queen*. Reissued as *A Hot Finish. (Edgar in the grandstands)*

**Twenty Minutes of Love** (4/20/14) **D:** Joseph Madden. Supervised by Mack Sennett. **C:** Charlie Chaplin, Minta Durfee, Chester Conklin, Gordon Griffith, Joseph Swickard, Emma Clifton, Edgar Kennedy. **L:** 2-reels **P:** Keystone/Mutual *(A lover in the park)*.

**Caught in a Cabaret** (4/27/14) **D:** Mabel Normand **C:** Charlie Chaplin, Mabel Normand, Alice Davenport, Harry McCoy, Chester Conklin, Mack Swain, Minta Durfee, Alice Howell, Hank Mann, Gordon Griffith, Phyllis Allen, Joseph Swickard, Wallace MacDonald, Edgar Kennedy. **L:** 2-reels **P:** Keystone/Mutual **Note:** Reissued as *The Jazz Waiter (Café proprietor)*.

**Our Country Cousin** (6/6/14) **D:** _ **C:** Edgar Kennedy. **L:** 1-reel **P:** Keystone/Mutual. **Note:** Working title: *Rube Elopement*

**Knockout, The** (6/11/14) **D:** Charles Avery/Roscoe Arbuckle/Mack Sennett. **C:** Charlie Chaplin, "Fatty" Arbuckle, Mabel Normand, Minta Durfee, Mack Swain, Eric Campbell, Mack Sennett, Ford Sterling, Al St. John, Hank Mann, George "Slim" Summerville, Charles Parrott [Charley Chase], Edgar Kennedy. **L:** 2-reels **P:** Keystone/Mutual. **Note:** Fatty is a heavyweight boxer and fights Kennedy, Charlie is the referee. Charlie appears rather briefly in the second reel of this Fatty Arbuckle comedy. Reissued as *The Pugilist* and *Counted Out.* Working title: *Fighting Demon. (As Cyclone Flynn, the champion boxer)*.

**Mabel's Busy Day** (6/13/14) **D:** Charles Chaplin/Mabel Normand **C:** Mabel Normand, Charlie Chaplin, Chester Conklin, Harry McCoy, Charley Chase, George "Slim" Summerville, Al St. John, Billie Bennett, Wallace MacDonald and Edgar Kennedy as one of the cops. **L:** 1-reel **P:** Keystone/Mutual. **Note:** Working title: *Weine Story.* A.K.A.: *Charlie and the Sausages, Hot Dogs,* and *Love and Lunch. (Hot dog eater)*

**Sky Pirate, The** (7/18/14) **D:** Roscoe Arbuckle **C:** "Fatty" Arbuckle, Edgar Kennedy **L:** 1-reel. **P:** Keystone/Mutual **(Villain)**

**Killing Horace** (10/1/14) **D:** _ **C:** Charles Murray, Edgar Kennedy **L:** 1-reel **P:** Keystone/Mutual *(Rival)*

**Those Love Pangs** (10/10/14) **D:** Charles Chaplin **C:** Charlie Chaplin, Chester Conklin, Vivian Edwards, Cecile Arnold, Norma Nichols, Harry McCoy, Edgar Kennedy **L:** 1-reel. **P:** Keystone/Mutual. **Note:** A.K.A.: *Busted Hearts (As the girl's friend)*.

**Gentlemen of Nerve** (10/29/14) **D:** Charles Chaplin **C:** Mabel Normand, Charlie Chaplin, Chester Conklin, Mack Swain, Charley Chase, Phyllis Allen, George "Slim" Summerville, Edgar Kennedy. **L:** 1-reel **P:** Keystone/Mutual. **Note:** Working title: *Attending the Races.* A.K.A.: *Charlie at the Races* and *Some Nerve (Cop)*.

**Love Thief, The** (10/22/14) **D:** _ **C:** Chester Conklin, Edgar Kennedy **L:** 1-reel **P:** Keystone/Mutual

**Curses! They Remarked** (11/5/14) **D:** Dell Henderson **C:** Chester Conklin, Edgar Kennedy, Charlie Murray, Slim Summerville, Charles Parrott [Charley Chase], Nick Cogley **L:** 1-reel. **P:** Keystone/Mutual

**Incompetent Hero, An** (11/12/14) **D:** Roscoe Arbuckle **C:** "Fatty" Arbuckle, Minta Durfee, Al St. John, Edgar Kennedy **L:** 1-reel **P:** Keystone/Mutual *(Jealous neighbor)*

**Tillie's Punctured Romance (feature)** (11/14/14) **D:** Mack Sennett **C:** Marie Dressler, Charlie Chaplin, Mabel Normand, Mack Swain, Charles Bennett, Charles Murray, Chester Conklin, Charles Parrott [Charley Chase], Harry McCoy, Minta Durfee, Phyllis Allen, Alice Davenport, Alice Howell, George "Slim" Summerville, Al St. John, Wallace MacDonald, Hank Mann, Edward Sutherland, Joe Bordeaux, Gordon Griffith, Billie Bennett, Edgar Kennedy. **L:** 6-reels **P:** Keystone/Mutual. **Note:** The very first full-length feature comedy ever produced. *(As the restaurant owner also a butler).*

**Noise of Bombs, The** (11/19/14) **D:** Charles Parrot [Charley Chase] **C:** Charles Murray, Edgar Kennedy, Chester Conklin, Slim Summerville, Al St. John, Eddie Cline, Harry McCoy. **L:** 1-reel **P:** Keystone/Mutual. **Note:** Working title: *The Blackhanders (As the Chief of Police).*

**Leading Lizzy Astray** (11/30/14) **D:** Roscoe Arbuckle **C:** "Fatty" Arbuckle, Minta Durfee, Mack Swain, Edgar Kennedy **L:** 1-reel **P:** Keystone/Mutual *(Chauffeur)*

**Getting Acquainted** (12/5/14) **D:** Charles Chaplin **C:** Charlie Chaplin, Mabel Normand, Phyllis Allen, Mack Swain, Cecile Arnold, Harry McCoy, Edgar Kennedy. **L:** 1-reel **P:** Keystone/Mutual. *(Keystone Kop)*

**Ambrose's First Falsehood** (12/12/14) **D:** Dell Henderson **C:** Phyllis Allen, Charley Chase, Minta Durfee, Slim Summerville, Mack Swain, Edgar Kennedy **L:** ___ **P:** Keystone/Mutual *(Café proprietor)*

# 1915

**Giddy, Gay and Ticklish** (1/7/15) **D:** Charles Avery **C:** Syd Chaplin, Phyllis Allen, Edgar Kennedy **L:** 1-reel **P:** Keystone/Mutual *(Manicurist's boyfriend)*

**Fatty's New Role** (2/1/15) **D:** Roscoe Arbuckle **C:** "Fatty" Arbuckle, Minta Durfee, Al St. John, Hank Mann, Edgar Kennedy **L:** 1-reel **P:** Keystone/Mutual. *(As a rich cigar smoker)*

**Forced Bravery** (2/20/15) **D:** George O. Nicholls **C:** Fred Mace, Phyllis Allen, Nick Cogley, Edgar Kennedy. **L:** 1-reel **P:** Keystone/Mutual.

**Ambrose's Sour Grapes** (3/1/15) **D:** Walter Wright **C:** Mack Swain, Cecile Arnold, Mae Busch, Chester Conklin, Louise Fazenda, Harry Gribbon, Edgar Kennedy. **L:** 2-reels **P:** Keystone/Mutual. **Note:** Working title: *Twin Story   (Jealous husband)*

**Fatty's Reckless Fling** (3/4/15) **D:** Roscoe Arbuckle **C:** "Fatty" Arbuckle, Minta Durfee, Edgar Kennedy **L:** 1-reel **P:** Keystone/Mutual *(Jealous husband)*

**That Little Band of Gold** (3/15/15) **D:** Roscoe Arbuckle **C:** "Fatty" Arbuckle, Dixie Chene, Alice Davenport, Vivian Edwards, Mabel Normand, Al St. John, Ford Sterling, Charles Parrott [Charley Chase], Bobby Dunn, Slim Summerville, Hank Mann, Edgar Kennedy. **L:** 2-reels. **P:** Keystone/Mutual *(A diner)*

**His Luckless Love** (4/19/15) **D:** Dell Henderson **C:** Vivian Edwards, Frank Opperman, Syd Chaplin, Chester Conklin, Edgar Kennedy **L:** 1-reel **P:** Keystone/Mutual *(Maid's boyfriend)*

**Wished on Mabel** (4/19/15) **D:** Roscoe Arbuckle **C:** Mabel Normand, "Fatty" Arbuckle, Edgar Kennedy **L:** 1-reel **P:** Keystone/Mutual. **Note:** Filmed at San Francisco's Golden Gate Park. *(Cop)*

**Mabel's Willful Way** (5/11/15) **D:** Roscoe Arbuckle **C:** Mabel Normand, "Fatty" Arbuckle, Edgar Kennedy. **L:** 2-reels **P:** Keystone/Mutual **Note:** Filmed at Oakland's Idora Park. Working title: *Park Story   (As Fatty's rival for Mabel)*

**Miss Fatty's Seaside Lovers** (5/15/15) **D:** Roscoe Arbuckle **C:** "Fatty" Arbuckle, Harold Lloyd, Edgar Kennedy **L:** 1-reel **P:** Keystone/Mutual

**Fatty's Plucky Pup** (6/10/15) **D:** Roscoe Arbuckle **C:** "Fatty" Arbuckle, Josephine Stevens, Al St. John, Edgar Kennedy. **L:** 2-reels **P:** Keystone/Mutual. **Note:** Working title: *Dog and Villain Story (Con man)*

**Tools of Providence** (7/7/15) **D:** William S. Hart **C:** William S. Hart, Rhea Mitchell, Frank Borzage, Walter Whitman, Edgar Kennedy **L:** 2-reels **P:** Bronco. **Note:** Reissued as *Dakota Dan.*

**Fatty's Tintype Tangle** (7/26/15) **D:** Roscoe Arbuckle **C:** "Fatty" Arbuckle, Louise Fazenda, Frank Hayes, Luke the dog, Edgar Kennedy. **L:** 2-reels **P:** Keystone/Mutual *(Jealous husband)*

**Battle of Ambrose and Walrus, The** (8/16/15) **D:** Walter Wright **C:** Dora Rodgers, Chester Conklin, Mack Swain, Vivian Edwards, Harry McCoy, Nick Cogley, Harry Bernard, Edgar Kennedy **L:** 2-reels **P:** Keystone/Mutual

**No One to Guide Him** (8/30/15) **D:** Charles Avery **C:** Syd Chaplin, Slim Summerville, Edgar Kennedy **L:** 2-reels **P:** Keystone/Mutual *(A dark stranger)*

**Game Old Knight, A** (11/7/15) **D:** F. Richard Jones **C:** Charles Murray, Louise Fazenda, Harry McCoy, George "Slim" Summerville, Cecile Arnold, Edgar Kennedy **L:** 2-reels **P:** Triangle-Keystone. **Note:** Edgar is bald in this one *(Executioner)*

**Fickle Fatty's Fall** (11/14/15) **D:** Roscoe Arbuckle **C:** "Fatty" Arbuckle, Ivy Crosthwaite, Alice Davenport, Bobby Vernon, May Emory, Guy Woodward, Minta Durfee, Phyllis Allen, Al St. John, Glen Cavender, Fritz Schade, Bobby Dunn, Edgar Kennedy **L:** 2-reels **P:** Triangle-Keystone

**Janitor's Wife's Temptation, A** (12/5/15) **D:** Dell Henderson **C:** Fred Mace, Marta Golden, Betty Marsh, Harry Gribbon, Joe Jackson, Little Billy Gilbert, Edgar Kennedy **L:** 2-reels **P:** Triangle-Keystone

**Village Scandal, The** (12/12/15) **D:** Roscoe Arbuckle **C:** "Fatty" Arbuckle, Raymond Hitchcock, Flora Zabelle, Al St. John, Harry McCoy, Edgar Kennedy **L:** 2-reels **P:** Triangle-Keystone

**Great Vacuum Robbery, The** (12/12/15) **D:** F. Richard Jones **C:** Charles Murray, Louise Fazenda, George "Slim" Summerville, Harry Booker, Dixie Chene, Wayland Trask, Edgar Kennedy. **L:** 2-reels **P:** Triangle-Keystone *(Thief)*

**Fatty and the Broadway Stars** (12/19/15) **D:** Roscoe Arbuckle **C:** "Fatty" Arbuckle, Al St. John, Mack Sennett, Mack Swain, Weber and Fields, William Collier, Joe Jackson, Fred Mace, Minta Durfee, Mae Busch, Slim Summerville, Chester Conklin, Hank Mann, Charles Murray, Ford Sterling, Polly Moran, the Keystone Kops, Edgar Kennedy. **L:** 2-reels **P:** Triangle-Keystone. **Note:** Reissued as *Fatty's Dream.*

# 1916

**His Hereafter** (2/6/16) **D:** F. Richard Jones **C:** Charles Murray, Louise Fazenda, Harry Booker, Pat Kelly, Myrtle Lind, Wayland Trask, Edgar Kennedy. **L:** 2-reels **P:** Triangle-Keystone. **Note:** Working title: *Murray's Mix-Up. (Bouncer)*

**Bucking Society** (4/16/16) **D:** Harry Williams/William Campbell **C:** Chester Conklin, George "Slim" Summerville, Edgar Kennedy. **L:** 2-reels **P:** Triangle-Keystone.

**His Bitter Pill** (4/30/16) **D:** Fred Fishback **C:** Mack Swain, Louella Maxam, Ella Haines, Edgar Kennedy. **L:** 2-reels **P:** Triangle-Keystone *(Diamond Dan)*

**Her Marble Heart** (5/7/16) **D:** F. Richard Jones **C:** Louise Fazenda, Charles Murray, Nick Cogley, Edgar Kennedy **L:** 2-reels **P:** Triangle-Keystone *(Lawyer)*

**Ambrose's Cup of Woe** (6/10/16) **D:** Fred Fishback/Herman Raymaker **C:** Mack Swain, May Emory, Paul Jacobs, Joseph Swickard, Edgar Kennedy **L:** 2-reels **P:** Triangle-Keystone *(Artist)*

**Madcap Ambrose** (7/16/16)  **D:** Fred Fishback  **C:** Mack Swain, Polly Moran, Mai Wells, Frank Hayes, May Emory, Louis Morrison, Edgar Kennedy  **L:** 2-reels  **P:** Triangle-Keystone  *(Boarder)*

**Bombs** (10/8/16)  **D:** Frank Griffin  **C:** Charles Murray, Louise Fazenda, Mary Thurman, Harry Booker, Wayland Trask, Edgar Kennedy  **L:** 2-reels  **P:** Triangle-Keystone  *(Tony Peanutty)*

**Scoundrel's Toll, The** (ll/9/16)  **D:** Glen Cavender  **C:** Mary Thurman, Dale Fuller, Gene Rogers, Raymond Griffith, Edgar Kennedy  **L:** 2-reels  **P:** Triangle-Keystone *(Peter X. Bush, Streetcar Superintendent)*

# 1917

**Blue Streak, The (feature)** (3/19/17)  **D:** William Nigh  **C:** William Nigh, Violet Palmer, Ruth Thorp, Ned Finley, Edward Roseman, Danny Sullivan, Edgar Kennedy  **L:** 5-reels  **P:** Fox

**Her Fame and Shame** (3/25/17)  **D:** Frank Griffin  **C:** Charles Murray, Louise Fazenda, Polly Moran, George "Slim" Summerville, Sylvia Ashton, Harry Booker, Frank Opperman, Edgar Kennedy.  **L:** 2-reels  **P:** Triangle-Keystone  *(Theatre troupe cashier)*

**Oriental Love** (5/27/17)  **D:** Walter Wright  **C:** Ora Carew, Joseph Belmont, Joseph Callahan, Nick Cogley, Sid Smith, Andy Anderson, Blanche Payson, Edgar Kennedy  **L:** 2-reels  **P:** Triangle-Keystone  *(Hindu)*

**Whose Baby?** (6/8/17)  **D:** Clarence Badger  **C:** Bobby Vernon, Phyllis Haver, Gloria Swanson, Tom Kennedy, Edgar Kennedy.  **L:** 2-reels  **P:** Triangle-Keystone  *(Detective)*

**Hero for a Minute, A** (6/12/17)  **D:** Robert Kerr  **C:** Bobby Dunn, Katherine Young, Edgar Kennedy.  **L:** 2-reels  **P:** L-KO/Universal

**Skidding Hearts** (6/17/17)  **D:** Walter Wright  **C:** Ora Carew, Joseph Baldy Belmont, Mal St. Clair, Blanche Payson, Edgar Kennedy  **L:** 2-reels  **P:** Triangle-Keystone

# 1918

**Watch Your Neighbor** (2/3/18)  **D:** Victor Heeman  **C:** Billy Armstrong, Harry Booker, Clifford Bowes, Bert Gillespie, Charlie Murray, Ben Turpin, Edgar Kennedy.  **L:** 2-reels  **P:** Sennett/Paramount *(Innocent stranger)*

**Roaming Bathtub, The** (2/21/18)  **D:** Frank C. Griffin  **C:** Edgar Kennedy, William Franey, Jack Cooper.  **L:** 2-reels  **P:** Fox-Sunshine

**Scholar, The** (4/1/18)  **D:** Arvid Gilstrom  **C:** Billy West, Oliver Hardy, Blanche Payson, Edgar Kennedy  **L:** 2-reels  **P:** Louis Burstein

**Her Screen Idol** (6/13/18) **D:** Eddie Cline **C:** Glen Cavender, Jack Cooper, Louise Fazenda, Ford Sterling, Ben Turpin, Edgar Kennedy **L:** 2-reels **P:** Sennett-Paramount *(Movie Villain)*

**She Loved Him Plenty** (8/18/18) **D:** F. Richard Jones **C:** Ben Turpin, Charles Lynn, Marie Prevost, Edgar Kennedy **L:** 2-reels **P:** Sennett-Paramount *(Alf, a tough guy)*

**Mickey (feature)** (8/18/18) **D:** F. Richard Jones/James Young **C:** Mabel Normand, Wheeler Oakman, Lew Cody, George Nichols, Minta Durfee, Laura Lavarnie, Tom Kennedy, Edgar Kennedy. **L:** 7-reels **P:** Mabel Normand Feature Film Company/ Sennett Studios. *(As a bookie, also shotgun rider)*

**Self Made Lady** (9/18/18) **D:** David Kirkland **C:** Dot Farley, Bobby Vernon, Edgar Kennedy **L:** 2-reels. **P:** Fox-Sunshine

# 1919

**Yankee Doodle in Berlin (feature)** (3/20/19) **D:** F. Richard Jones **C:** Bothwell Browne, Ford Sterling, Mal St. Clair, Bert Roach, Marie Prevost, Charles Murray, Ben Turpin, Heinie Conklin, Eddie Foy, Ed Kennedy, Chester Conklin, Bobby Dunn, James Finlayson, Harry Gribbon, Sennett Bathing Girls **L:** 5-reels **P:** Sennett/Sol Lesser *(German soldier)*

**Love's False Faces** (5/25/19) **D:** F. Richard Jones **C:** Jack Ackroyd, Billy Armstrong, Chester Conklin, James Finlayson, Eddie Gribbon, Marie Prevost, Ben Turpin, Edgar Kennedy. **L:** 2-reels **P:** Sennett/Paramount *(Saloon manager)*

**Hearts and Flowers** (6/8/19) **D:** Eddie Cline/Mack Sennett **C:** Jack Ackroyd, Billy Armstrong, Louise Fazenda, Virginia Fox, Phyllis Haver, Ford Sterling, Edgar Kennedy. **C:** 2-reels **P:** Sennett/Paramount *(Pete, Fazenda's brother)*

**No Mother to Guide Him** (1919) **D:** Mal St. Clair **C:** Ben Turpin, Chas. Lynn, Myrtle Lind, Edgar Kennedy **L:** 2-reels **P:** Sennett/ Paramount *(Loudmouth in audience)*

**Among Those Present** (7/20/19) **D:** Ray Grey/Erle C. Kenton **C:** Lois Boyd, Eddie Gribbon, Phyllis Haver, Charlie Murray, Ford Sterling, Edgar Kennedy. **L:** 2-reels **P:** Sennett/Paramount *(Café Manager)*

**Treating 'em Rough** (8/3/19) **D:** Frederick W. Jackman **C:** Louise Fazenda, Baldy Belmont, Pat Kelly, Billy Bevan, Ford Sterling, Jack Ackroyd, Teddy the Dog, Ed Kennedy. **L:** 2-reels **P:** Sennett/Paramount *(Pete, a city slicker)*

**Up in Alf's Place** (1919) **D:** F. Richard Jones **C:** Charlie Murray, Harriet Hammond, Charlotte Mineau, Edgar Kennedy **L:** 2-reels **P:** Sennett/Paramount **(A Bolshevik)**

# 1920

**Her Naughty Wink** (2/21/20) **D:** __ **C:** Edgar Kennedy, William Franey, Ethel Teare **L:** 2-reels **P:** Fox-Sunshine.

**Daredevil Jack (Serial)** (3/8/20 to 6/15/20) **D:** W.S. Van Dyke **C:** Jack Dempsey, Josie Sedgwick, Herschel Mayall, Ruth Langston[Langdon], Al Kaufman, Lon Chaney, Edgar Kennedy (uncredited) **L:** 2-reels after the initial chapter, 33-reels total **P:** Astra Film Corp./Pathe' *Chapter #1: "The Mysterious Bracelets." #2: The Ball of Death." #3: "Wheels of Fate." #4: "Shanghaied." #5: "The Race for Glory." #6: "A Skirmish of Wits." #7: "A Blow in the Dark." #8: "Blinding Hate." #9: "Phantoms of Treachery." #10: "Paths of Destruction." #11: "Flames of Wrath." #12: "The Unseen Menace." #13: "Bating the Trap." #14: "A Terrible Vengeance." #15: "The Triple Chase."*

**Lightweight Lover, A** (4/3/20) **D:** Roy Del Ruth **C:** Jack Cooper, Edgar Kennedy, Marvel Rea **L:** 2-reels **P:** Fox-Sunshine

**Through the Keyhole** (7/5/20) **D:** Roy Del Ruth **C:** Edgar Kennedy. Glen Cavender, Dave Morris **L:** 2-reels **P:** Fox-Sunshine

**You Tell 'em, Lions, I'll Roar** (9/6/20) **D:** William H. Watson **C:** Dave Morris, Glen Cavender, Century Lions, Edgar Kennedy **L:** 2-reels **P:** Universal

**Chase Me** (10/16/20) **D:** Roy Del Ruth **C:** Edgar Kennedy, Olive Tell, Glen Cavender, Dave Morris **L:** 2-reels **P:** Fox-Sunshine

**Huntsman, The** (11/28/20) **D:** John G. Blystone **C:** Clyde Cook, Edgar Kennedy **L:** 2-reels. **P:** Fox-Sunshine.

# 1921

**Chauffeur, The** (2/12/21) **D:** William Fox **C:** Clyde Cook, Edgar Kennedy **L:** 2-reels **P:** Fox

**Puppets of Fate** (3/28/21) **D:** Dallas M. Fitzgerald **C:** Viola Dana, Francis McDonald, Jackie Saunders, Fred Kelsey, Edgar Kennedy **L:** 6-reels **P:** Metro *(Mike Reynolds)*

**Jockey, The** (5/21/21) **D:** John G. Blystone **C:** Clyde Cook, Edgar Kennedy **L:** 2-reels **P:** Fox

**Toreador, The** (9/2/21) **D:** Jack Blystone [John G. Blystone] **C:** Clyde Cook, Edgar Kennedy, Jim Donnelly, Lois Scott **L:** 2-reels **P:** Fox-Sunshine

**All Wrong** (9/8/21) **D:** John G. Blystone **C:** Clyde Cook, Edgar Kennedy **L:** 1-reel **P:** Fox-Sunshine

**Guide, The** (9/11/21) **D:** __ **C:** Clyde Cook, Edgar Kennedy **L:** 2-reels **P:** Fox *(Girl's father)*

**Skirts** (feature) (10/4/21) **D:** Hampton Del Ruth **C:** Clyde Cook, Harry Booker, Glen Cavender, Buster Keaton, George "Slim" Summerville, Chester Conklin, Polly Moran, Bobby Dunn, Tom Kennedy, Edgar Kennedy **L:** 5-reels **P:** Fox Films Corporation. **Note:** Hampton Del Ruth was the brother of Roy.

# 1922

**Leather Pushers, The** (series) (1/11/22 to 12/1/24) **D:** Edward Laemmle/Harry Pollard **C:** Reginald Denny, Sam Ryan, Hayden Stevenson, Billy Sullivan, Phil Salvador, Edgar Kennedy (who allegedly appeared in all 24 chapters). **L:** 2-reels each. **P:** Universal Pictures. *Chapter #1: "Let's Go." #2: "Round Two." #3: "Payment Through the Nose." #4: "A Fool and His Money." #5: "Taming of the Shrewd." #6: "Whipsawed." #7: Young King Cole." #8: "He Raised Kane." #9: "Chickasa Bone Crusher." #10: "When Kane Met Abel." #11: "Strike Father Strike Son." #12: "Joan of Newark." #13: "Wandering Two." #14: "Widow's Mite." #15: "Don Coyote." #16: "Something for Nothing." #17: "Columbia the Gem of the Ocean." #18: "Barnaby's Grudge." #19: "The Kid from Madrid." #20: "He Loops to Conquer." #21: "Girls Will Be Girls." #22: "A Tough Tenderfoot." #23: "Swing Bad the Sailor." #24: "Big Boy Blue." (As Ptomaine Tommy, the fighting camp cook).*

**Edgar's Little Saw** (4/5/22) **D:** ___ **C:** Edgar Kennedy, Johnny Jones **L:** 1-reel **P:** Vitagraph. **Note:** May have been a parody of the "Edgar Pomeroy" series of the time.

**Oh, Daddy** (4/15/22) **D:** Roy Del Ruth **C:** Billy Bevan, Mildred June, Edgar Kennedy **L:** 1-reel. **P:** Sennett/First National

**Eskimo, The** (8/7/22) **D:** Slim Summerville **C:** Clyde Cook, Edgar Kennedy **L:** 1-reel **P:** Fox-Sunshine.

**Lazy Bones** (11/5/22) **D:** John G. Blystone **C:** Clyde Cook, Edgar Kennedy **L:** 2-reels **P:** Fox-Sunshine

**Fresh Heir** (12/10/22) **D:** Edgar Kennedy **C:** Edgar Kennedy **L:** 2-reels **P:** Fox

**High and Dry** (12/24/22) **D:** Slim Summerville **C:** Clyde Cook, Edgar Kennedy **L:** 2-reels **P:** Fox-Sunshine

# 1923

**Cyclist, The** (8/19/23) **D:** Slim Summerville **C:** Clyde Cook, Edgar Kennedy **L:** 2-reels. Fox-Sunshine.

**Little Girl Next Door, The** (feature) **D:** W.S. Van Dyke **C:** Edward Kennedy (A.K.A. Edgar) **L:** 6-reels **P:** Blair Coan Productions

**Wet and Weary** (11/18/23) **D:** Slim Summerville **C:** Edgar Kennedy **L:** 2-reels **P:** Fox-Sunshine

# 1924

**Broncho Express, The** (2/10/24) **D:** Slim Summerville **C:** Clyde Cook, Edgar Kennedy **L:** 2-reels **P:** Fox

**Night Message, The (feature)** (3/17/24) **D:** Perley Poore Sheehan **C:** Howard Truesdell, Gladys Hulette, Charles Cruz, Margaret Seddon, Edgar Kennedy **L:** 5-reels **P:** Universal **Note:** A.K.A.: *Innocent (Lem Beeman)*

**Misfit, The** (3/23/24) **D:** Clyde Cooke/Albert Austin **C:** Clyde Cook, Edgar Kennedy **L:** 2-reels **P:** Educational

**Hot Air** (6/22/24) **D:** Norman Taurog **C:** Edgar Kennedy, Lois Moran, Ruth Hiatt, Jack Lloyd, Otto Fries. **L:** 2-reels **P:** Educational

**Racing for Life (feature)** (8/1/24) **D:** Henry MacRae **C:** William Fairbanks, Eva Novak, Edgar Kennedy **L:** 5-reels **P:** C.B.C. *(Tom Grady)*

**Battling Fool, The (feature)** (8/1/24) **D:** W.S. Van Dyke **C:** William Fairbanks, Pat Harmon, Eva Novak, Fred Butler, Laura Winton, Edgar Kennedy **L:** 5-reels **P:** Columbia

**Wall Street Blues** (8/1/24) **D:** Del Lord **C:** Billy Bevan, Andy Clyde, Vernon Dent, Sunshine Hart, Edgar Kennedy **L:** 2-reels **P:** Sennett/Pathe' *(Crook)*

**All's Swell on the Ocean** (8/18/24, Chapter #5) **D:** Erle C. Kenton **W:** Scott Darling **C:** Jack Dempsey, Hayden Stevenson, George Ovey, Frank Hagney, Edgar Kennedy, Gertrude Ralston **L:** 2-reel **P:** Universal. **Note:** 10-chapter serial, part of the "Fight and Win" series starring Jack Dempsey.

# 1925

**Golden Princess, The (feature)** (5/10/25) **D:** Clarence Badger **C:** Betty Bronson, Neil Hamilton, Phyllis Haver, Edgar Kennedy. **L:** 9-reels **P:** Paramount Pictures. **Note:** Melodrama of California goldmine. Remake of *Tennessee's Partner* (1916). *(Grizzly Bill)*

**Paths to Paradise (feature)** (6/29/29) **D:** Clarence Badger **C:** Betty Compson, Raymond Griffith, Tom Santschi, Bert Woodruff, Fred Kelsey, Edgar Kennedy **L:** 7-reels **P:** Famous Players-Lasky/Paramount *(Night Watchman)*

**Cupid's Boots** (7/25/25) **D:** Edgar Kennedy **W:** Frank Capra **C:** Ralph Graves, Thelma Hill, Andy Clyde, Edgar Kennedy **L:** 2-reels **P:** Sennett/Pathe

**Trouble with Wives (feature)** (9/28/25) **D:** Malcolm St. Clair **C:** Florence Vidor, Tom Moore, Esther Ralston, Ford Sterling, Lucy Beaumont, Edgar Kennedy **L:** 7-reels **P:** Famous Players-Lasky/Paramount *(Detective)*

**People vs. Nancy Preston (feature)** (11/1/25) **D:** Tom Forman **C:** John Bowers, David Butler, Frankie Darro, Marguerite De La Motte, Alphonse Ethier, Ray Gallagher, Mary Gordon, Ed Kennedy **L:** 7-reels **P:** Hunt Stromberg Productions/ P.D.C. *(Gloomy Gus)*

**His People** (feature) (11/28/25) **D:** Edward Sloman **C:** Rudolph Schildkraut. Rosa Rosanova, George Lewis, Jean Johnson, Kate Price, Bobby Gordon, Edgar Kennedy. **L:** 9-reels **P:** Universal Pictures. **Note:** Edgar has a scene as a boxing promoter. A.K.A.: *Proud Heart. (Thomas Nolan)*

# 1926

**Oh! What a Nurse! (feature)** (3/7/26) **D:** Charles Reisner **C:** Sydney Chaplin, Patsy Ruth Miller, Gayne Whitman, Matthew Betz, Edith Yorke, David Torrence, Pat Hartigan, Raymond Wells, Henry Barrows, Edgar Kennedy. **L:** 7-reels **P:** Warner Brothers **Note:** Sequel to *Charley's Aunt. (Eric Johnson)*.

**My Old Dutch** (feature) (5/26/26) **D:** Lawrence Trimble **C:** Jean Hersholt, May McAvoy, Pat O'Malley, Cullen Landis, Edgar Kennedy **L:** 8-reels **P:** Universal Pictures. **Note:** Based on a famous British song title *(Bill Sproat, King of the Coasters)*

**Wet Paint (feature)** (7/26) **D:** Arthur Rosson **C:** Raymond Griffith, Helene Costello, Bryant Washburn, Natalie Kingston, Henry Kolker, Edgar Kennedy **L:** 6-reels **P:** Paramount *(Detective)*

**Across the Pacific (feature)** (10/2/26) **D:** Roy Del Ruth **C:** Monte Blue, Myrna Loy, Jane Winton, Edgar Kennedy **L:** 7-reels **P:** Warner Bros. **Note:** Edgar has a death scene. *(Corporal R. Van)*.

**Better 'Ole, The (feature)** (10/5/26) **D:** Charles Reisner **C:** Sydney Chaplin, Doris Hill, Jack Ackroyd, Harold Goodwin, Theodore Lorch, Tom Kennedy, Kewpie Morgan, Edgar Kennedy **L:** 9-reels **P:** Warner Bros. *(Corporal Quint)*.

**Private Izzy Murphy (feature)** (10/30/26) **D:** Lloyd Bacon **C:** George Jessel, Patsy Ruth Miller, Vera Gordon, Nat Carr, William Strauss, Edgar Kennedy **L:** 8-reels **P:** Warner Bros.

**Going Crooked** (feature) (12/12/26) **D:** George Melford **C:** Bessie Love, Oscar Shaw, Gustav von Seyffertitz, Edgar Kennedy **L:** 6-reels **P:** Fox.

# 1927

**Finger Prints (feature)** (1/8/27) **D:** Lloyd Bacon **C:** Louise Fazenda, Myrna Loy, William Demarest, John T. Murray, Helene Costello, Edgar Kennedy **L:** 7-reels **P:** Warner Bros. *(As a stuttering coroners assistant)*

**Gay Old Bird, The (feature)** (2/26/27) **D:** Herman Raymaker **C:** Louise Fazenda, Jane Winton, William Demarest, John Stepping, Frances Raymond, Edgar Kennedy **L:** 7-reels **P:** Warner Bros. *(Chauffeur)*

**Wrong Mr. Wright, The (feature)** (2/27/27) **D:** Scott Sidney **C:** Jean Hersholt, Enid Bennett, Dorothy Devore, Edgar Kennedy **L:** 7-reels **P:** Universal *(Detective)*

**Wedding Bill$ (Feature)** (5/7/27) **D:** Erle C. Kenton **C:** Raymond Griffith, Anne Sheridan, Hallam Cooley, Iris Stuart, Vivien Oakland, Tom S. Guise, Louis Stern, John Steppling, Edgar Kennedy **L:** 6-reels **P:** Paramount **Note:** Anne Sheridan not to be confused with later Warner Bros. actress, Ann. *(Detective)*

**Chinese Parrot, The (feature)** (10/23/27) **D:** Paul Leni **C:** Marian Nixon, Florence Turner, Hobart Bosworth, Edmund Burns, Captain Albert Conti, K. Sojin, Fred Esmelton, George Kuwa, George "Slim" Summerville, Dan Mason, Anna May Wong, Etta Lee, Jack Trent, Edgar Kennedy **C:** 7-reels **P:** Universal *(As Maydorf)*

# 1928

**Leave 'em Laughing** (1/28/28) **D:** Clyde A. Bruckman **C:** Stan Laurel, Oliver Hardy, Charlie Hall, Viola Richard, Dorothy Coburn, Stanley "Tiny" Sandford, Sam Lufkin, Edgar Dearing, Al Hallet, Jack V. Lloyd, Otto Fries, Jack Hill, Edgar Kennedy **L:** 2-reels **P:** Roach/MGM *(Laurel & Hardy series)* **(Kennedy the cop)**

**Dumb Daddies** (2/4/28) **D:** Hal Yates **C:** Max Davidson, Edgar Kennedy, Thelma Hill, Spec O'Donnell **L:** 2-reels **P:** Roach/MGM *(All Star series)*

**Family Group, The** (2/18/28) **D:** Fred Guiol **C:** Charley Chase, Gertrude Astor, Edgar Kennedy **L:** 2-reels **P:** Roach/MGM. *(Charley Chase series)* **(Photographer)**

**Finishing Touch, The** (2/25/28) **D:** Clyde A. Bruckman **C:** Stan Laurel, Oliver Hardy, Dorothy Coburn, Sam Lufkin, Edgar Kennedy **L:** 2-reels **P:** Roach/MGM. *(Laurel & Hardy series)* **(Kennedy the cop)**.

**Limousine Love** (4/14/28) **D:** Fred Guiol **C:** Charley Chase, Viola Richard, Edgar Kennedy **L:** 2-reels **P:** Roach/MGM. *(Charley Chase series)* **(Hitchhiker)**

**Fight Pest, The** (5/28/28) **D:** Fred Guiol **C:** Charley Chase, Edgar Kennedy, Edna Marion, Bull Montana **L:** 2-reels **P:** Roach/MGM. *(Charley Chase series)*

**Imagine My Embarrassment** (9/1/28) **D:** Hal Yates **C:** Charley Chase, Anita Garvin, Vivien Oakland, Edgar Kennedy **L:** 2-reels **P:** Roach/MGM *(Charley Chase series)*

**Should Married Men Go Home?** (9/8/28) **D:** James Parrott **C:** Stan Laurel, Oliver Hardy, Edna Marian, Viola Richard, Jack Hill, Dorothy Coburn, Lyle Tayo, Chet Brandenburg, Sam Lufkin, Charlie Hall, Edgar Kennedy **L:** 2-reels **P:** Roach/MGM.

*(Laurel & Hardy series)* *(As a golfer with a grass divot on his head)*

**Is Everybody Happy?** (9/29/28) **D:** Hal Yates **C:** Charley Chase, Dell Henderson, Edgar Kennedy **L:** 2-reels **P:** Roach/MGM *(Charley Chase series)*

**All Parts** (10/27/28) **D:** Hal Yates **C:** Charley Chase, Edgar Kennedy **L:** 2-reels **P:** Roach/MGM. *(Charley Chase series)*

**Two Tars** (11/3/28) **D:** James Parrott **C:** Stan Laurel, Oliver Hardy, Thelma Hill, Ruby Blaine, Charlie Rogers, Clara Guiol, Jack Hill, Charlie Hall, Edgar Dearing, Harry Bernard, Sam Lufkin, Baldwin Cooke, Charles McMurphy, Ham Kinsey, Lyle Tayo, Edgar Kennedy **L:** 2-reels **P:** Roach/MGM. *(Laurel & Hardy series)* *(As a motorist)*

**Boy Friend, The** (11/10/28) **D:** Leo McCarey **C:** Max Davidson, Gordon Elliott, Marion Byron, Fay Holderness, Edgar Kennedy **L:** 2-reels **P:** Roach/MGM. *(All Star series)*

**Booster, The** (11/24/28) **D:** Hal Yates **C:** Charley Chase, Edgar Kennedy **L:** 2-reels **P:** Roach/MGM. *(Charley Chase series)*

**Feed 'em and Weep** (12/8/28) **D:** Fred Guiol **C:** Max Davidson, Marion Bryon, Anita Garvin, Charlie Hall, Edgar Kennedy **L:** 2-reels **P:** Roach/MGM. *(All Star series)*

**Pair of Tights, A** (12/10/28) **D:** Hal Yates **C:** Anita Garvin, Marion Byron, Stuart Erwin, Charlie Hall, Spec O'Donnell, Edgar Kennedy **L:** 2-reels **P:** Roach/MGM. *(All Star series)* *(Anita's "boyfriend")*

**Chasing Husbands** (12/22/28) **D:** James Parrott **C:** Charley Chase, Edgar Kennedy, Gertrude Astor, Jean Harlow **L:** 2-reels **P:** Roach/MGM. *(Charley Chase series)*

**Going Ga-ga** (12/27/28) **D:** James W. Horne **C:** Anita Garvin, Marion Byron, Max Davidson, Edgar Kennedy **L:** 2-reels **P:** Roach/MGM *(All Star series)*

# *1929*

**Off to Buffalo** (2/4/29) **D:** James Horne **C:** Charley Chase, Vivien Oakland, Anita Garvin, Dell Henderson, Edgar Kennedy **L:** 2-reels **P:** Roach/MGM *(Charley Chase series)*

**When Money Comes** (3/2/29) **D:** Hal Roach **C:** Edgar Kennedy, Charlie Rogers **L:** 2-reels **P:** Roach/MGM *(All Star series)*

**Why is a Plumber?** (3/11/29) **D:** Hal Roach **C:** Edgar Kennedy, Jean Harlow, Eddie Dunn, Gertrude Sutton **L:** 2-reels **P:** Roach/MGM *(All Star series)*

**Trent's Last Case (feature)** (3/31/29) **D:** Howard Hawks **C:** Raymond Griffith, Marceline Day, Raymond Hatton, Donald Crisp, Anita Garvin, Ed Kennedy. **L:** 6-reels **P:** Fox *(Inspector Murch)*

**Unaccustomed as We Are** (5/4/29) **D:** Lewis Foster **C:** Stan Laurel, Oliver Hardy, Mae Busch, Thelma Todd, Edgar Kennedy . **L:** 2-reels **P:** Roach/MGM. **Note:** L&H's first talkie. *(Laurel & Hardy series) (Kennedy the cop)*

**Hurdy-Gurdy** (5/11/29) **D:** Hal Roach/Leo McCarey **C:** Max Davidson, Thelma Todd, Edgar Kennedy, Eddie Dunn. **L:** 2-reels **P:** Roach/MGM. **Note:** First sound film made at the Roach Studios, but released after *Unaccustomed as We Are*. *(All Star series) (Kennedy the cop)*

**Thundering Toupees** (5/25/29) **D:** Robert F. McGowan **C:** Edgar Kennedy, Vivien Oakland, Jean Harlow, Eddie Dunn, Mickey Daniels **L:** 2-reels **P:** Roach/MGM

**Madam Q** (6/8/29) **D:** Hal Roach **C:** Edgar Kennedy, Charley Rogers, Eddie Dunn, Elinor Vanderveer, Frank Alexander, Gertrude Sutton **L:** 2-reels **P:** Roach/MGM *(All Star series) (Judge)*

**Dad's Day** (7/29/29) **D:** Hal Roach **C:** Edgar Kennedy, Gertie Messinger, Eddie Dunn, Ben Hall, Irma Harrison. **L:** 2-reels **P:** Roach/MGM. *(All Star series) (Edgar as Dad)*

**Big Squawk, The** (7/29/29) **D:** Warren Doane **C:** Edgar Kennedy **L:** 2-reels. **P:** Roach/MGM. *(All Star series)*

**Perfect Day** (8/10/29) **D:** James Parrott **C:** Stan Laurel, Oliver Hardy, Kay Deslys, Isabelle Keith, Harry Bernard, Lyle Tayo, Baldwin Cooke, Charley Rogers, Edgar Kennedy, Buddy the dog **L:** 2-reels. **P:** Roach/MGM. *(Laurel & Hardy series) (As the gouty-footed Uncle Edgar)*

**Hotter Than Hot** (8/26/29) **D:** Lewis R. Foster **C:** Harry Langdon, Thelma Todd, Frank Austin, Edith Kramer, Edgar Kennedy **L:** 2-reels **P:** Roach/MGM. *(Harry Langdon series)*

**Crazy Feet** (8/26/29) **D:** Warren Doane **C:** Charley Chase, Thelma Todd, Eddie Dunn, Anita Garvin, Charlie Hall, Edgar Kennedy **L:** 2-reels **P:** Roach/MGM *(Charley Chase series)*

**They Had to See Paris (feature)** (9/18/29) **D:** Frank Borzage **C:** Will Rogers, Irene Rich, Marguerite Churchill, Owen Davis, Jr., Fifi D'Orsay, Ivan Lebedeff, Marcelle Coreene, Rex Bell, Christiane Yves, Bob Kerr, Marcia Manon, Andre Cheron, Gregory Gay, Edgar Kennedy. **L:** 97 minutes **P:** Fox. **Note:** Will Rogers' first talking picture. *(Ed Eggers)*

**Welcome Danger (feature)** (10/12/29) **D:** Malcolm St.Clair (silent version)/Clyde Bruckman (sound version) **C:** Harold Lloyd, Barbara Kent, Noah Young, Charles Middleton, William Walling, James Wang, Douglas Haig, Edgar Kennedy. **L:** 115 minutes **P:** Paramount. **Note:** Completed as a silent film then almost entirely re-shot as Lloyd's first talkie. *(Desk Sergeant)*

**Bacon Grabbers** (10/19/29) **D:** Lewis R. Foster **C:** Stan Laurel, Oliver Hardy, Jean Harlow, Charlie Hall, Bobby Dunn, Eddie Baker, Sam Lufkin, Harry Bernard, Ham Kinsey, Cy Slocum, Buddy the dog, Edgar Kennedy **L:** 2-reels. **P:** Roach/MGM. **Note:** Edgar's wife is played by Jean Harlow! *(Laurel & Hardy series)* *(Radio owner)*

**Moan & Groan, Inc.** (12/7/29) **D:** Robert F. McGowan **C:** Our Gang: Allen "Farina" Hoskins, Mary Ann Jackson, Jackie Cooper, Bobby "Wheezer" Hutchins, Norman "Chubby" Chaney, Betty Jane Beard, Jay R. Smith, Bobby Mallon, and Pete the Pup; Max Davidson, Edgar Kennedy **L:** 2-reels **P:** Roach/MGM *(Our Gang series)* *(Kennedy the cop)*

**Angora Love** (12/14/29) **D:** Lewis R. Foster **C:** Stan Laurel, Oliver Hardy, Charlie Hall, Harry Bernard, Charley Young, Edgar Kennedy **L:** 2-reels **P:** Roach/MGM. *(Laurel & Hardy series)* *(Landlord)*.

**Great Gobs** (12/28/29) **D:** Warren Doane **C:** Charley Chase, Linda Loredo, Mildred Costello, William Guiler, Edgar Kennedy **L:** 2-reels **P:** Roach/MGM. *(Charley Chase series)*

# *1930*

**Head Guy, The** (1/1/30) **D:** Fred Guiol **C:** Harry Langdon, Thelma Todd, Nancy Dover, Eddie Dunn, Edgar Kennedy **L:** 2-reels **P:** Roach/MGM. *(Harry Langdon series)*

**Night Owls** (1/4/30) **D:** James Parrott **C:** Stan Laurel, Oliver Hardy, James Finlayson, Anders Randolph, Harry Bernard, Charles McAvoy, Edgar Kennedy **L:** 2-reels **P:** Roach/MGM *(Laurel & Hardy series)* *(Kennedy the Cop)*

**Help Wanted, Female** (1/11/30) **D:** Ralph Ceder **C:** Arthur Housman, Daphne Pollard, Edgar Kennedy **L:** 2-reels **P:** Pathe' **Note:** Edgar teams w/ Houseman as "a couple of boiglers." *(As Gunner)*

**Shivering Shakespeare** (1/25/30) **D:** Anthony Mack **C:** Our Gang: Jackie Cooper, Allen "Farina" Hoskins, Norman "Chubby" Chaney, Mary Ann Jackson, Bobby "Wheezer" Hutchins, Donald Haines, Edith Fellows, Gordon Thorpe, Fletcher Tolbert, Jack McHugh, Georgie Billings, Johnny Aber, Douglas "Turkie Egg" Greer, Bobby Mallon, and Pete the Pup; Gertrude Sutton, Mickey Daniels, Carlton Griffin, Lyle Tayo, Ham Kinsey, Edgar Kennedy **L:** 2-reels **P:** Roach/MGM. **Note:** Pie-throwing climax. *(Our Gang series)* *(Kennedy the cop)*

**Next Door Neighbors** (1/28/30) **D:** Harry Sweet **C:** Arthur Housman, Edgar Kennedy **L:** 2-reels **P:** Pathe'

**Real McCoy, The** (2/1/30) **D:** Warren Doane **C:** Charley Chase, Thelma Todd, Charlie Hall, Nelson McDowell, Edgar Kennedy **L:** 2-reels. **P:** MGM-Roach *(Charley Chase series)* **(Kennedy the cop)**

**First Seven Years, The** (3/1/30) **D:** Robert F. McGowen **C:** Our Gang: Jackie Cooper, Donald "Speck" Haines, Mary Ann Jackson, Norman "Chubby" Chaney, Allen "Farina" Hoskins, Bobby "Wheezer" Hutchins, and Pete the Pup; Otto Fries, Joy Winthrop, Edgar Kennedy **L:** 2-reels **P:** Roach/MGM **Note:** Edgar tells Jackie how to get a girl. *(Our Gang series)* **(Kennedy the cop)**

**Big Kick, The** (3/29/30) **D:** Warren Doane **C:** Harry Langdon, Nancy Dover, Bob Kortman, Sam Lufkin, Baldwin Cooke, Charles McAvoy, Eddie Baker, Edgar Kennedy **L:** 2-reels **P:** Roach/MGM. *(Harry Langdon series)*

**When the Wind Blows** (4/5/30) **D:** James W. Horne **C:** Our Gang: Jackie Cooper, Bobby "Wheezer" Hutchins, Mary Ann Jackson, Allen "Farina" Hoskins, Norman "Chubby" Chaney, Betty Jane "Hector" Beard and Pete the Pup; Charles McAvoy, Mary Gordon, Chet Brandenburg, David Sharpe, Edgar Kennedy **L:** 2-reels **P:** Roach/ MGM **Note:** "Say, nothing ever happens when I'm on the beat!" *(Our Gang series)* **(Kennedy the cop)**

**All Teed Up** (4/19/30) **D:** Edgar Kennedy **C:** Charley Chase, Thelma Todd, Tenen Holtz, Dell Henderson, Carl Stockdale, Nelson McDowell, Harry Bowen, Edgar Kennedy **L:** 2-reels **P:** Roach/MGM *(Charley Chase series)* **(Thelma's dad)**

**Fifty Million Husbands** (5/24/30) **D:** Edgar Kennedy **C:** Charley Chase, Tiny Sandford, Charlie Hall, Edgar Kennedy **L:** 2-reels **P:** Roach/MGM *(Charley Chase series)*

**Girl Shock** (8/23/30) **D:** James W. Horne **C:** Charley Chase, Carmen Guerrero, Jerry Mandy, Elinor Vandivere, Caesar Varoni, Catherine Courney, Edgar Kennedy **L:** 2-reels **P:** Roach/MGM. *(Charley Chase series)*

**Doctor's Orders** (9/13/30) **D:** Arch B. Heath **C:** Mickey Daniels, Grady Sutton, David Sharpe, Mary Kornman, Dorothy Granger, Gertie Messinger, Tiny Sandford, Edgar Kennedy. **L:** 2-reels **P:** Roach/MGM *(The Boy Friends series)* **(Mary's uncle)**

**Dollar Dizzy** (10/4/30) **D:** James W. Horne **C:** Charley Chase, Thelma Todd, James Finlayson, Dorothy Granger, Charlie Hall, Dick Granger, Ted Strobach, Dorothy Dix, Eda Shumacher, Ann Levis, Lorema Carr, Edgar Kennedy **L:** 3-reels **P:** Roach/ MGM. *(Charley Chase series)*

**Bigger and Better** (10/25/30) **D:** Edgar Kennedy **C:** Mickey Daniels, Grady Sutton, David Sharpe, Mary Kornman, Dorothy Granger, Gertie Messinger, Dell Henderson,

Dick Granger, Jim Granger, Edgar Kennedy. **L:**  2-reels **P:** Roach/MGM.  (*The Boy Friends series*)

**Looser Than Loose**  (11/15/30)  **D:** James W. Horne **C:**  Charley Chase, Thelma Todd, Dorothy Granger, Dell Henderson, Wilfred Lucas, Eddie Dunn, Gordon Douglas, Edgar Kennedy **L:** 2-reels  **P:** Roach/MGM. *(Charley Chase series)*

**Blood and Thunder** (11/30/30) **D:** George Stevens **C:** Edgar Kennedy  **L:** 2-reels  **P:** Roach/MGM

**Ladies Last** (12/6/30) **D:** George Stevens **C:**  Mickey Daniels, Grady Sutton, Mary Kornman, Dorothy Granger, Edgar Kennedy. **L:** 2-reels **P:**  Roach/MGM *(The Boy Friends series)*

# 1931

**Stage Struck** (1/18/31) **D:** Albert Ray **C:**  Walter Catlett, Heinie Conklin, Ruth Etting, Edgar Kennedy **L:** 2-reels **P:** Pathe' ("Checker" Comedy)

**It Happened in Hollywood** (2/4/31) **D:**  Ralph Ceder **C:** Edgar Kennedy **L:** 2-reels **P:** Universal ("Red Star Comedy")

**Hot Wires** (2/22/31) **D:** Harry Sweet **C:**  Daphne Pollard, Franklin Pangborn, Donald Haines, Edgar Kennedy **L:** 2-reels **P:**  Pathe'

**High Gear**  (2/28/31)  **D:** George Stevens **C:** Mickey Daniels, Grady Sutton, David Sharpe, Mary Kornman, Gertie Messinger, Betty Bolen, Harry Bernard, Tiny Sandford, Edgar Kennedy. **L:** 3-reels **P:** Roach/MGM  *(The Boy Friends series)* *(Kennedy the cop)*

**Humanettes No. 8** (3/7/31) **D:**  **C:** Edgar Kennedy **L:** 1-reel **P:** RKO (**Hard boiled Sgt.**)

**Rough House Rhythm**  (4/5/31)  **D:** Harry Sweet **C:** Edgar Kennedy, Florence Lake, Franklin Pangborn, Claud Allister. **L:**  2-reels **P:**  RKO. **Note:** The Kennedys move into a "modern" bungalow. *(A Whoopie Comedy, a forerunner to the Average Man series)*

**Love Fever**  (4/11/31) **D:** Robert McGowan **C:** Thelma Todd, Mickey Daniels, Grady Sutton, David Sharpe, Mary Kornman, Gertie Messinger, Dorothy Granger, Eddie Dunn, Edgar Kennedy. **L:** 2-reels **P:** Roach/MGM. *(The Boy Friends series)* *(Kennedy the cop)*

**Quick Millions (feature)** (4/17/31) **D:** Rowland Brown **C:** Spencer Tracy, Marguerite Churchill, Sally Eilers, Bob "Bazooka" Burns, Edgar Kennedy, George Raft. **L:** 7-reels **P:** Fox

**All Gummed Up** (5/24/31) **D:** Harry Sweet **C:** Edgar Kennedy, Florence Lake, Louise Carver, Georgie Billings. **L:** 2-reels  **P:** RKO/Educational. *(A Whoopee Comedy, a*

forerunner to the *Average Man* series)

**Lemon Meringue** (8/3/31)  **D:** Harry Sweet **C:** Edgar Kennedy, Florence Lake, Dot Farley, William Eugene. **L:** 2-reels **P:** RKO. **Note:** The Kennedys open a luncheonette with a pie-throwing melee. The first official entry of the *Average Man series*. **(Luncheonette Owner)**

**Clean Up on the Curb, A** (9/12/31) **D:** Lloyd French **C:** Edgar Kennedy **L:** 2-reels **P:** RKO

**Thanks Again** (10/5/31)  **D:** Harry Sweet **C:** Edgar Kennedy, Florence Lake, Dot Farley, William Eugene, Jerry Drew. **L:** 2-reels **P:** RKO. *(Average Man* series)

**Bad Company (feature)** (11/8/31)  **D:** Tay Garnett **C:** Helen Twelvetrees, Ricardo Cortez, John Garrick, Paul Hurst, Frank Conroy, Frank McHugh, Kenneth Thomson, Emma Dunn, William V. Mong, Wade Boteler, Al Herman, Harry Carey, Robert Keith, Edgar Kennedy. **L:** 75 minutes **P:** RKO/Pathe' **Note:** Edgar provides comedy relief in this crime drama. *(Buff)*

**Camping Out** (12/14/31)  **D:** Harry Sweet **C:** Edgar Kennedy, Florence Lake, Dot Farley, William Eugene, Walter Catlett. **L:** 2-reels **P:** RKO. *(Average Man series)*

**Don't Divorce Him** (1931)  **D:** William Watson **C:** Clyde Cook, Vernon Dent, Edgar Kennedy **L:** 2-reels **P:** Al Christie "Tuxedo Comedies" **(A doctor)**

**Moonlight and Monkey Business** (1931)  **D:** Mark Sandrich **C:** Nick Basil, Henry Armetta, Monte Collins, Edgar Kennedy **L:** 2-reels **P:** RKO

# 1932

**Bon Voyage** (2/22/32)  **D:** Harry Sweet **L:** Edgar Kennedy, Florence Lake, Dot Farley, William Eugene, Jerry Mandy, Renee Torres, Charlie Hall. **L:** 2-reels **P:** RKO. **Note:** Edgar was scripted to sing in this short. *(Average Man series)*

**Carnival Boat (feature)** (3/21/32)  **D:** Albert S. Rogell **C:** Bill Boyd, Fred Kohler, Ginger Rogers, Hobart Bosworth, Harry Sweet, Marie Prevost, Charlie Sellon, Eddie Chandler, Walter Percival, Edgar Kennedy **L:** 61 minutes **P:** RKO/Pathe **Note:** Edgar in a brief brawl. *(Baldy)*

**He's a Honey** (4/17/32)  **D:** Walter Graham  **C:** Bobby Vernon, Eleanor Hunt, Harry Barris, Helen Mann, Edgar Kennedy  **L:** 2-reels  **P:** Educational   *(As Helen's dad)*

**Mother-In-Law's Day** (4/25/32)  **D:** Harry Sweet **C:** Edgar Kennedy, Florence Lake, Dot Farley, William Eugene, Isabelle Withers, Eddie Boland, Georgie Billings, Andre Cheron. **L:** 2-reels **P:** RKO *(Average Man series)*

**Westward Passage (feature)** (5/27/32) **D:** Robert Milton **C:** Ann Harding, Laurence Oliver, Irving Pichel, ZaSu Pitts, Irene Purcell, Bonita Granville, Don Alvarado, Ethel Griffies, Juliette Compton, Florence Lake, Edgar Kennedy **L:** 75 minutes **P:** RKO/Pathe *(Elmer)*

**Spot on the Rug, The** (5/15/32) **D:** Del Lord **C:** Billy Bevan, Marjorie Kane, Edgar Kennedy, Bud Jamison **L:** 2-reels **P:** Sennett/ Educational

**Now's the Time** (6/12/32) **D:** Harry J. Edwards **C:** Harry Barris, Mary Carlisle, Edgar Kennedy **L:** 2-reels **P:** Al Christie

**Giggle Water** (6/27/32) **D:** Harry Sweet **C:** Edgar Kennedy, Florence Lake, Dot Farley, William Eugene, Eddie Boland. **L:** 2-reels **P:** RKO. *(Average Man series)*

**Golf Chump, The** (8/5/32) **D:** Harry Sweet **C:** Edgar Kennedy, Florence Lake, Dot Farley, William Eugene. **L:** 2-reels **P:** RKO. *(Average Man series)*

**Hold 'em Jail** (feature) (9/16/32) **D:** Norman Taurog **C:** Bert Wheeler, Robert Woolsey, Edna May Oliver, Betty Grable, Robert Armstrong, Roscoe Ates, Warren Hymer, Paul Hurst, G. Pat Collins, Stanley Blystone, Jed Prouty, Spencer Charters, Edgar Kennedy **L:** 74 minutes **P:** RKO. **Note:** Betty Grable plays Edgar's daughter *(Warden Elmer)*

**Parlor, Bedroom and Wrath** (10/14/32) **D:** Harry Sweet **C:** Edgar Kennedy, Florence Lake, Dot Farley, William Eugene, Lucy Beaumont, Arthur Housman. **L:** 2-reels **P:** RKO *(Average Man series)* *(Apartment dweller)*

**Little Orphan Annie (feature)** (11/4/32) **D:** John Robertson **C:** Mitzi Green, Buster Phelps, May Robson, Matt Moore, Kate Lawson, Sidney Bracey, Edgar Kennedy. **L:** 70 minutes **P:** RKO **Note:** Based on Harold Gray's famous comic strip. Edgar is shaved bald. *(Daddy Warbucks)*

**Rockabye (feature)** (11/25/32) **D:** George Cukor/George Fitzmaurice **C:** Constance Bennett, Joel McCrea, Paul Lukas, Jobyna Howland, Walter Pidgeon, Clara Blandick, Walter Catlett, June Filmer, Edgar Kennedy **L:** 67 minutes **P:** RKO/Pathe *(Driver)*.

**Fish Feathers** (12/16/32) **D:** Harry Sweet **C:** Edgar Kennedy, Florence Lake, Dot Farley, William Eugene, Maude Treux, Tom Kennedy. **L:** 2-reels **P:** RKO *(Average Man series)* *(Fisherman)*

**Penguin Pool Murder, The (feature)** (12/25/32) **D:** George Archainbaud **C:** Edna May Oliver, James Gleason, Mae Clarke, Robert Armstrong, Donald Cook, Clarence H. Wilson, Oscar Piper, Mary Mason, Rochelle Hudson, Guy Usher, James Donlan, Joe Hermano, William LeMaire, Gustav von Seyffertitz, Edgar Kennedy. **L:** 70 minutes **P:** RKO **Note:** Kennedy's hair had not yet grown in from his last film, *Little Orphan Annie. A.K.A.: The Penguin Pool Mystery (Donovan the Detective)*

**Never the Twins Shall Meet** (1932) **D:** Harold Schwartz **C:** Roscoe Ates, Monte Collins, Billy Gilbert, Edgar Kennedy. **L:** 2-reels **P:** RKO *(Mr. Carp)*

# 1933

**Art in the Raw** (2/24/33) **D:** Harry Sweet **C:** Edgar Kennedy, Florence Lake, Dot Farley, William Eugene, Franklin Pangborn, Mona Ray. **L:** 2-reels **P:** RKO *(Average Man series)* *(Artist)*

**Scarlet River (feature)** (3/10/32) **D:** Otto Brower **C:** Tom Keene, Dorothy Wilson, Creighton Chaney [Lon Chaney, Jr.], Betty Furness, Hooper Atchley, Roscoe Ates, Yakima Canutt, James [Jim] Mason, Jack Raymond, Billy Butts, Edgar Kennedy, and {in cameos], Myrna Loy, Joel McCrea, Bruce Cabot,. **L:** 62 minutes **P:** RKO *(As the frustrated film director, Sam Gilroy)*

**Merchant of Menace, The** (4/21/33) **D:** Harry Sweet **C:** Edgar Kennedy, Florence Lake, Dot Farley, William Eugene, Nat Carr, Dorothy Granger. **L:** 2-reels **P:** RKO *(Average Man series)* *(Store owner)*

**Diplomaniacs (feature)** (4/29/33) **D:** William A. Seiter **C:** Bert Wheeler, Robert Woolsey, Marjorie White, Phyllis Barry, Louis Calhern (practically reprising his role from *Duck Soup*), Hugh Herbert, Charlie Hall, Charles Coleman, Richard Carle, Dewey Robinson, Neely Edwards, Billy Bletcher, William Irving, Vernon Dent, Constantine Romanoff, Carrie Daumery, Grace Hayle, Artie Ortega, Blackie Whiteford, Harry Schultz, Dick Alexander, John Kelly, Edgar Kennedy **L:** 76 minutes **P:** RKO. **Note:** Last scene in blackface. *(As a robed Commissioner)*

**Son of the Border (feature)** (5/5/33) **D:** Lloyd Nosler **C:** Tom Keene, Julie Haydon, David Durand, Creighton Chaney [Lon Chaney, Jr.], Charles King, Al Bridge, Claudia Coleman, Edgar Kennedy. **L:** 55 minutes **P:** RKO.

**Professional Sweetheart (feature)** (6/9/33) **D:** William A. Seiter **C:** Ginger Rogers, Norman Foster, ZaSu Pitts, Frank McHugh, Allen Jenkins, Gregory Ratoff, Lucien Littlefield, Franklin Pangborn, Sterling Holloway, Edgar Kennedy. **L:** 68 minutes **P:** RKO *(As Kelsey of the Kelsey Dishrag Company)*

**Good Housewrecking** (6/16/33) **D:** Harry Sweet **C:** Edgar Kennedy, Florence Lake, Dot Farley, William Eugene, Arthur Housman, Jane Darwell, Bud Jamison. **L:** 2-reels **P:** RKO **Note:** Originally titled *Inferior Decorations*. *(Average Man series)* *(Interior designer)*

**Quiet, Please** (8/11/33) **D:** George Stevens **C:** Edgar Kennedy, Florence Lake, Dot Farley, William Eugene, Charles Dow Clark, Al Hill, Fred Kelsey, Bud Jamison. **L:** 2-reels **P:** RKO *(Average Man series)* *(Wellington Firearms salesman)*

**Cross-Fire (feature)** (8/15/33) **D:** Otto Brower **C:** Tom Keene, Betty Furness, Edward Phillips, Lafe McKee, Nick Cogley, Jules Cowles, Tom Brown, Murdock MacQuarrie,

Stanley Blystone, Edgar Kennedy. **L:** 54 minutes **P:** RKO **Note:** Cast includes original Keystone Kop Nick Cogley. *(Ed Wimpy)*

**Tillie and Gus** (feature) (9/27/33) **D:** Francis Martin **C:** W.C. Fields, Alison Skipworth, Baby LeRoy, Jacqueline Wells [Julie Bishop], Clifford Jones, Clarence Wilson, George Barbier, Barton MacLane, Robert McKenzie, Maston Williams, Edgar Kennedy. **L:** 58 minutes **P:** Paramount **Note:** "Do you have anything to say before I hang you?" *(Judge Elmer)*

**King for a Night** (feature) (10/30/33) **D:** Kurt Neumann **C:** Chester Morris, Helen Twelvetrees, Alice White, John Miljan, Dorothy Granger, Maxie Rosenbloom, Edgar Kennedy **L:** 78 minutes **P:** Universal. *(Jim the Policeman)*

**What Fur** (11/3/33) **D:** George Stevens **C:** Edgar Kennedy, Florence Lake, Dot Farley, William Eugene, Treva Lawler, Nat Carr, Charlie Hall. **L:** 2-reels **P:** RKO **Note:** Florence buys an expensive fur coat, while Ed has troubles of his own with a blackmail photo. *(Average Man* series) *(Photographer)*

**Duck Soup** (feature) (11/17/33) **D:** Leo McCarey **C:** Groucho, Harpo, Chico, Zeppo Marx, Margaret Dumont, Louis Calhern, Raquel Torres, Edmund Breese, William Worthington, Edwin Maxwell, Leonid Kinskey, Verna Hillie, George MacQuarrie, Fred Sullivan, Davison Clark, Charles Middleton, Eric Mayne, Edgar Kennedy **L:** 68 minutes **P:** Paramount **Note:** Edgar holds his own with Chico and Harpo *(Lemonade vendor).*

**Grin and Bear It** (12/29/33) **D:** George Stevens **C:** Edgar Kennedy, Florence Lake, Dot Farley, William Eugene, Fred Kelsey. **L:** 2-reels **P:** RKO. *(Average Man* series)

# 1934

**All of Me** (feature) (2/1/34) **D:** James Flood **C:** Fredric March, Miriam Hopkins, George Raft, Helen Mack, Nella Walker, William Collier, Jr., Gilbert Emery, Blanche Frederici, Kitty Kelly, Guy Usher, John Marston, Edgar Kennedy. **L:** 70 minutes **P:** Paramount *(A guard)*

**Love on a Ladder** (3/2/34) **D:** Sam White **C:** Edgar Kennedy, Florence Lake, Dot Farley, William Eugene, Jean Fontaine. **L:** 2-reels **P:** RKO *(Average Man series)* *(Fireman)*

**Heat Lightning** (feature) (3/7/34) **D:** Mervyn LeRoy **C:** Aline MacMahon, Ann Dvorak, Preston Foster, Lyle Talbot, Glenda Farrell, Frank McHugh, Ruth Donnelly, Theodore Newton, Jane Darwell, Edgar Kennedy. **L:** 63 minutes **P:** Warner Bros. *(Husband)*

**Twentieth Century** (feature) (5/3/34) **D:** Howard Hawks **C:** John Barrymore, Carole Lombard, Walter Connolly, Roscoe Karns, Etienne Girardot, Ralph Forbes, Charles Levison [Lane], Dale Fuller, Herman Bing, Lee Kohlmar, Edgar Kennedy. **L:** 91 minutes **P:** Columbia *(McGonigle, a private eye)*

**Wrong Direction** (5/18/34) **D:** Alf Goulding **C:** Edgar Kennedy, Florence Lake, Dot Farley, William Eugene, Nat Carr, Jean Fontaine, Bud Jamison. **L:** 2-reels **P:** RKO **Note:** One of the best of the series *(Average Man series)* *(Film Director)*

**Murder on the Blackboard (feature)** (6/15/34) **D:** George Archainbaud **C:** Edna May Oliver, James Gleason, Bruce Cabot, Gertrude Michael, Tully Marshall, Frederik Vogeding, Regis Toomey, Jackie Searle, Barbara Fritchie, Gustav von Seyffertitz, Tom Herbert, Jed Prouty, Edgar Kennedy **L:** 71 minutes **P:** RKO *(Detective Sgt. Donahue)*

**Money Means Nothing (feature)** (6/15/34) **D:** Christy Cabanne **C:** Wallace Ford, Gloria Shea, Maidel Turner, Betty Blythe, Richard Tucker, Vivien Oakland, Tenen Holtz, Edward Tamblyn, Ann Brody, Olah Hytten, Edgar Kennedy **L:** 64 minutes **P:** Monogram *(As Green)*

**In-Laws Are Out** (6/29/34) **D:** Sam White **C:** Edgar Kennedy, Florence Lake, Dot Farley, William Eugene, Jean Fontaine. **L:** 2-reels **P:** RKO *(Average Man series)*

**We're Rich Again (feature)** (7/13/34) **D:** William A. Seiter **C:** Reginald Denny, Joan Marsh, Edna May Oliver, Billie Burke, Grant Mitchell, Marian Nixon, Larry "Buster" Crabbe, Gloria Shea, Otto Yamaoka, Lenita Lane, Dick Elliott, Andres de Segurola, Edgar Kennedy. **L:** 73 minutes **P:** RKO *(Healy)*

**Blasted Event, A** (9/7/34) **D:** Alf Goulding **C:** Edgar Kennedy, Florence Lake, Dot Farley, Jack Rice. **L:** 2-reels **P:** RKO **Note:** The first appearance in the series of Jack Rice *(Average Man series)* *(Office worker)*

**King Kelly of the U.S.A.** (feature) (9/15/34) **D:** Leonard Fields **C:** Guy Robertson, Irene Ware, Franklin Pangborn, Joyce Compton, Ferdinand Gottschalk, William von Brincken, Lorin Raker, Otis Harlan, Bodil Rosing, Edgar Kennedy **L:** 66 minutes **P:** Monogram *(Edgar plays the sidekick)*

**Gridiron Flash (feature)** (10/26/34) **D:** Glenn Tryon **C:** Eddie Quillan, Betty Furness, Grant Mitchell, Grady Sutton, Joseph Sauers [Joe Sawyer], Allen Wood, Margaret Dumont, Lucien Littlefield, Edgar Kennedy. **L:** 62 minutes **P:** RKO **Note:** A.K.A.: *Luck of The Game.*

**Kid Millions (feature)** (11/10/34) **D:** Roy Del Ruth **C:** Eddie Cantor, Ethel Merman, Ann Sothern, George Murphy, Warren Hymer, Berton Churchill, Edgar Kennedy. **L:** 90 minutes **P:** Goldwyn/UA *(As Herman, one of Eddie's brothers)*

**Poisoned Ivory** (11/16/34) **D:** Alf Goulding **C:** Edgar Kennedy, Florence Lake, Dot Farley, Jack Rice, William Augustine. **L:** 2-reels **P:** RKO *(Average Man series)*

**Marines Are Coming, The** (feature) (11/20/34) **D:** David Howard **C:** William Haines, Esther Ralston, Conrad Nagel, Armida, Hale Hamilton, George Regas, Edgar Kennedy. **L:** 73 minutes **P:** Mascot *(Buck Martin, Haines' butler/chauffeur)*

**Silver Streak, The (feature)** (11/30/34) **D:** Thomas Atkins **L:** Sally Blane, Charles Starrett, Hardie Albright, William Farnum, Irving Pichel, Arthur Lake, Theodore von Eltz, Guinn Williams, Doris Dawson, Edgar Kennedy **L:** 85 minutes **P:** RKO *(O'Brien)*

**Flirting with Danger (feature)** (12/1/34) **D:** Vin Moore **C:** Robert Armstrong, William Cagney, Marion Burns, Maria Alba, William von Brincken, Ernest Hilliard, Gino Corrado, Guy Usher, Edgar Kennedy. **L:** 69 minutes **P:** Monogram *(Jimmy Pierson)*

# 1935

**Bric-A-Brac** (1/18/35) **D:** Sam White **C:** Edgar Kennedy, Florence Lake, Dot Farley, Jack Rice, Walter Brennan. **L:** 2-reels **P:** RKO *(Average Man series)* *(Cabin builder)*

**Rendezvous at Midnight (feature)** (2/11/35) **D:** Christy Cabanne **C:** Ralph Bellamy, Valerie Hobson, Catherine Doucet, Irene Ware, Helen Jerome Eddy, Kathlyn Williams, Vivien Oakland, Purnell Pratt, W.P. Carleton, William Arnold, Gail Arnold, William Ruhl, James Bush, Arthur Vinton, Edgar Kennedy **L:** 60 minutes **P:** Universal. *(As Mahoney)*

**Living on Velvet (feature)** (3/2/35) **D:** Frank Borzage **C:** Kay Francis, George Brent, Warren William, Russell Hicks, Maude Turner Gordon, Samuel S. Hinds, Edgar Kennedy. **L:** 80 minutes **P:** Warner Bros./First National *(As a counterman)*

**South Seasickness** (3/29/35) **D:** Arthur Ripley **C:** Edgar Kennedy, Florence Lake, Dot Farley, Jack Rice, Adrian Rosley **L:** 2-reels **P:** RKO *(Average Man series) (Boat builder)*

**Cowboy Millionaire, The (feature)** (4/25/35) **D:** Edward F. Cline **C:** George O'Brien, Evelyn Bostock, Alden Chase, Maude Allen, Dan Jarrett, Lloyd Ingraham, Dean Benton, Thomas Curran, Edgar Kennedy. **L:** 65 minutes **P:** Atherton/Fox. **Note:** "El Repozo welcomes you." *(As Persimmon, O'Brien's sidekick)*

**Sock Me to Sleep** (5/17/35) **D:** Ben Holmes **C:** Edgar Kennedy, Florence Lake, Dot Farley, Jack Rice, Tom Kennedy. **L:** 2-reels **P:** RKO *(Average Man series) (Salesman)*

**Night at the Biltmore Bowl, A** (6/21/35) **D:** Alf Goulding **C:** Betty Grable, Bert Wheeler, Joy Hodges, Lucille Ball, Anne Shirley, Preston Foster, Jimmie Grier Orchestra, Edgar Kennedy. **L:** 2-reels **P:** RKO.

**Edgar Hamlet** (7/5/35) **D:** Arthur Ripley **C:** Edgar Kennedy, Dot Farley, Jack Rice. **L:** 2-reels **P** RKO *(Average Man series)*

**Woman Wanted (feature)** (8/2/35) **D:** George B. Seitz **C:** Maureen O'Sullivan, Joel McCrea, Adrienne Ames, Lewis Stone, Louis Calhern, Robert Greig, Leonard Fields, Noel Madison, Granville Bates, William B. Davidson, Gertrude Short, Edgar Kennedy **L:** 70 minutes **P:** MGM *(Sweeney)*

**In Love at 40**  (8/30/35)  **D:** Arthur Ripley **C:** Edgar Kennedy, Florence Lake, Dot Farley, Jack Rice, Curley Wright.  **L:**  2-reels **P:**  RKO *(Average Man series)*

**Little Big Shot**  (feature) (9/7/35)  **D:**  Michael Curtiz **C:**  Sybil Jason, Glenda Farrell, Robert Armstrong, Edward Everett Horton, Jack LaRue, Edgar Kennedy **L:** 78 minutes **P:** Warner Brothers *(Onderdonk)*

**Thousand Dollars a Minute, A** (feature) (10/22/35)  **D:** Aubrey Scotto **C:** Roger Pryor, Leila Hyams, Purnell Pratt, William Austin, Herman Bing, Ian Wolfe, Edgar Kennedy  **L:** 70 minutes  **P:** Republic *(McCarthy)*

**Happy Tho' Married**  (11/1/35)  **D:** Arthur Ripley **C:**  Edgar Kennedy, Florence Lake, Dot Farley, Jack Rice.  **L:**  2-reels **P:** RKO
*(Average Man series)*

**In Person** (feature)  (11/22/35)  **D:** William A. Seiter **C:** George Brent, Ginger Rogers, Alan Mowbray, Grant Mitchell, Samuel S. Hinds, Joan Breslau, Edgar Kennedy  **L:** 90 minutes  **P:** RKO

**Bride Comes Home, The**  (feature) (12/25/35)  **D:** Wesley Ruggles **C:** Claudette Colbert, Fred MacMurray, Robert Young, William Collier, Sr., Donald Meek, Richard Carle, Johnny Arthur, Bob McKenzie, Eddie Dunn, Kate MacKenna, James Conlin, Edward Gargan, Tom Kennedy, Edgar Kennedy. **L:** 82 minutes **P:**  Paramount **Note:** Louella Parsons said in her column, "Edgar Kennedy is marvelous as the small town justice of the peace." *(Henry McCarthy)*

# 1936

**Gasoloons** (1/3/36)  **D:** Arthur Ripley **C:** Edgar Kennedy, Florence Lake, Dot Farley, Jack Rice, Charles Withers, Dickie Jones, Brandon Hurst, Pearl Eaton  **L:**  2-reels  **P:** RKO **Note:**  First time Edgar slow-burns at fade-out    *(Average Man series)*

**It's Up to You** (1/4/36)  **D:**  Christy Cabanne **C:**  Edgar Kennedy, Ray Jones, Maxine Doyle, Vivien Oakland.  **L:** 55 minutes. **Note:** Standard Oil (Industrial Film). Unclear if released theatrically or only used as a promotional film for Standard Oil.  *(Elmer Block, the station attendant)*

**Return of Jimmy Valentine, The** (feature) (2/22/36)  **D:** Lewis D. Collins **C:**  Roger Pryor, Charlotte Henry, Robert Warwick, James Burtis, J. Carrol Naish, Lois Wilson, Wade Boteler, Gayne Whitman, Dewey Robinson, Hooper Atchley, George Chesebro, Charles Wilson, Franklin Parker, Harry Bowen, Lane Chandler, Jack Mack, Gertrude Messinger, Lucille Ward, Edgar Kennedy. **L:** 67 minutes **P:**  Republic **Note:** A.K.A.: *Jimmy Valentine (As Callahan)*

**Will Power**  (3/6/36)  **D:** Arthur Ripley **C:** Edgar Kennedy, Florence Lake, Dot Farley, Jack Rice, Kitty McHugh, Hamson Green, Harry Bowen. **L:**  2-reels **P:** RKO *(Average Man series) (Salesman)*

**Robin Hood of El Dorado** (feature)   (3/13/36)   **D:** William Wellman **C:** Warner Baxter, Margo, Bruce Cabot, Ann Loring, J. Carrol Naish, Eric Linden, Charles Trowbridge, Harvey Stephens, Ralph Remley, Soledad Jimenez, George Regas, Francis McDonald, Kay Hughes, Paul Hurst, Boothe Howard, Harry Woods, Edgar Kennedy. **L:** 86 minutes **P:** MGM   *(Sheriff Judd)*

**Small Town Girl** (feature) (4/10/36)   **D:** William Wellman **C:** Janet Gaynor, Robert Taylor, Binnie Barnes, James Stewart, Lewis Stone, Elizabeth Patterson, Frank Craven, Andy Devine, Isabel Jewell, Charley Grapewin, Agnes Ayres, Nella Walker, Robert Greig, Mary Forbes, Willie Fung, Douglas Fowley, Richard Carle, Frank Sully, Buster Phelps, Robert Livingston, Edward Norris, Eddie Kane, Charles Wilson, Edgar Kennedy. **L:** 72 minutes **P:** MGM **Note:** A.K.A.: *One Horse Town (Captain Mack)*

**High Beer Pressure** (5/8/36)   **D:** Leslie Goodwins **C:** Edgar Kennedy, Florence Lake, Dot Farley, Jack Rice, Tiny Sandford.   **L:** 2-reels **P:** RKO *(Average Man series)*

**Fatal Lady** (feature) (5/15/36)   **D:** Edward Ludwig **C:** Mary Ellis, Walter Pidgeon, Ruth Donnelly, Norman Foster, John Halliday, Alan Mowbray, Samuel S. Hinds, Ward Bond, Irene Franklin, Jean Rouverol, Edgar Kennedy. **L:** 77 minutes **P:** Paramount *( Rudy)*

**San Francisco** (feature) (6/26/36)   **D:** W.S. Van Dyke II **C:**  Clark Gable, Jeanette MacDonald, Spencer Tracy, Jack Holt, Jessie Ralph, Ted Healy, Shirley Ross, Al Shean, Margaret Irving, Harold Huber, William Ricciardi, Kenneth Harlan, Roger Imhof, Charles Judels, Russell Simpson, Bert Roach, Warren B. Hymer, Edgar Kennedy. **L:** 115 minutes.  **P:** MGM   *(Edgar as the frustrated process-serving Sheriff )*

**Dummy Ache** (7/10/36)   **D:** Leslie Goodwins **C:** Edgar Kennedy, Florence Lake, Dot Farley, Jack Rice, Harry Bowen, George Lewis, Lucille Ball, Bobby Burns. **L:** 2-reels **P:** RKO **Note:**  Nominated for an Academy Award, losing to Our Gang's *Board of Education*. *(Average Man series)*

**Yours for the Asking** (feature) (8/19/36)   **D:**  Alexander Hall **C:** George Raft,  Ida Lupino, Dolores Costello, James Gleason, Lynne Overman, "Skeets" Gallagher, Robert Gleckler, Louis Natheaux, Ralph Remley, Betty Blythe, Olive Tell, Charles Requa, Edgar Kennedy **L:** 74 minutes  **P:** Paramount *(As Bicarbonate)*

**Vocalizing** (10/23/36) **D:** Leslie Goodwins **C:** Edgar Kennedy.  **L:** 2-reels  **P:** RKO **Note:**  Edgar sings! Remade by Leon Errol as *Seeing Nellie Home. (Average Man series)*

**Mad Holiday** (feature) (11/13/36)   **D:** George B. Seitz **C:** Elissa Landi, Edmund Lowe, ZaSu Pitts, Edmund Gwenn, Ted Healy, Gustav von Seyffertitz, Walter Kingsford, Edgar Kennedy **L:** 71 minutes **P:** MGM   *(Donovan)*

**Three Men on a Horse** (feature) (11/21/36)   **D:**  Mervyn LeRoy **C:** Frank McHugh, Sam Levene, Joan Blondell, Teddy Hart, Guy Kibbee, Carol Hughes, Allen Jenkins,

Eddie Anderson, Paul Harvey, George Chandler, Harry Davenport, Edgar Kennedy. **L:** 85 minutes **P:** Warner Bros. *(Harry, the bartender)*

# 1937

**Hillbilly Goat** (l/1/37) **D:** Leslie Goodwins **C:** Edgar Kennedy, Si Jenks, Fern Emmett. **L:** 2-reels **P:** RKO *(Average Man series)*     *(Eastern Wholesale Electrical Appliances Salesman)*

**Edgar and Goliath** (1/l/37) **D:** Leslie Goodwins **C:** Edgar Kennedy, Florence Lake, Billy Franey, Frank O'Connor, Dick Rush, Stanley Blystone. **L:** 2-reels **P:** RKO *(Average Man series)*

**When's Your Birthday?** (feature) (2/19/37) **D:** Harry Beaumont **C:** Joe E. Brown, Marian Marsh, Margaret Hamilton, Frank Jenks, Fred Keating, Maude Eburne, Suzanne Kaaren, Minor Watson, Don Rowan, Granville Bates, Charles Judels, Edgar Kennedy. **L:** 77 minutes **P:** RKO *(Mr. Basscombe)*

**Bad Housekeeping** (3/5/37) **D:** Leslie Goodwins **C:** Edgar Kennedy, Vivien Oakland, Franklin Pangborn. **L:** 2-reels **P:** RKO *(Average Man series)*

**Locks and Bonds** (4/15/37) **D:** Leslie Goodwins **C:** Edgar Kennedy, Bill Franey, Eddie Dunn. **L:** 2-reels **P:** RKO *(Average Man Series)*

**Star Is Born, A** (feature) (4/20/37) **D:** William Wellman **C:** Fredric March, Janet Gaynor, Adolphe Menjou, May Robson, Andy Devine, Lionel Stander, Franklin Pangborn, Edgar Kennedy. **L:** 111 minutes **P:** Selznick/United Artists *(**Pop Randall, hotel clerk**)*

**Dumb's the Word** (6/11/37) **D:** Leslie Goodwins **C:** Edgar Kennedy, Vivien Oakland, Billy Franey, Eddie Dunn. **L:** 2-reels **P:** RKO *(Average Man series)* .

**Tramp Trouble** (8/7/37) **D:** Leslie Goodwins **C:** Edgar  Kennedy, Vivien Oakland, Billy Franey, Billy Benedict, Lloyd Ingraham, Ed Dunn. **L:** 2-reels **P:** RKO *(Average Man series) (**Markham & Co. Architect**)*

**Morning, Judge** (9/24/37) **D:** Leslie Goodwins **C:** Edgar Kennedy, Agnes Ayres, Billy Franey, George Irving, Harry Bowen, Bud Jamison. **L:** 2-reels **P:** RKO *(Average Man series)*

**Super-Sleuth** (feature) (1937) **D:** Ben Stoloff **C:** Jack Oakie, Ann Sothern, Eduardo Ciannelli, Joan Woodbury, Bradley Page, Edgar Kennedy. **L:** 70 minutes **P:** RKO *(**Lt. Garrison**)*

**Double Wedding** (feature) (10/15/37) **D:** Richard Thorpe **C:** William Powell, Myrna Loy, John Beal, Florence Rice, Sidney Toler, Katherine Alexander, Barnett Parker, Mary

Gordon, Jessie Ralph, Priscilla Lawson, Edgar Kennedy. **L:** 87 minutes  **P:** MGM *(Spike)*

**True Confession (feature)** (12/24/37) **D:** Wesley Ruggles **C:** Carole Lombard, Fred MacMurray, John Barrymore, Una Merkel, Porter Hall, Lynne Overman, Irving Bacon, Fritz Feld, Edgar Kennedy **L:** 85 minutes  **P:** Paramount  *(Darsey)*

**Other Fella, The** (1937) **D:** __ **C:** Edgar Kennedy, Jane Darwell. **L:** 8 minutes **Note:** Industrial short. "Chevrolet is at it again, this time utilizing the comic relief of comedian Edgar Kennedy to teach reckless drivers to see themselves on the road." Edgar plays five different roles, as obnoxious drivers. Edgar sings "I'm Sitting on Top of the World" while driving.

# 1938

**Hollywood Hotel (feature)** (1/15/38) **D:** Busby Berkeley **C:** Dick Powell, Rosemary Lane, Lola Lane, Ted Healy, Johnnie "Scat" Davis, Alan Mowbray, Frances Langford, Louella Parsons, Hugh Herbert, Glenda Farrell, Ronald Reagan, Mabel Todd, Allyn Joslyn, Grant Mitchell, Fritz Feld, Edgar Kennedy, Raymond Paige and His Orchestra. **L:** 109 minutes  **P:** Warner Bros.  **Note:** The song "Hooray for Hollywood" is the number everyone remembers from this film, but the song, "Let That Be a Lesson to You" is memorable, especially when Dick Powell and Ted Healy do the "Slow-Burn," much to Edgar's dismay.  *(Callaghan, the owner of a drive-in restaurant)*

**Ears of Experience** (1/28/38) **D:** Leslie Goodwins **C:** Edgar Kennedy, Florence Lake, Billy Franey, Richard Lane, Jack Rice, Landers Stevens .**L:** 2-reels **P:** RKO *(Average Man series)*.

**Black Doll, The** (feature) (1/30/38) **D:** Otis Garrett **C:** Donald Woods, Nan Grey, C. Henry Gordon, Doris Lloyd, John Wray, Addison Richards, Holmes Herbert, William Lundigan, Syd Saylor, Edgar Kennedy. **L:** 66 minutes  **P:** Universal *(As a bullheaded country Sheriff)*

**False Roomers** (3/26/38) **D:** Leslie Goodwins **C:** Edgar Kennedy, Constance Bergen, Billy Franey, James Finlayson, Jack Rice. **L:** 2-reels **P:** RKO **Note:** Fin plays Edgar's uncle. *(Average Man series)* .

**Kennedy's Castle** (5/28/38) **D:** Leslie Goodwins **C:** Edgar Kennedy, Vivian Tobin, Ed Dunn, Billy Franey, J.P. McGowan, Bud Jamison. **L:** 2-reels **P:** RKO  *(Average Man series)* *(Contractor)*

**Fool Coverage** (7/15/38) **D:** Leslie Goodwins **C:** Edgar Kennedy, Vivien Oakland, Billy Franey, Robert E. Keane, Max Wagner. **L:** 2-reels **P:** RKO **Note:** Original script title was *Sunday Driver*. *(Average Man series)* *(DMV Clerk)*

**Beaux and Errors** (10/7/38) **D:** Charles E. Roberts **C:** Edgar Kennedy, Vivien Oakland, Billy Franey, Ed Dunn, Eva McKenzie. **L:** 2-reels **P:** RKO *(Average Man series)* .

**Clean Sweep, A** (12/2/38) **D:** Charles E. Roberts **C:** Edgar Kennedy, Vivien Oakland, Billy Franey, Ed Dunn, Billy Franey, John Dilson, Tiny Sandford, Lillian Miles. **L:** 2-reels **P:** RKO. **Note:** *I Love Lucy* fans will recognize the vacuum sales pitch *(Average Man series)* (**Bank employee/vacuum salesman**)

**Peck's Bad Boy with the Circus (feature)** (12/2/38) **D:** Edward F. Cline **C:** Tommy Kelly, Ann Gillis, Billy Gilbert, Benita Hume, Spanky McFarland, Grant Mitchell, Louise Beavers, Nana Bryant, William Demarest, Wade Boteler, Harry Stubbs, Fay Helm, Edgar Kennedy. **L:** 78 minutes **P:** RKO **Note:** First and only time Edgar and Spanky worked together. Kennedy and Gilbert steal the show at the conclusion. *(Lion tamer)*

**Scandal Street (feature)** (12/11/38) **D:** James Hogan **C:** Lew Ayres, Louise Campbell, Roscoe Karns, Porter Hall, Virginia Weidler, Elizabeth Patterson, Cecil Cunningham, Lucien Littlefield, Carl "Alfalfa" Switzer, Louise Beavers, Edgar Kennedy **L:** 62 minutes **P:** Paramount *(Daniel Webster Smith)*

**Charlie McCarthy, Detective (feature)** (12/22/38) **D:** Frank Tuttle **C:** Edgar Bergen, Robert Cummings, Constance Moore, John Sutton, Louis Calhern, Samuel S. Hinds, Warren Hymer, Harold Huber, Edgar Kennedy. **L:** 78 minutes **P:** Universal *(Inspector Dailey)*

**Hey! Hey! U.S.A.** (feature) (12/26/38, U.K.) **D:** Marcel Varnel **C:** Will Hay, David Burns, Eddie Rynan, Fred Duprez, Paddy Reynolds, Tommy Bupp, Arthur Goulett, Gibb McLaughlin, Eddie Pola, Peter Gawthorne. **L:** 92 minutes **P:** Gainsborough Pictures (British). **Note:** Sometimes referred to as *Chicago Ben.* Charlie Hall plays a Chicago mobster *(Bugs Leary)*

# *1939*

**Maid to Order** (1/27/39) **D:** Charles E. Roberts **C:** Edgar Kennedy, Vivien Oakland, Billy Franey, Minerva Urecal, Tom Dempsey. **L:** 2-reels **P:** RKO (*Average Man series*)

**Clock Wise** (3/24/39*)* **D:** Charles E. Roberts **C:** Edgar Kennedy, Vivien Oakland, Billy Franey, Fred Kelsey, Harry Harvey, James Morton **L:** 2-reels **P:** RKO (*Average Man* series).

**Baby Daze** (5/19/39) **D:** Charles E. Roberts **C:** Edgar Kennedy, Vivien Oakland, Billy Franey, Don Brodie, Lillian Miles. **L:** 2-reels **P:** RKO (*Average Man series*)

**It's a Wonderful World** (feature) (5/19/39) **D:** W. S. Van Dyke **C:** Claudette Colbert, James Stewart, Guy Kibbee, Nat Pendleton, Frances Drake, Ernest Truex, Richard Carle, Sidney Blackmer, Andy Clyde, Cliff Clark, Cecil Cunningham, Hans Conried, Grady Sutton, Edgar Kennedy **L:** 86 minutes **P:** MGM *(Lieutenant Meller)*

**Feathered Pests** (7/14/39) **D:** Charles E. Roberts **C:** Edgar Kennedy, Vivien Oakland, Billy Franey, Eva McKezie, Dix Davis, Tim Davis, Derry Deane, Sonny Bupp. **L:** 2-reels **P:** RKO (*Average Man series*)

**Act Your Age** (10/6/39) **D:** Charles E. Roberts **C:** Edgar Kennedy, Vivien Oakland, Billy Franey, Robert Graves, Larry Steers. **L:** 2-reels **P:** RKO *(Average Man series)* *(Treasurer of Barnes & Co. Investments)*

**Everything's on Ice** (feature) (10/6/39) **D:** Erle C. Kenton. **C:** Irene Dare, Roscoe Karns, Lynne Roberts, Eric Linden, Bobby Watson, George Meeker, Maxine Stewart, Wade Boteler, Paul Winchell, Edgar Kennedy. **L:** 65 minutes **P:** RKO *(Joe Barton)*

**Little Accident** (feature) (10/27/39) **D:** Charles Lamont **C:** Hugh Herbert, Baby Sandy [Sandra Lee Henville], Florence Rice, Richard Carlson, Ernest Truex, Joy Hodges, Etienne Girardot, Anne Gwynne, Peggy Moran, Charles D. Brown, Fritz Feld, Arthur Q. Bryan, Virginia Sale, Ruth Gillette, Milton Kibbee, Mary Field, Minerva Urecal, Dave Willock, Fay McKenzie, Marjorie "Babe" Kane, Edgar Kennedy. **L:** 70 minutes **P:** Universal *(Paper hanger)*

**Laugh It Off** (feature) (12/1/39) **D:** Albert S. Rogell **C:** Johnny Downs, Constance Moore, Cecil Cunningham, Hedda Hopper, Janet Beecher, Marjorie Rambeau, Tom Dugan, William Demarest, Chester Clute, Horace MacMahon, Paula Stone, Jack Norton, Edgar Kennedy. **L:** 64 minutes **P:** Universal *(Judge McGuinnis)*

**Kennedy the Great** (12/8/39) **D:** Charles E. Roberts **C:** Edgar Kennedy, Vivien Oakland. Billy Franey, Robert Graves, Barbara Jo Allen [Vera Vague], Keith Kenneth. **L:** 2-reels **P:** RKO *(Average Man series)*

**Start the Music** (1939) **D:** Jean Yarbrough **C:** Edgar Kennedy, Billy Franey. **L:** 2-reels **P:** Jam Handy **Note:** "Story about a Standard Oil Service station owner and his cost-cutting measures that are not meeting company approval. The stingy owner is worried about his station and what a station!" This obscure industrial film also featured William Franey as Elmer's long lost uncle. *(Elmer, the station owner)*

# 1940

**Slightly at Sea** (2/9/40) **D:** Harry D'Arcy **C:** Edgar Kennedy, Vivien Oakland, Billy Franey, Jack Rice, Robert Graves, Charlie Hall, Tiny Sandford. **L:** 2-reels **P:** RKO. *(Average Man series)*

**Mutiny in the County** (5/3/40) **D:** Harry D'Arcy **C:** Edgar Kennedy, Vivien Oakland, Billy Franey, James Morton, Fred Kelsey **L:** 2-reels **P:** RKO *(Average Man series)*

**Sandy Is a Lady** (feature) (5/21/40) **D:** Charles Lamont. **C:** Baby Sandy, Nan Grey, Eugene Pallette, Tom Brown, Mischa Auer, Billy Gilbert, Fritz Feld, Anne Gwynne, Richard Lane, Charles Wilson, Edgar Kennedy. **L:** 62 minutes **P:** Universal. *(Officer Rafferty)*

**Margie** (feature) (9/7/40) **D:** Otis Garrett/Paul Gerard Smith. **C:** Tom Brown, Nan Grey, Mischa Auer, Allen Jenkins, Joy Hodges, Wally Vernon, Eddie Quillan, Horace MacMahon, Frank Faylen, Andy Devine, Edgar Kennedy. **L:** 59 minutes **P:** Universal *(Chauncey)*

**Who Killed Aunt Maggie?** (feature) (11/1/40)  **D:** Arthur Lubin **C:** John Hubbard, Wendy Barrie, Elizabeth Patterson, Onslow Stevens, Joyce Compton, Walter Abel, Mona Barrie, Willie Best, Milton Parsons, Tom Dugan. Edgar Kennedy. **L:** 70 minutes **P:** Republic *(Sheriff Gregory)*

**Li'l Abner** (feature) (11/1/40)  **D:** Albert S. Rogell **C:** Granville Owen, Martha O'Driscoll, Mona Ray, Johnnie Morris, Buster Keaton, Billie Seward, Kay Sutton, Maude Eburne, Bud Jamison, Dick Elliott, Johnny Arthur, Walter Catlett, Lucien Littlefield, Chester Conklin, Mickey Daniels, Doodles Weaver, Edgar Kennedy. **L:** 73 minutes **P:** Vogue/RKO **Note:** Based on Al Capp's popular comic strip characters. Milton Berle co-wrote the title song. *(Cornelius Cornpone)*

**Sandy Gets Her Man** (feature) (11/8/40) **D:** Otis Garrett/Paul Gerard Smith. **C:** Baby Sandy, Paul Smith, Stuart Erwin, Una Merkel, William Frawley, Edward Brophy, Jack Carson, Wally Vernon, Bert Roach, Edgar Kennedy. **L:** 74 minutes **P:** Universal **Note:** William Frawley plays the police chief. *(Fire Chief Galvin).*

**Dr. Christian Meets the Women** (8/5/40)  **D:** William McGann **C:** Jean Hersholt, Dorothy Lovett, Rod LaRocque, Frank Albertson, Marilyn Merrick [Lynn Merrick], Maude Eburne, Veda Ann Borg,, Heinie Conklin, Phyllis Kennedy, Edgar Kennedy. **L:** 65 minutes RKO **Note:** Edgar as the local grocery store owner. *(Dr. Christian* series) *(George Browning)*

**Quarterback, The** (feature) (1940) **D:** H. Bruce Humberstone **C:** Wayne Morris, Virginia Dale, Lillian Cornell, Alan Mowbray, Jerome Cowan, Rod Cameron, William Frawley, Edgar Kennedy. **L:** 74 minutes **P:** Paramount *(Pops)*

**Remedy for Riches** (feature) (1940) **D:** Erle C. Kenton **C:** Jean Hersholt, Dorothy Lovett, Jed Prouty, Walter Catlett, Robert Baldwin, Maude Eburne, Margaret McWade, Warren Hull, Renie Riano, Edgar Kennedy. **L:** 60 minutes **P:** RKO *(Dr. Christian* series) *(George Browning, the shopkeeper)*

**'Taint Legal** (5/25/40) **D:** Harry D'Arcy **C:** Edgar Kennedy, Vivien Oakland, Billy Franey, Arthur O'Connell, Robert Graves. **L:** 2-reels **P:** RKO *(Average Man series)*

**Sunk by the Census** (9/6/40) **D:** Harry D'Arcy **C:** Edgar Kennedy, Vivien Oakland, Billy Franey, Anita Garvin, Jody Gilbert, Clara Blore. **L:** 2-reels **P:** RKO *(Average Man series) (Census taker)*

**Trailer Tragedy** (10/18/40) **D:** Harry D'Arcy **C:** Edgar Kennedy, Vivien Oakland, Billy Franey, Tiny Sandford, Charlie Hall, Tom Dempsey. **L:** 2-reels **P:** RKO *(Average Man series)*

**Drafted in the Depot** (12/20/40) **D:** Lloyd French **C:** Edgar Kennedy, Vivien Oakland, Billy Franey, Phil Arnold, Ralph Dunn, Frank O'Connor, Warren Jackson. **L:** 2-reels **P:** RKO *(Average Man* series)

# 1941

**Bride Wore Crutches, The (feature)** (1941)  **D:** Shepard Traube **C:** Lynne Roberts, Ted [Michael] North, Robert Armstrong, Lionel Stander, Richard Lane, Grant Mitchell, Edmund McDonald, Horace MacMahon, Anthony Caruso, Edgar Kennedy **L:** 54 minutes **P:** 20th Century-Fox. *(Capt. McGuire)*

**Mad About Moonshine** (2/21/41) **D:** Harry D'Arcy **C:** Edgar Kennedy, Vivien Oakland, Billy Franey, Fran O'Connor, Kay Vallon. **L:** 2-reels **P:** RKO **Note:** Pop thinks he's inherited a luxurious Sothern manor, but it's just a dust-laden dump. *(Average Man series)* *(Plantation owner)*

**It Happened All Night** (4/4/41) **D:** Charles E. Roberts, **C:** Edgar Kennedy, Vivien Oakland, Billy Franey, Ernie Adams, Donald Kerr, Ed Foster. **L:** 2-reels **P:** RKO **Note:** Billy Franey died after making this short; it was released posthumously. *(Average Man series)* *(Night watchman)*

**Too Many Blondes (feature)** (5/23/41) **D:** Thornton Freeland **C:** Rudy Vallee, Helen Parrish, Lon Chaney, Jr., Shemp Howard, Eddie Quillan, Iris Adrian, Edgar Kennedy. **L:** 60 minutes **P:** Universal *(Hotel Manager)*

**Apple in His Eye, An** (6/6/41) **D:** Harry D'Arcy **C:** Edgar Kennedy, Vivien Oakland, Charlie Hall, Harry Harvey. **L:** 2-reels **P:** RKO *(Average Man series)*

**Blondie in Society (feature)** (7/17/41) **D:** Frank R. Strayer **C:** Penny Singleton, Arthur Lake, Larry Simms, Jonathan Hale, Danny Mummert, William Frawley, Chick Chandler, Irving Bacon, Bill Goodwin, Edgar Kennedy. **L:** 77 minutes. **P:** Columbia **Note:** A.K.A.: *Henpecked. (Blondie* series*) (Doctor)*

**Westward Ho-Hum** (9/15/41) **D:** Clem Beauchamp **C:** Edgar Kennedy, Sally Payne, Jack Rice, Glenn Strange, Ernie Adams, Ethan Laidlaw. **L:** 2-reels **P:** RKO **Note:** The family has bought a hotel in a ghost town. *(Average Man series)*

**I'll Fix That** (10/7/41) **D:** Charles E. Roberts **C:** Edgar Kennedy, Sally Payne, Jack Rice, John Dilson, Harry Harvey, Ken Christy, Charlie Hall, Curly Wright, Charlie Delaney. *(Average Man series)* **L:** 2-reels **P:** RKO *(Water heater installer)*

**Public Enemies (feature)** (10/30/41) **D:** Albert S. Rogell **C:** Phillip Terry, Wendy Barrie, William Frawley, Marc Lawrence, Nana Bryant, Willie Fung, Paul Fix, Russell Hicks, Tim Ryan, Duke York, Peter Leeds, Guy Usher, Sammy McKim, Arthur Housman, Edgar Kennedy **L:** 66 minutes **P:** Republic *(Biff)*

**Quiet Fourth, A** (12/19/41) **D:** Harry D'Arcy **C:** Edgar Kennedy, Sally Payne, Jack Rice, Pat Taylor, Frankie Ward, Charlie Hall. **L:** 2-reels **P:** RKO *(Average Man series)*

# *1942*

**Pardon My Stripes** (feature) (1/26/42)  **D:** John H. Auer  **C:** Bill Henry, Shelia Ryan, Harold Huber, Paul Hurst, Cliff Nazarro, Tom Kennedy, Edwin Stanley, Dorothy Granger, George McKay, Edgar Kennedy.  **L:** 64 minutes  **P:** Republic  *(Warden Bingham)*

**Screen Snapshots, Series 21, #6** (2/12/42)  **L:** 1-reel  **P:** Columbia  **Note:** Edgar as part of an all-star cast as one of the Comedians vs. The Leading Men baseball game.

**Inferior Decorator** (4/13/42)  **D:** Clem Beauchamp  **C:** Edgar Kennedy, Sally Payne, Dot Farley, Jack Rice, Eddie Kane, Keith Hitchcock, Isabel LeMal.  **L:** 2-reels  **P:** RKO *(Average Man series)*

**In Old California** (feature) (5/31/42)  **D:** William McGann  **C:** John Wayne, Edgar Kennedy, Binnie Barnes, Albert Dekker, Helen Parrish, Patsy Kelly, Dick Purcell, Harry Shannon.  **L:** 88 minutes  **P:** Republic  *(Kegs McKeever, Wayne's sidekick)*

**There's One Born Every Minute** (feature) (6/26/42) **D** Harold Young **C:** Hugh Herbert, Peggy Moran, Tom Brown, Guy Kibbee, Catherine Doucet, Scott Jordan, Gus Schilling, Elizabeth Taylor, Charles Halton, Renie Riano, Carl "Alfalfa" Switzer, Edgar Kennedy. **L:** 59 minutes  **P:** Universal  **Note:** Ten-year-old Elizabeth Taylor's film debut. *(Moe Carson)*

**Snuffy Smith, Yard Bird** (feature) (6/26/42)  **D:** Edward F. Cline  **C:** Bud Duncan, Sarah Padden, Doris Linden, Andria Palmer, J.Farrell MacDonald, Jimmie Dodd, Edgar Kennedy.  **L:** 67 min. **P:** Monogram **Note:** G.B.: *Snuffy Smith.* A.K.A.: *Private Snuffy Smith. (Sgt. Smith)*

**Hillbilly Blitzkrieg** (feature) (8/14/42)  **D:** Roy Mack **C:** Bud Duncan, Edgar Kennedy, Cliff Naxarro, Doris Linden, Lucien Littlefield, Alan Baldwin, Nicolle Andre, Jimmie Dodd.  **L:** 63 minutes  **P:** Monogram  **Note:** Sequel to *Snuffy Smith, Yard Bird.* This film concludes with Duncan and Kennedy riding on a bomb, 23 years before Slim Pickens did the same in *Dr. Strangelove.* A.K.A.: *Enemy Round-up. (Sgt. Gatling)*

**Heart Burn** (1942)  **D:** Harry D'Arcy  **C:** Edgar Kennedy, Sally Payne, Jack Rice, Dot Farley, Archie Twitchell, Darryl Hickman, Roy Butler.  **L:** 2-reels  **P:** RKO *(Average Man series)*

**Cooks and Crooks** (6/5/42)  **D:** Henry James  **C:** Edgar Kennedy, Sally Payne, Dot Farley, Jack Rice, Ann Summers, Marten Lamont, John McGuire, Lew Kelly, Lillian Randolph.**L:** 2-reels **P:** RKO **Note:** This one's bloody awful. *(Average Man series)* *(Amateur Detective)*

**Two for the Money** (8/14/42)  **D:** Lloyd French  **C:** Edgar Kennedy, Florence Lake, Dot Farley, Jack Rice, Bryant Washburn, Mary Halsey, Gertrude Short, Johnny Berkes, Charlie Hall.  **L:** 2-reels  **P:** RKO *(Average Man series)*

**Rough on Rents** (10/30/42) **D:** Ben Holmes **C:** Edgar Kennedy, Florence Lake, Dot Farley, Jack Rice, Bud Jamison, Dorothy Granger, Martin Lamont, Charlie Hall, Gertrude Astor, Max Wagner, Kernan Cripps. **L:** 2-reels **P:** RKO **Note:** One of the best in the series. The "Little Menace" in a zoot suit. (*Average Man series*)

**Duck Soup** (12/18/42) **D:** Ben Holmes **C:** Edgar Kennedy, Florence Lake, Dot Farley, Jack Rice **L:** 2-reels. RKO (*Average Man series*)

# 1943

**Cosmo Jones - Crime Smasher (feature)** (1/29/43) **D:** James Tinling **C:** Frank Graham, Gale Storm, Richard Cromwell, Mantan Moreland, Gwen Kenyon, Herbert Rawlinson, Tristram Coffin, Vince Barnett, Emmett Vogan, Maxine Leslie, Mauritz Hugo, Edgar Kennedy. **L:** 62 minutes **P:** Monogram *(Cop)*

**Hold Your Temper** (2/5/43) **D:** Lloyd French **C:** Edgar Kennedy, Irene Ryan, Dot Farley, Jack Rice **L:** 2-reels **P:** RKO(*Average Man series*)

**Falcon Strikes Back, The (feature)** (3/24/43) **D:** Edward Dmytryk **C:** Tom Conway, Harriet Hilliard, Jane Randolph, Cliff Edwards, Rita Corday, Wynne Gibson, Edgar Kennedy **L:** 66 minutes **P:** RKO **Note:** Off camera death scene. (*The Falcon* series) *(Smiley Dugan)*

**Indian Signs** (3/26/43) **D:** Charles E. Roberts **C:** Edgar Kennedy, Irene Ryan, Dot Farley, Jack Rice. **L:** 2-reels **P:** RKO **Note:** Irene Ryan played the wife in this one. She became better known as "Granny" in the *Beverly Hillbillies* television show twenty years later. (*Average Man series*)

**Air Raid Wardens (feature)** (4/30/43) **D:** Edward Sedgwick **C:** Stan Laurel, Oliver Hardy, Edgar Kennedy, Jacqueline White, Horace [Stephen] McNally, Donald Meek **L:** 67 minutes **P:** MGM *(Joe Bledsoe)*

**Hot Foot** (5/14/43) **D:** Ben Holes **C:** Edgar Kennedy, Pauline Drake, Dot Farley, Jack Rice, Bud Jamison, Jimmy Farley. **L:** 2-reels **P:** RKO (*Average Man Series*)

**Hitler's Madman (feature)** (6/10/43) **D:** Douglas Sirk **C:** Patricia Morison, John Carradine, Alan Curtis, Ralph Morgan, Howard Freeman, Ludwig Stossel, Al Shean, Ava Gardner, Edgar Kennedy. **L:** 84 minutes **P:** MGM/PRC **Note:** Edgar plays a sly hero and is executed at the grisly ending. *(Nepomuk, the hermit)*

**Girl from Monterey, The (feature)** (10/4/43) **D:** Wallace Fox **C:** Armida, Jack LaRue, Terry Frost, Anthony Caruso, Veda Ann Borg, Charles Williams, Edgar Kennedy. **L:** 62 minutes **P:** PRC **Note:** Edgar is the fight promoter *(Doc Hogan)*

**Crazy House (feature)** (10/4/43) **D:** Edward F. Cline **C:** Ole Olsen, Chic Johnson, Martha O'Driscoll, Patric Knowles, Cass Daley, Percy Kilbride, Leighton Noble, Thomas Gomez,

Ray Walker, Robert Emmett Keane, Franklin Pangborn, Chester Clute, with Alan Curtis, Allan Jones, Billy Gilbert, Richard Lane, Hans Conried, Shemp Howard, Leo Carrillo, Lon Chaney, Jr., Andy Devine, Robert Paige, the Glenn Miller Singers with Marion Hutton, Edgar Kennedy, Count Basie and his Orchestra, the Delta Rhythm Boys, Basil Rathbone and Nigel Bruce as Sherlock Holmes and Dr. Watson. **L:** 80 minutes **P:** Universal *(Judge)*

**Not on My Account** (9/17/43) **D:** Charles E. Roberts **C:** Edgar Kennedy, Pauline Drake, Dot Farley, Jack Rice **L:** 2-reels **P:** RKO *(Average Man series)*

**Unlucky Dog** (11/12/43) **D:** Ben Holmes **C:** Edgar Kennedy, Pauline Drake, Dot Farley, Jack Rice, Harrison Green, Mary Jane Halsey, Eddie Borden. **L:** 2-reels **P:** RKO *(Average Man series)*

# 1944

**Prunes and Politics** (1/7/44) **D:** Ben Holmes **C:** Edgar Kennedy, Pauline Drake, Dot Farley, Jack Rice, Hugh Beaumont, Harrison Green, Barbara Hale, Russell Wade. **L:** 2-reels **P:** RKO  *Note:* Edgar runs for office. TV's *Leave it to Beaver* dad, Beaumont, plays a reporter. *(Average Man series)*

**Love Your Landlord** (3/3/44) **D:** Charles E. Roberts **C:** Edgar Kennedy, Florence Lake, Claire Carleton, Tom Kennedy, Russell Hopton, Lloyd Ingraham, Harry Harvey, Harry Tyler, Emory Parnell, Bud Jamison. **L:** 2-reels **P:** RKO *(Average Man series)*

**Radio Rampage** (3/28/44) **D:** Charles E. Roberts **C:** Edgar Kennedy, Florence Lake, Dot Farley, Jack Rice, Tom Kennedy, Russell Hopton, Charlie Hall, Mary Jane Halsey, Emory Parnell, Lee Trent. **L:** 2-reels **P:** RKO *(Average Man series)*

**Great Alaskan Mystery, The** (serial) (4/25/44) **D:** Ray Taylor/Lewis D. Collins. **C:** Milburn Stone, Marjorie Weaver, Samuel S. Hinds, Martin Kosleck, Ralph Morgan, Fuzzy Knight, Harry Cording, Anthony Warde, Edgar Kennedy. **L:** Chapter 1 is 3-reels, subsequent chapters, 2-reels. **P:** Universal **Note:** A group of people go to Alaska in search of ore to be used with a new defensive weapon. Edgar gets the girl at the end. Serial in 13 chapters. *(Bosun)*

**It Happened Tomorrow** (feature) (5/28/44) **D:** Rene Clair **C:** Dick Powell, Linda Darnell, Jack Oakie, Edward Brophy, George Cleveland, Sig Rumann, Edgar Kennedy. **L:** 84 minutes **P:** United Artists *(Inspector Mulrooney)*

**Kitchen Cynic, The** (6/25/44) **D:** Hal Yates **C:** Edgar Kennedy, Florence Lake, Jack Rice, Sarah Edwards, Emory Parnell, Teddy Infuhr, Bert Moorehouse. **L:** 2-reels **P:** RKO *(Average Man series)*

**Feather Your Nest** (10/24/44) **D:** Hal Yates **C:** Edgar Kennedy, Florence Lake, Dot Farley, Jack Rice, Emory Parnell, Maxine Semon, Lee Trent, Bryant Washburn. **L:** 2-reels **P:** RKO *(Average Man series)*

# 1945

**Alibi Baby** (l/5/45) **D:** Hal Yates **C:** Edgar Kennedy, Florence Lake, Elaine Riley, Emory Parnell, Minerva Urecal, Jim Jordan, Jr., Sammy Blum, Baby Dickie. **L:** 2-reels **P:** RKO *(Average Man series)*

**Sleepless Tuesday** (2/23/45) **D:** Hal Yates **C:** Edgar Kennedy, Florence Lake, Dot Farley, Jack Rice, Edmund Glover, Carl Kent, Sam Blum. **L:** 2-reels **P:** RKO *(Average Man series)*

**Anchors Aweigh (feature)** (7/14/45) **D:** George Sidney **C:** Frank Sinatra, Kathryn Grayson, Gene Kelly, Dean Stockwell, Jose Iturbi, Pamela Britton, Rags Ragland, Henry O'Neill, Billy Gilbert, Carlos Ramirez, Grady Sutton, Sharon McManus, Edgar Kennedy **L:** 140 minutes **P:** MGM *(Police Captain)*

**Captain Tugboat Annie (feature)** (7/14/45) **D:** Phil Rosen **C:** Jane Darwell, Charles Gordon, Mantan Moreland, Pamela Blake, Hardie Albright, H.B. Warner, Jack Norton, Barton Yarborough, Fritz Feld, Joe Crehan, Robert Elliott, Edgar Kennedy. **L:** 70 minutes **P:** Republic **Note:** The female title role was originally supposed to be played by Louise Fazenda. *(Captain Bullwinkle)*

**What, No Cigarettes?** (7/13/45) **D:** Hal Yates **C:** Edgar Kennedy, Florence Lake, Dot Farley, Jack Rice, Jimmy Conlin, Tom Noonan, Jason Robards, Emory Parnell, Paul Brooks, Gwen Crawford, Robert Anderson, Sam Blum, George Holmes. **L:** 2-reels **P:** RKO *(Average Man series)*

**It's Your Move** (8/10/45) **D:** Hal Yates **C:** Edgar Kennedy, Florence Lake, Dot Farley, Jack Rice, Maxine Semon, Larry Wheat, Gwen Crawford, Edmund Glover, Sam Blum. **L:** 2-reels **P:** RKO **Note:** This is the one where Edgar and brother carry a washing machine up a long flight of stairs. *(Average Man series)*

**You Drive Me Crazy** (9/7/45) **D:** Hal Yates **C:** Edgar Kennedy, Florence Lake, Jack Rice, Emory Parnell, Eddie Kane, Dick Elliott, Betty Gillette, Jack Wheat. **L:** 2-reels **P:** RKO *(Average Man* series)

**Big Beef, The** (10/l/45) **D:** Charles E. Roberts **C:** Edgar Kennedy, Florence Lake, Dot Farley, Jack Rice, Emory Parnell, Harry Harvey, Eddie Kane, Tom Noonan, Bob Manning, Paul Brooks. **L:** 2-reels **P:** RKO *(Average Man series)*

**Mother-in-Law's Day** (12/745) **D:** Hal Yates **C:** Edgar Kennedy, Florence Lake, Jack Rice, Dot Farley, Dick Elliott, Sarah Edwards, Bess Flowers. **L:** 2-reels **P:** RKO *(Average Man series)*

# 1946

**Trouble or Nothing** (1/25/46) **D:** Hal Yates **C:** Edgar Kennedy, Florence Lake, Dot Farley, Jack Rice, Dick Elliott, Harry Woods, Joe Devlin, Harry Harvey. **L:** 2-reels **P:** RKO *(Average Man series)*

**Wall Street Blues** (7/12/46) **D:** Hal Yates **C:** Edgar Kennedy, Florence Lake, Dot Farley, Jack Rice, Robert Smith, Charlie Hall, Ralph Dunn, Harry Strang. **L:** 2-reels **P:** RKO (*Average Man series*)

**Motor Maniacs** (7/26/46) **D:** Wallace Grissell **C:** Edgar Kennedy, Florence Lake, Dot Farley, Jack Rice, Tom Kennedy, Robert Smith. **L:** 2-reels **P:** RKO (*Average Man series*)

**Noisy Neighbors** (9/20/46) **D:** Hal Yates **C:** Edgar Kennedy, Florence Lake, Dot Farley, Jack Rice, Dick Wessel, Harry Harvey. **L:** 2-reels **P:** RKO (*Average Man series*)

**I'll Build It Myself** (10/18/46) **D:** Hal Yates **C:** Edgar Kennedy, Florence Lake, Dot Farley, Jack Rice, Jason Robards, Harry Strang, Robert Bray. **L:** 2-reels **P:** RKO (*Average Man series*)

**Social Terrors** (12/18/46) **D:** Charles E. Roberts **C:** Edgar Kennedy, Florence Lake, Jack Rice, Dot Farley, Chester Clute, Phyllis Kennedy, Paul Maxey, Vivien Oakland. **L:** 2-reels **P:** RKO (*Average Man series*)

# 1947

**Do Or Diet** (2/10/47) **D:** Hal Yates **C:** Edgar Kennedy, Florence Lake, Dot Farley, Jack Rice, Dick Wessel, Cy Ring, Bryant Washburn, Jason Robards. **L:** 2-reels **P:** RKO (*Average Man series*) (**Factory worker**)

**Sin of Harold Diddlebock, The (feature)** (4/4/47) **D:** Preston Sturges **C:** Harold Lloyd, Frances Ramsden, Jimmy Conlin, Raymond Walburn, Arline Judge, Lionel Stander, Rudy Vallee, Edgar Kennedy. **L:** 89 minutes **P:** RKO/Howard Hughes **Note:** Reissued as *Mad Wednesday*. *Jake the Bartender*)

**Heading for Trouble** (6/20/47) **D:** Hal Yates **C:** Edgar Kennedy, Florence Lake, Dot Farley, Jack Rice, Lee Frederick, Robert Bray. **L:** 2-reels **P:** RKO (*Average Man series*)

**Host to a Ghost** (7/18/47) **D:** Hal Yates **C:** Edgar Kennedy, Florence Lake, Jack Rice, Dot Farley, Chester Clute, Ida Moore. **L:** 2-reels **P:** RKO (*Average Man series*)

**Television Turmoil** (8/15/47) **D:** Hal Yates **C:** Edgar Kennedy, Florence Lake, Dot Farley, Jack Rice, Eddie Dunn, Dick Elliott. **L:** 2-reels **P:** RKO (*Average Man series*)

**Heaven Only Knows (feature)** (9/12/47) **D:** Albert S. Rogell **C:** Robert Cummings, Brian Donlevy, Marjorie Reynolds, Bill Goodwin, Stuart Erwin, Edgar Kennedy. **P:** United Artists **Note:** Edgar in a dramatic death scene. (*Jud*)

**Mind Over Mouse** (11/21/47) **D:** Hal Yates **C:** Edgar Kennedy, Florence Lake, Dot Farley, Jack Rice, Max the Mouse. **L:** 2-reels **P:** RKO (*Average Man series*)

# 1948

**Brother Knows Best** (1/2/48) **D:** Hal Yates **C:** Edgar Kennedy, Florence Lake, Dot Farley, Jack Rice, Paul Maxey, Harry Strang. **L:** 2-reels **P:** RKO *(Average Man series)*

**No More Relatives** (2/6/48) **D:** Hal Yates **C:** Edgar Kennedy, Florence Lake, Dot Farley, Jack Rice, Walter Long. **L:** 2-reels **P:** RKO *(Average Man series)*

**How to Clean House** (5/14/48) **D:** Charles E. Roberts **C:** Edgar Kennedy, Florence Lake, Jack Rice, Dot Farley, Iris Adrian, Harry Harvey, Anne O'Neal, Charlie Hall. **L:** 2-reels **P:** RKO *(Average Man series)*

**Dig That Gold** (6/25/48) **D:** Hal Yates **C:** Edgar Kennedy, Florence Lake, Jack Rice, Dick Wessel, Robert Bray. **L:** 2-reels **P:** RKO *(Average Man series)*

**Home Canning** (8/16/48) **D:** Hal Yates **C:** Edgar Kennedy, Florence Lake, Jack Rice, Dot Farley, Vivien Oakland, Charlie Hall. **L:** 2-reels **P:** RKO *(Average Man series)*

**Contest Crazy** (10/l/148) **D:** Hal Yates **C:** Edgar Kennedy, Florence Lake, Jack Rice, Dot Farley, Paul Maxey. **L:** 2-reels **P:** RKO **Note:** Final film in *Average Man series,* Edgar can still burn. *(Ruff-Ruff Dog Food Company Employee)*

**Unfaithfully Yours (feature)** (12/10/48) **D:** Preston Sturges **C:** Rex Harrison, Linda Darnell, Kurt Kreuger, Barbara Lawrence, Rudy Vallee, Robert Greig, Lionel Stander, Julius Tannen, Alan Bridge, Edgar Kennedy **L:** 105 minutes **P:** 20th Century-Fox *(Detective Sweeney)*

# 1949

**My Dream Is Yours (feature)** (4/15/49) **D:** Michael Curtiz **C:** Doris Day, Jack Carson, Eve Arden, Lee Bowman, Adolphe Menjou, Edgar Kennedy. **L:** 101 minutes **P:** Warner Bros. *(As Doris Day's Uncle Charlie)*

**NOTE:** For plot synopses on the above films, the author recommends the following books:

*The Great Movie Shorts* by Leonard Maltin
*Leonard Maltin's Movie & Video Guide*
*Smile When the Raindrops Fall* by Brian Anthony and Andy Edmonds
*Laurel and Hardy - The Magic Behind the Movies* by Randy Skretvedt
*The Little Rascals: The Life and Times of Our Gang* by Leonard Maltin and Richard Bann

*Edgar was in the following foreign titles that should be considered separate productions:*

**Ladrones** (Spanish)  *Night Owls*
**I Ladroni** (Italian) *Night Owls*
**El Jugador de Golf** (Spanish)  *All Teed Up*
**Le Jouer de Golf**  (French)  *All Teed Up* **Note:  Believed to be dubbed over**
**Los Pequenos Papas** (Spanish) *The First Seven Years*
**Los Fantasmas**  (Spanish) *When the Wind Blows*
**Bon Voyage** (Spanish)
**Huye, Faldas!** (Spanish) *Girl Shock*
**Gare La Bombe!** (French) *Looser Than Loose*

Author Richard Braff (*The Braff Silent Film Working Papers*) indicated that the below Keystone titles included Edgar Kennedy.  There are no other existing scripts, reviews, photos or films available to confirm that fact.

**Hoffmeyer's Legacy** * (12/23/12  **D:** Mack Sennett **C:** Ford Sterling, Fred Mace, Edgar Kennedy, Alice Davenport, Mack Sennett.  **L:** 1-reel  **P:** Keystone/Mutual.

**Heinze's Resurrection** * (2/13/13)  **D:** Mack Sennett **C:** Mabel Normand, Ford Sterling, Fred Mace, Nick Cogley, Betty Schade, Edgar Kennedy **L:** 1-reel **P:** Keystone/Mutual.

**Mabel's Heroes** *  (2/17/13)   **D:** George Nichols **C:** Mabel Normand, Mack Sennett, Ford Sterling, Fred Mace, Hank Mann, Nick Cogley, Edgar Kennedy **L:**  1-reel **P:** Keystone/Mutual.

**Landlord's Troubles, A** * (2/20/13)  **D:** George O. Nicholls **C:**  Fred Mace, Edgar Kennedy, Al St. John, Henry Lehrman, Mack Sennett, Ford Sterling. **L:** 1/2-reel **P:** Keystone/Mutual.

# FILM CLIPS OF EDGAR KENNEDY ARE IN THE FOLLOWING:

## 1933
**Kickin' the Can Around**  (Clark and McCullough short*).*

## 1948
**Variety Time  (feature) D:** Hal Yates. **C:** Jack Parr (Host), Hans Conried, Leon Errol, Jack Rice, Dot Farley, Florence Lake, Jason Robards, Pat Rooney, Dorothy Granger, Jack Norton, Minerva Urecal. **Note:**  Includes the entire Edgar Kennedy short *I'll Build It Myself.*

# 1958

**Golden Age of Comedy, The**    Compilation by Robert Youngston  **Note:**  Features Chaplin, Laurel & Hardy, Keystone Kops, et al.

# 1960

**When Comedy Was King**    Compilation by Robert Youngston.  **Note:**  Includes the second reel of *A Pair of Tights,* featuring the famous ice-cream dropping scene.

# 1963

**Sound of Laughter, The**    Compilation (hosted by Ed Wynn)  **Note:**  *Stock footage of Educational Pictures comedies.*

# 1965

**Laurel and Hardy's Laughing 20's**  *Compilation by Robert Youngston.*  **Note:**  Stan Laurel, Oliver Hardy, Charley Chase, James Finlayson, Anita Garvin.

# 1968

**Further Perils of Laurel and Hardy, The**    Compilation  by Robert Youngston.  **Note:**  Laurel and Hardy, Charley Chase, Max Davidson, James Finlayson.

# 1970

**Four Clowns, The**    Compilation by Robert Youngston.  **Note:**  Edgar in a Charley Chase segment, *Limousine Love.*

# 1989

**Cinema Paradiso (feature)** *(Italian) The Knockout*

## FILMS DIRECTED BY EDGAR KENNEDY:

# 1922

**His Wife's Son**  (4/23/22)  **D:** Edgar Kennedy  **L:** 2-reels  **P:** Fox-Sunshine

**Safe in the Safe** (6/18/22)  **D:** Edgar Kennedy  **L:** 2-reels  **P:** Fox-Sunshine

**Step Lively Please** (10/15/22)  **D:** Edgar Kennedy  **L:** 2-reels  **P:** Fox-Sunshine

**Fresh Heir, The** (12/10/22)  **D:** Edgar Kennedy  **L:** 2-reels  **P:** Fox-Sunshine

# 1924

**Love's Sweet Piffle** (11/16/24) **D**: Edgar Kennedy. **C**: Ralph Graves, Vernon Dent, Billy Bevan **L**: 2-reels **P**: Sennett/Pathe

**Three Foolish Weeks** (9/14/24) **D**: Edgar Kennedy. **C**: Ben Turpin, Madeline Hurlock, Billy Bevan, William Lowery, Judy King **L**: 2-reels **P**: Sennett/Pathe

**Reel Virginian, The** (10/26/24) **D**: Edgar Kennedy/Reggie Morris. **W**: Arthur Ripley/Frank Capra. **C**: Ben Turpin, Alice Day. Christian J. Frank, Coy Watson **L**: 2-reels **P**: Sennett/Pathe

# 1925

**Cupid's Boots** (7/26/25) **D**: Edgar Kennedy **C**: Ralph Graves, Thelma Hill, Christian J. Frank, Andy Clyde **L**: 2-reels **P**: Sennett/Pathe

**Marriage Circus, The** (4/11/25) **D**: Edgar Kennedy/Reggie Morris. **W**: Frank Capra/Vernon Smith. **C**: Ben Turpin, Madeline Hurlock, Sunshine Hart, Louise Carver, William C. Lawrence, Edgar Kennedy **L**: 2-reels **P**: Keystone/Pathe

# 1926

**For Cryin' Out Loud!** (11/1/26) **D**: Edgar Kennedy **C**: Neely Edwards **L**: 2-reels **P**: Universal Bluebird

**Hot Dog** (2/8/26) **D**: Edgar Kennedy **C**: Arthur Lake **L**: 2-reels **P**: Universal Bluebird

**Olga's Boatman** (10/11/26) **D**: Edgar Kennedy **C**: Neely Edwards **L**: 2-reels **P**: Universal Bluebird

**Prep School** (1/18/26) **D**: Edgar Kennedy **C**: Arthur Lake **L**: 2-reels **P**: Universal Bluebird

**Separated Sweethearts** (5/24/26) **D**: Edgar Kennedy **C**: Arthur Lake **L**: 2-reels **P**: Universal Bluebird

**Couple of Skates, A** (4/28/26) **D**: Edgar Kennedy **C**: Neely Edwards **L**: 2-reels **P**: Universal Bluebird

**Two Dollars Please** (9/20/26) **D**: Edgar Kennedy **C**: Neely Edwards, Bert Roach **L**: 2-reels **P**: Universal Bluebird

# 1927

**Do or Diet** (6/13/26) **D**: Edgar Kennedy **C**: Charles Puffy, Elsie Tarron **L**: 2-reels **P**: Universal

# 1928

**You're Darn Tootin'**  **D:**  E. Livingston Kennedy [Edgar Kennedy] **C:** Stan Laurel, Oliver Hardy, Charlie Hall, William Irving, Ham Kinsey, Christian J. Frank  **L:** 2-reels  **P:** Roach/MGM

**From Soup to Nuts**  **D:**  E. Livingston Kennedy [Edgar Kennedy] **C:** Stan Laurel, Oliver Hardy, Anita Garvin, Tiny Sandford **L:** 2-reels  **P:** Roach/MGM

# 1930

**All Teed Up**  (4/19/30) **D:**  Edgar Kennedy **C:** Charley Chase, Thelma Todd, Edgar Kennedy, Tenen Holtz, Dell Henderson **L:** 2-reels  **P:** Roach/MGM

**Bigger and Better** (10/25/30  **D:**  Edgar Kennedy **C:** Mickey Daniels, Grady Sutton, David Sharpe, Mary Kornman, Dorothy Granger, Gertie Messinger, Dell Henderson **L:** 2-reels  **P:** Roach/MGM (*The Boy Friends* series)

# 1932

**Blondes by Proxy** (4/11/32) **D:** Edgar Kennedy **C:** Louis John Bartels **L:** 2-reels **P:** RKO (*Traveling Man* series)

# Bibliography

Anthony, Brian & Edmonds Andy. *Smile When the Raindrops Fall*, Scarecrow Press, 1998

Blake, Michael F. *Lon Chaney—The Man Behind the Thousand Faces*, The Vestal Press, 1993

Braff, Richard E. *The Universal Silents*, McFarland & Co., 1999

Braff, Richard E. *Braff Silent Short Film Working Papers, The*, McFarland & Co., 1998

Bronson, William. *Earth Shook, the Sky Burned, The*. Doubleday & Co. 1959

Brooks, Leo. *The Laurel & Hardy Stock Company*, Blotto Press. 1997

Bruskin, David N. *Behind the Three Stooges: The White Brothers*, A Directors Guild of America Publication. 1990, 1993

Cahn, William. *The Laugh Makers*, Bramhall House. 1951

Cannom, Robert C. *Van Dyke and the Mythical City Hollywood*, Murray & Gee, Inc. 1948

Capra, Frank. *The Name Above the Title*, Macmillian. 1971

Clark, Donald Thomas. *Monterey County Place Names*, Kestrel Press. 1991

D'Agostino, Annette M. *Filmmakers in The Moving Picture World*, McFarland & Co., 1997

Dempsey, Jack & Dempsey, Barbara Piattelli. *Dempsey*, Harper & Row, 1977

Edmonds, Andy. *Frame-Up*, Avon Books, 1992

Fernett, Gene. *American Film Studios*, McFarland & Co., 1988

Flam, Jerry. *Hometown San Francisco*, Scottwall Associates. 1994

Fowler, Gene. *Father Goose*. New York: Covici-Fried Publishers. 1934

Jewell, Richard B. & Vernon Harbin. *The RKO Story*

Gagey, Edmond M. *The San Francisco Stage; A History*

Hansen, Glays & Condon, Emmet. *Denial of Disaster*

Kerr, Walter. *The Silent Clowns*, Alfred A. Knopf.

Lahue, Kalton C. and Brewer, Terry. *Kops and Custards: The Legend of Keystone Films*. Norman, OK: University of Oklahoma Press, 1968

Lahue, Kalton C. *Motion Picture Pioneer: The Selig Polyscope Company*. A.S. Barnes & Co., Inc., 1973

Lahue, Kalton C. *World of Laughter: The Motion Picture Comedy Short 1910-1930*. Norman, OK: University of Oklahoma Press. 1972.

Lahue, Kalton C. and Gill, Sam. *Clown Princes and Court Jesters*. New York: A.S. Barnes & Co., 1970.

Lahue, Kalton C. *Mack Sennett's Keystone; The Man, the Myth and the Comedies*, South Brunswick & New York: A.S. Barnes & Co. 1971

Langman, Larry. *Encyclopedia of American Film Comedy*, Garland Publishing, Inc. 1987

London, Jack. *Stories of Boxing*, Wm. C. Brown Publishers 1992

Maltin, Leonard. *The Great Movie Comedians*. New York: Crown Publishers, 1978.

Maltin, Leonard. *The Great Movie Shorts*. Bonanza Books, 1972

Maltin, Leonard & Richard Bann. *The Little Rascals: The Life and Times of Our Gang*. Crown, 1992

Maltin, Leonard. *Film Fan Monthly*. (*Newsletter*) December 1967

Mitchell, Glenn. *A-Z of Silent Film Comedy*. BT Batsford ltd-London, 1998

McCabe, John. *The Comedy World of Stan Laurel.* Doubleday & Co., 1974

Miller. *American Silent Film Comedies: An Illustrated Encyclopedia*

Motion Picture Almanac 1936-1937

Neibaur, James L. *RKO Features*, McFarland & Co., 1994

Okuda, Ted. *The Monogram Checklist*, McFarland & Co., Inc., 1987

O'Brien. *This is San Francisco*

Sennett, Mack. *King of Comedy.* New York: Doubleday, 1954

Sherk, Warren M. *The Films of Mack Sennett.* Scarecrow Press, 1998

Shumate, Albert. *A Visit to Rincon Hill and South Park.* Windgate Press, 1988

Schickel, Richard. *D.W. Griffith; An American Life*, Limelight Editions, 1984

Skretvedt, Randy. *Laurel and Hardy: The Magic Behind the Movies.* Moonstone Press, 1987

Smith, Ron. *Comic Support*

Spehr, Paul C. with Lundquist, Gunnar. *American Film Personnel and Company Credits, 1908-1920*, McFarland & Co., Inc. 1996

Twomey, Alfred E & McClure, Arthur I. *The Versatiles*, South Brunswick and New York: A.S. Barnes & Co. 1969

Watson, Coy Jr. *The Keystone Kid*, Santa Monica Press, 2001

# Magazine and Newspaper References

**MAGAZINE REFERENCES:**

*Motion Picture Magazine*
June 1919

*Motion Picture Magazine*
Feb. 1921

*Moving Picture World*
Oct. 17, 1925

*Moving Picture World*
Aug. 27, 1927

*Motion Picture News*
6-29-29

*Motion Picture Herald*
Jan. 20, 1934

*Motion Picture Herald*
Jan. 22, 1938

*World Film News*
July 1938

*U.S. Camera*
Aug. 1935

*Motion Picture Magazine*
Aug. 1942

*Moving Picture Herald*
May 1944

*Golf World*
Jan. 1948

**NEWSPAPER REFERENCES:**

*Marin Journal, The*
April 15, 1905

*Marin Journal, The*
Feb. 1909

*San Francisco Chronicle*
April 24, 1912

*San Francisco Chronicle*
April 27, 1912

*San Francisco Call-Bulletin*
April 27, 1912

*Sacramento Bee*
May 20, 1912

*Sacramento Union*
May 21, 1912

*San Francisco Chronicle*
Aug. 9, 1912

*San Francisco Chronicle*
Aug. 10, 1912

*San Francisco Chronicle*
Aug. 11, 1912

*San Francisco Chronicle*
Aug. 31, 1912

*San Francisco Chronicle*
Jan. 25, 1913

*Taft Newspaper*
Feb. 7-9, 1913

*Grizzly Bear, The*
Sept. 1913

*Los Angeles Record, The*
Nov. 23, 1914

*Oakland Tribune, The*
April 12, 1915

*Oakland Tribune, The*
April 17, 1915

*Los Angeles Evening Express*
Oct. 25, 1915

*Los Angeles Express, The*
Oct. 23, 1918

*Los Angeles Record*
Oct. 6, 1926

Hollywood Citizen News
Oct. 9, 1926

*Associated Press*
June 8, 1927

*Motion Picture News*
Oct. 6, 1929

*Louella Parsons*
May 1, 1931

*Jimmy Starr*
March 16, 1932

*Los Angeles Illustrated Daily News*
Sept. 19, 1932

*Los Angeles Evening Herald Express*
Sept. 7, 1933

*Los Angeles Evening Herald Express*
June 30, 1934

*Hollywood Citizen News*
May 4, 1933

*Los Angeles Evening Herald Express*
June 19, 1934

*Los Angeles Herald Express*
May 18, 1935

*Los Angeles Illustrated Daily News*
Feb. 14, 1936

*New York Times*
June 21, 1936

*Los Angeles Examiner*
Nov. 19, 1936

*Los Angeles Times*
8-15-37

*Hollywood Citizen News*
August 31, 1937

*San Francisco Examiner*
Nov. 8, 1937

*Los Angeles Examiner*
Dec. 19, 1937

*Los Angeles Examiner*
Dec. 24, 1937

*Los Angeles Examiner*
July 17, 1938

*New York Daily Mirror*
June 26, 1936

*Washington Post*
June 1936

*Los Angeles Examiner*
Sept. 3, 1936

*Los Angeles Times*
Aug. 15, 1937

*Motion Picture Herald*

*Motion Picture Herald*
Jan. 22, 1938

*San Francisco Examiner*
April 7, 1938

Hollywood Citizen News

*New York Times*
Dec. 11, 1940

*San Francisco Chronicle*
Sept. 16, 1939

*San Francisco Chronicle*
Sept. 17, 1939

*San Francisco Chronicle*
Sept. 18, 1939

*New York Times*
Aug. 2, 1942

*Berkley Daily Gazette*
Feb. 4, 1943

*Hollywood Citizen News*
Oct. 19, 1942

*San Francisco Examiner*
Aug. 23, 1944

*Washington Post*
July 5, 1945

*San Francisco Chronicle*
Jan 10-12, 1947

*Louella Parsons*
9-17-48

*Los Angles Times*
*Daily Mirror*
Nov. 13, 1948

*Los Angeles Times*
March 12, 1970

# Index

CPSIA information can be obtained
at www.ICGtesting.com
Printed in the USA
FSOW02n1052160916
25095FS